CREATIVITY TWENTY

A Photographic Review
Edited by Don Barron

ART DIRECTION BOOK COMPANY • New York 10016

Advertising Directions Volume 23

Designed by Jim Bennett
and Robin Resnick/Bennett

Copyright © 1991 Art Direction Book Company
10 East 39th Street, New York, NY 10016
All rights reserved

ISBN: 0-88108-088-8
ISBN for Creativity Annuals Standing Orders: 0-910-158-10-X
Library of Congress Catalog Card Number: 74-168254

Printed in Hong Kong

Distributors:
USA and Canada: Art Direction Book Company
Foreign Distributor
Hearst International
105 Madison Avenue, New York, NY 10016

CONTENTS

. . .The Art Director is the genre
artist of our time. His talent is
the eye and the mind for the
contemporary scene and his skill
the ability to depict his client's
product in terms of the immediate
moment.

From the Announcement for the First Creativity Show, 1970

CREATIVITY 20

This show pulled off an unusual surprise. Absent, 100%, is the "Parade of One" art directing style. It's as though the style never existed, though only three years ago most art directors solved assignments with their own individual solutions.

The excitement here is that you will see everyone from art directors to designers to package designers to cover designers and on and on all responding to problems identically. This is new, totally new, to current advertising art, now an art form some 70-75 years old. Some extent the significance is visible in the styles of art directors, as evidenced by art director shows, and the styles of designers, as evidenced by AIGA exhibitions, merging if only for now.

For the third consecutive year, "I'm just telling you the facts" style of visual advertising is seen throughout a Creativity Annual. What is developing is a kind of hard sell that was true some 50-60 years ago during the great depression. It's rather grim and merciless, though it would have you believe it is humorous. Well, it may be, but it's not the humor one usually expects from U.S. advertising. It is more ironic; even sardonic. It has an elitist touch that makes no bones about its appeals to the classes, rather than the masses.

This may not be the best environment for audacious art directing. There's just too much copy. This is not the era of "one picture is worth a thousand words". Quite the opposite—a thousand words equals one picture—is more like it. Second, clients seem to be demanding pounding, sledge hammer efforts.

Now, it's not impossible to art direct such messages with outstanding graphics, but the interest to do so doesn't seem to exist. The art director is being called upon to present the clients' products and services with the directness of a catalog sell.

To cope, art directors have rummaged through their bags of visual devices - and tricks - to come up with a startling display of skills, talent and knowledge of art, type, photography, illustration, design, etc.. In CREATIVITY 19, the art director's handiwork was plainly evident. In this Annual you have to look for it. This is not an Annual to flip through. It's a good show, but you may have to evaluate the entries very carefully.

For many years, we have also evaluated the entries in the various design categories. Our assessment for CREATIVITY 20 is:

Television commercials are, as always, excellent. The skill of communicating via the TV screen grows ever more apparent. The photography and music are great, and the story line, in most cases, exactly fits the product. Freshness, however, seems harder and harder to find. In the hundreds and hundreds of commercials we judged, only a few are not only competent but truly creative. Since communication depends to a great extent on repetition, the judges picked out about fifteen commercials that they truly enjoyed seeing over and over. Another way to reach the viewer is by shock—this the public service commercials have truly learned.

Consumer Advertising Strong, simple, uncomplicated, untricky. Photography is the dominant medium; illustration mostly line and decorative. The fractional units are on the fun side.

Trade Advertising Once a stepchild sort of design category, certainly isn't now. The campaigns show much thought, attention to detail, lots of tlc. Layouts are strong, clever, colorful, imaginative ... and beautiful. Type treatments are wow! Photography again very strong, but now there's no question that trade accounts are using more illustration. All in all, a very strong, uncomplicated, forceful group of award winners.

Posters are on the quiet side, and, as with so much in this show, simple and direct. Type and lettering is handled somewhat loosely but effectively. Again this year, art and illustration increased.

Annual Reports now reflect a cut back in budgets. The number of pages is down, as is the use of 4C. There seems to be a slight movement toward oblong formats. Covers, incidentally, are fantastic, perhaps to hide the smaller budgets.

Radio has gone home. As in down home. As in "This is Tom Bodett for Motel 6... We'll leave a light on for you." Folksy raconteurs are now the presenters-of-choice for everything from pesticides to insurance to, believe it or not, a New York City newspaper. The copy is razor sharp. Meanwhile, the snappy he/she dialogues have faded away—as has straight music. Humorous music, though not prevalent, remains very good. Again, note the subdued, muted quality.

Brochures/Catalogs Long an outstanding category, it has become an art form all unto itself. This year the entries are spectacular throughout, from concept to finish down to the smallest details.

House Organs Another great year for this category. In quality, they're now up to trade magazines and, in some instances, consumer books. It's quite remarkable that art directors and designers have created such a valuable source of new business in a span of a few years.

Magazine Covers Another design category of simpler, less frantic layouts. Photography still strong, but again, shows increasing competition from art and illustration.

Book Jackets display excellence in every medium—art, design, typography, photography and concept. Textbooks are also great.

Record Albums too, are great. They reflect an easy "Oh, what the hell" attitude and are the better for it. Art covers are particularly loose. The increasing number of CD and cassette covers show how well good design can fit within a small space.

Packaging While design here is trendless, it is also extremely functional; there is absolutely no gap between products and the designing to sell them; all work together. Design is somewhat muted, which is very surprising for a field existing on impulse buying. Not surprising is the eclecticism. Packaging uses everything—art, design, computer art, photography, type, anything. No favorites.

Calendars are handsome and, after many years of confused layouts, useful!

Promotion is alive with excellent designs and execution. It appeared that this category got all it asked for in terms of budgets. The entries do not seem to want for anything. Accordingly, many of them are expensive looking, yet display wise, not ostentatious, designing. The use of paper is splendid. As for shopping bags, even here, believe it or not, renderings are muted, subdued. However, they're beautiful.

Logotypes/Trademarks The trend, now 4-5 years old, towards illustrative design continues. The use of color is extensive, while clever intertwining is less. Quality is high.

Letterheads are one of the stars of this year's show. There is an excellent use of paper and beautifully designed envelopes. Color printing is outstanding with 2, 3, and 4 colors. There isn't any formula to design, although going off center does had an edge.

Corporate Identity Programs once were limited to the do's and don'ts of each corporation. In this show, that confinement is fading. The manuals are edging into promotional efforts. The winning entries were, as they should be, extremely professional.

Self Promotion Perhaps there's no better place to catch the spirit of the show than here. The entries are understated; a rarity in this part of the show. However, the quality of work is superb; nothing slipshod. Again visible is the slide from photography to art and design.

Photography/Illustration For the first time in some 20 years, photography shares the stage with art and illustration. It's still not equal billing, but it would be misrepresenting not to point out the continuing swing. Both enjoy a good year in this show, but one can't help noticing that advertising illustration now is decorative, realistic, line wash and is used for fashion, landscapes, portraits, product, etc..

Editorial like most of the show, is strong, clear-cut, uncomplicated presentations. Here the emphasis is on expert story telling.

Public Service Here there are effective efforts to present the messages without hysterics or cheap shots. Budgets, always a factor, are wisely used.

Typography Throughout this category the type treatments were outstanding. The expertise with which art directors and designers solve their problems is remarkable!

SUMMARY

This show highlights the sudden 100% disappearance of the once exuberant "Parade of One" style of art directing. In its place is a quiet, subdued collection of work in all the design categories. It is a startling unexpected development. Just to call it "The British Look" doesn't do it justice. What seems to be in the making is the prospect of exceptional art directing. The work in this show is simply too good to be relegated to but another turn on the wheel. The signal here is for a major upsurge in art directing.

DEMANDED BY AND CREATED FOR PERFECTIONISTS

HARMONIE

ARC DE TRUFFLES

Tracy McFarlane Art Director
Henry Wolf Photographer
Peter Rogers Copywriter
Peter Rogers Associates Agency
Baccarat Client
New York, NY

Heintje Moo Art Director
David Foo Photographer
Gordon Tan Typographer
Ketchum Advertising (S) Pte. Ltd. Agency
The Dynasty Hotel Singapore Client
Singapore

Gordon Bennett Art Director/Designer
Stephen Wilkes, Grant Peterson Photographers
Steven Landsberg Copywriter
Calet, Hirsch & Spector, Inc. Agency
Monsieur Henri Wines & Spirits, Ltd. Client
New York, NY

Priviet. Imported from Russia. Serious vodka you don't have to take too seriously.

9

Brian Kelly Art Director
Tom Marchini Creative Director
Victor Skrebneski Photographer
AC&R Advertising Agency
Estee Lauder Client
New York, NY

Ava Schlesinger Director
Anne Zaccardo, Ava Schlesinger Designers
Just Loomis Photographer
MADEMOISELLE Magazine Production
Christian Dior Client
New York, NY

Mike Calluori Art Director/Designer
Floewnxe Tischler Creative Director
Dan Smith Photographer
Retail Advertising Group Agency
Encore Shoe Corporation Client
New York, NY

Paul Ciavarra Art Director
Doug Law, Paul Ciavarra Designers
Jeffrey Stein Photographer
Paul Ciavarra Illustrator
Della Femina McNamee, Inc. Agency
Swank Client
Boston, MA

Donald Montgomery Art Director
Donna Cristina Creative Director
Adrienne Vittadini Designer
Andrea Blanch Photographer
Adrienne Vittadini Advertising Agency/Client
New York, NY

Carmine Coppola, Christopher Jarrin
 Art Directors
Karen McIver, Joanna Patton
 Creative Directors
Andrew MacPherson Photographer
Lotas Minard Patton McIver Agency
Jay Feinberg Client
New York, NY

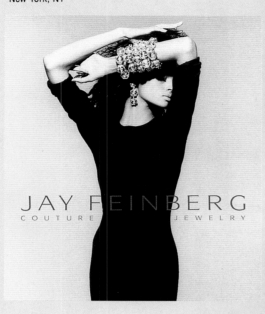

JAY FEINBERG
COUTURE   JEWELRY

Glen Jacobs, Paul Safsel Art Directors
Al Colello Creative Director
Tony Pezzullo Copywriter
Lintas:New York Agency
G.H. Bass & Company Client
New York, NY

Barbara A. Kwasnicki Art Director/Designer
Barbara L. Borejko Creative Director
Bruce Fields Photographer
Borejko Leibler/B Designed Ltd. Agency
Trifari Jewelry Client
New York, NY

Russ Hardin Art Director/Creative Director
Gordon Munro Photographer
Steve Raines Type Design
In-house Design Firm
Lord & Taylor Client
New York, NY

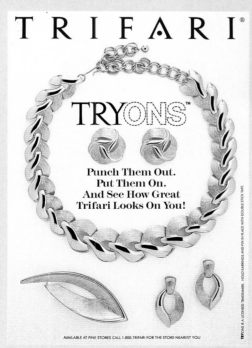

Michael Salisbury Art Director/Designer
Mike Funk Photographer
Terry Lamb, Pam Hamilton, Michael Salisbury
 Illustrators
Salisbury Communications Agency
Gotcha Sportswear Client
Torrance, California

Max Fujishima Art Director
Ed Velandria Designer
Joel Baldwin Photographer
DCA Advertising, Inc. Agency
Canon U.S.A., Inc. Client
New York, NY

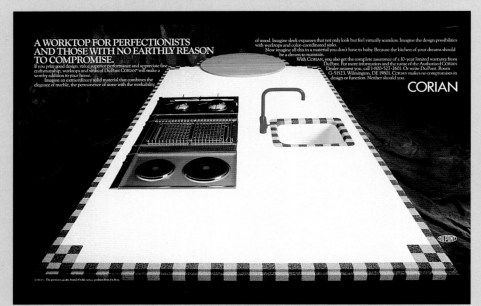

Mickey Tender Art Director/Designer
Ted Regan Executive Creative Director
Joe Standart Photographer
W.W. Ayer, Inc. Agency
E.I. DuPont de Nemours & Co., Inc. Client
New York, NY

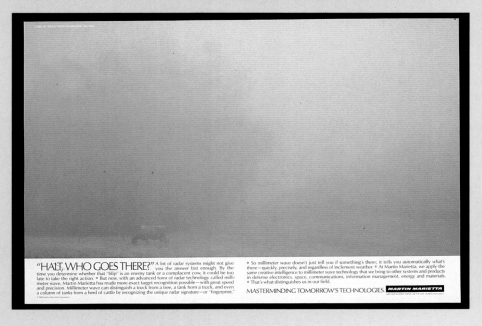

Don Schramed Art Director
Burgess Blevins Photographer
Elise Kolaja Copywriter
VanSant Dugdale Advertising Agency
Martin Marietta Client
Baltimore, MD

A classic inspiration.

Ray-Ban

CLASSIC ROUND METALS Sunglasses by Bausch & Lomb

Suggested Poster Design

Kathy Cairo/Buck & Pulleyn
  Art Director/Designer
Brian Sprouse/GKPL Photographer
Jack Bliss Illustrator
Buck & Pulleyn, Inc. Agency
Bausch & Lomb Inc. Client
Rochester, NY

Ann Bodlund Art Director
Anette Norman, Ann Bodlund Designers
Jan Bengtsson Photographer
Storm & Co. Agency
Riksost Client
Stockholm, Sweden

Mark Fuller Art Director
Jim Erickson Photographer
Steve Bassett Copywriter
The Martin Agency Agency
Blue Cross/Blue Shield of Virginia Client
Richmond, VA

John Klimo Art Director
Roz Rubenstein Creative Director
Olof Wahlund Photographer
RR&J Advertising, Inc. Agency
John Paul Mitchell Systems Client
New York, NY

Sharon L. Occhipinti Art Director/Designer
Steven White Photographer
Robert Dale Illustrator
Bertrand Garbassi Copywriter
DDB Needham Agency
Seagrams - Crown Royal Client
New York, NY

14

Madeleine Bissonnette Art Director
Wayne Johnson Copywriter
Publicite Martin, Inc. Agency
Port de Montreal Client
Montreal, Quebec, Canada

THE NEW FRAGRANCE FOR MEN

YVESSAINTLAURENT

Jérôme Faillant-Dumas Art Director
Yves Saint Laurent Designer/Illustrator
Jean Baptiste Mondino Photoghapher
Yves Saint Laurent Perfumes Client
Neuilly Sur Seine, France

R E F L E C T I O N S   O F   G R A N D E U R.

To send a gift of Grand Marnier® Liqueur (except where prohibited by law) call 1-800-243-3787
Product of France. Made with fine cognac brandy 40% alc/vol (80 proof). © 1989 Carillon Importers, Ltd., Teaneck, NJ.

Arnie Arlow Art Director
Gervasio Gallardo Illustrator
TBWA Advertising, Inc. Agency
Carillon Importers, Ltd. Client
New York, NY

Les Broude Art Director
Angelo Avlonitis Photographer
Merlin Grant Copywriter
McCann Agency
Times Media Limited Client
Sandton, South Africa

PARA CABELLO HERMOSO,
SOLO AÑADA AGUA.

Es sencillo. Pert Plus® tiene una fórmula exclusiva que combina
champú y acondicionador, todo en uno. Esto significa un cabello suave, limpio y brillante
en un sólo paso. Lo único que hay que hacer es añadir agua.

L A   B E L L E Z A   D E   L O   S E N C I L L O

Jorge Ballara Art Director
Susan Kinast Photographer
Jorge Ballara Copywriter
Leo Burnett USA Agency
Procter & Gamble Client
Deerfield, IL

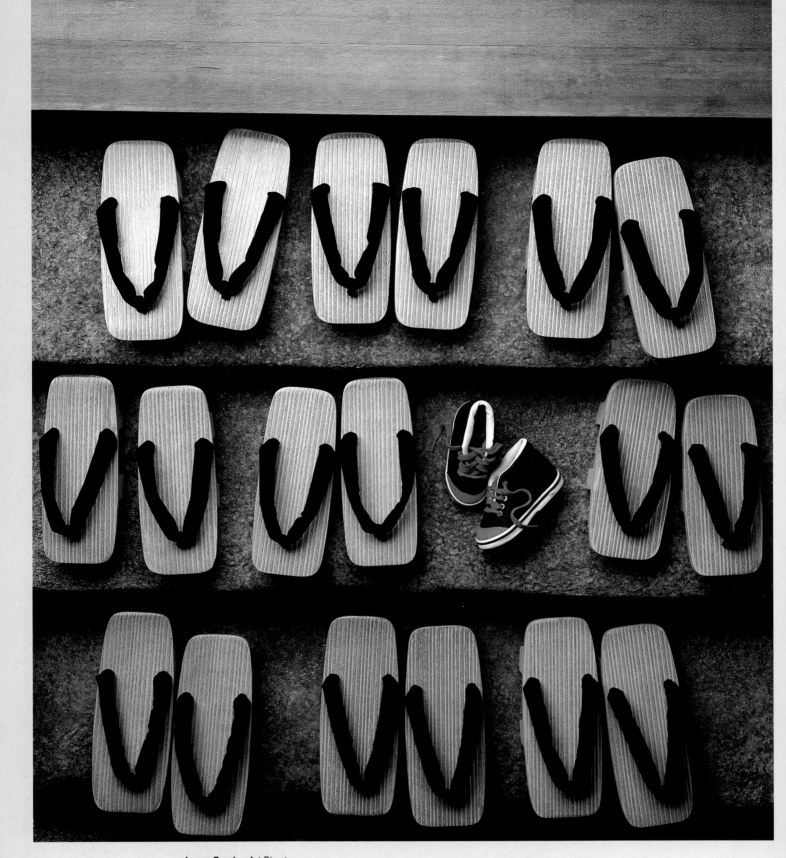

James Dearing Art Director
Ivan Horvath Creative Director
Terry Heffernan Photographer
Holly Stewart Stylist
Ogilvy & Mather/LA Agency
Pan Pacific Hotels & Resorts Client
San Francisco, CA

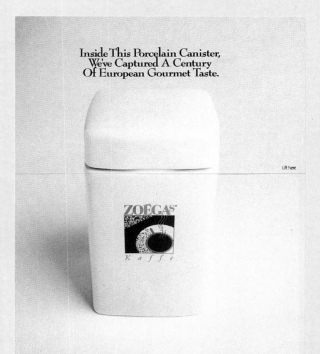

Inside This Porcelain Canister,
We've Captured A Century
Of European Gourmet Taste.

Enjoy Gourmet European Coffee For Just $5.00
And Receive Our Glazed Porcelain Canister, Free.

Introducing ZOÉGAS Kaffe
Home Delivery Service.
Sweden's Finest Gourmet Coffees
Since 1886 Are Now Delivered
Fresh To Your Door.

Jeff Kemhadjian Art Director
Paul Zink Creative Director
Jeff Li Photographer
Lisa Fielding Copywriter
Krupp/Taylor Agency
Hill Bros. Client
Los Angeles, CA

Next Time You Buy Carpet, Consider Our Point Of View.

Claude Shade Art Director
Stephanie Arnold, Jim Jolliffe Copywriters
TBWA Kerlick Switzer Agency
Monsanto Wear-Dated Carpet Client
St. Louis, MO

We're helping the economy
take off.

Barry Moss Art Director/Designer
Bruce Illidge Copywriter
IHJ Advertising Pty. Ltd. Agency
Air Pacific Client
Suva, Fiji Islands

Jagdish Prabhu Art Director
Bob Shriber Producer
Linda Kaplan, Charlie Gennarelli
  Creative Directors
Karen Abbate Copywriter
J. Walter Thompson Agency
Bell Atlantic Client
New York, NY

If getting the right information system
is an uphill battle,
let Bell Atlantic show you the ropes.

17

Karl Shaffer Art Director
Marc A. Williams Creative Director
Joseph A. Puhy Group Creative Director
Anthony Arciero Photographer
Young & Rubicam, Inc. Agency
Lincoln-Mercury Division Client
Detroit, MI

Gustavo Sanchez Art Director
Pablo Conde Designer
Angel Ortiz Photographer
Tiempo BBDO. Agency
Pepsi-Cola Espana Client
Madrid, Spain

Diane Meier Art Director/Designer
Ken Skalski Photographer
Robert Merola Illustrator
Meier Advertising, Inc. Agency
Kalkin & Co. Client
New York, NY

Paul Hargreaves Art Director
Craig Love, Lawrie Walton Designer
Dennis Hitchcock Photographer
Lintas:New Zealand Agency
Unilever NZ, Limited Client
Wellington, New Zealand

Arpad C. Makay Art Director/Designer
Francis Giacobetti Photographer
James Lyons Copywriter
H&M Graphics Design Firm
James R. Lyons, Plastic Surgical Center Client
Wallingford CT

Få se nu.
Går till allt, det gör ju grönsaker.
Och där finns alla nyttiga vitaminer.
Och säkert en massa fiber.

Okej, men det är ingen grönsak.
Det är snarare en brun sak.
Som innehåller i stort sett
allt nyttigt du behöver.
Smakar underbart.
Mättar gott.
Är till 99% fettfri.
Har noll kolesterol.
Just det.
Potatis.

Faktum är att du skulle kunna
leva sunt på nästan bara potatis.
Tro det eller ej.
Det säger det mesta om
vilken fantastisk liten knöl det är.
Om du slarvar med maten
ibland, så har vi ett gott råd.
Ät potatis oftare.
Det är lika välgörande för
kroppen som för plånboken.

POTATIS
Allt i ett skal.

Peer Eriksson Art Director/Designer
Ola Lager Photographer
Philip Ostberg Copywriter
Soren Blanking AB Agency
SPI-Swedish Potato Growers Association Client
Malmoe, Sweden
"Goes with Everything"

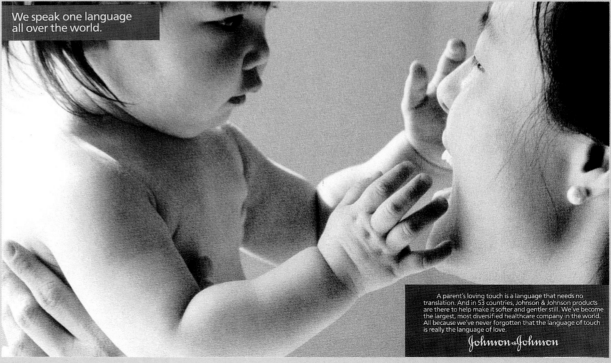

We speak one language
all over the world.

A parent's loving touch is a language that needs no translation. And in 53 countries, Johnson & Johnson products are there to help make it softer and gentler still. We've become the largest, most diversified healthcare company in the world. All because we've never forgotten that the language of touch is really the language of love.

Johnson & Johnson

Tom Peck Art Director
Cary Lemkowitz Copywriter
Young & Rubicam New York Agency
Johnson & Johnson Client
New York, NY

Sure and Natural.
Because life doesn't
stop for your period.
Period.

The only thin maxi
with a unique thin layer

ALL YOU NEED WITH A PAIR OF BLUE JEANS.

ALL STARS. ALL YOU NEED.

Lynn Pratts Mercado Art Director
Bonnie Harris Copywriter
Young & Rubicam New York Agency
Johnson & Johnson Client
New York, NY

Peter Favat, Don Pogany Art Directors
Dwight Olmsted Photographer
Mary Olmsted Stylist
Ingalls, Quinn & Johnson Agency
Converse Client
Boston, MA

IN THIS AGE OF
televangelists who sin,
politicians who lie,
athletes who cheat,
billionaires who evade
taxes, movie stars
who assault policemen,
baseball managers
who gamble and teen
idols who make home
movies...
isn't it nice to know
there's still one thing
that's completely pure.

Mazola Corn Oil.
No additives.
No preservatives.
No cholesterol.
100% PURE CORN OIL.

Michael McLaughlin Art Director
Rick McKechnie Photographer
Stephen Creet Copywriter
MacLaren:Lintas,Inc. Agency
Best Foods Client
Toronto, Canada

Consumer SMALL SPACE

Isn't life delicious?

Sam Gulisano Art Director
Grant Peterson Photographer
Rob Austin, Scott Rosenblit Copywriters
FCB/Leberkatz Agency
Lifesavers Client
New York, NY

Sharon Brady, Jane Rubini Art Directors
Barry Holniker Photographer
Sara Slater Copywriter
W.B. Doner & Company Agency
The Maryland Ballet Client
Baltimore, MD

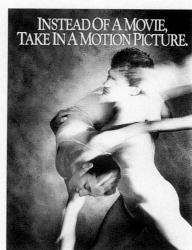

INSTEAD OF A MOVIE, TAKE IN A MOTION PICTURE.

Witness "The Awakening," an exciting production by the Maryland Ballet, based on the novel by Kate Chopin. Performances of "Bouquet" featuring prima ballerina Michelle Lucci will be February 16th at 8 p.m., 17th at 2 and 8 p.m. and 18th at 4 p.m. at the Baltimore Museum of Art. Don't miss a single breathtaking scene. *The Maryland Ballet*
For ticket information, call 576-2400.

Harold Woodridge Art Director/Designer
Ken Reid Photographer
Mark Aronson Copywriter
BBDO Chicago Agency
Central Telephone of Centel Corporation Client
Chicago, IL

ESTA ES
TU CAMISETA

Maratón
Löwenbräu
1º de Mayo

Ven! Ponte tu camiseta Lowenbrau
porque tú también puedes ganar,
pues hay RD$22,000.00 en premios,
para todos los vencedores.

EXTRACTO DE MALTA
Löwenbräu
La auténtica malta alemana

Juan Antonio
Acosta Hernandez
Art Director/Designer/Illustrator
Leo Burnett, Inc., Dominican Republic Agency
Cerveceria Nacional Domincana CXA Client
Villas de Loiza, Dominican Republic

George Noszgah Art Director
Sally Patterson Copywriter
Brouillard Communications Agency
American Gas Association Client
New York, NY

Harriet Walley, Stacy Mannheim Art Directors
Stacy Mannheim Designer
David Behl Photographer
Harriet Walley Associates Agency
Place des Antiquaires Client
New York, NY

Place des Antiquaires
The International Center of Arts and Antiques

More than 40 galleries specializing in antique European
& American furniture, paintings, marble and bronze
sculptures, Antiquities, Oriental works of art, antique and
period jewelry, art nouveau, art deco, ceramics &
glass, copper & brass, Russian paintings,
works of art & icons, silver, books and
manuscripts, autographs, maps, prints, dolls,
automata and toys,
rugs & tapestries,
pipes & canes,
scientific and
marine
instruments,
objects of
vertu: gold boxes,
ivories & fans.

*(Detail) One of a pair
of Napoleon I candelabras
from The Chateau of
Fontainbleu, dark
and gilt bronze,
circa 1810.
Gallery –
Russissimoff*

Open to the public
Monday through
Saturday
11am to 6pm

Place des Antiquaires
125 East 57th Street
New York, NY 10022
tel: 212.758.2900

22

"Home is where the heart is."
—Pliny the Elder

John Follis Art Director/Designer
John Follis, Brian Kelley Copywriters
Follis & Verdi, New York Agency
Adrienne Meltzer & Associates Client
New York, NY

Dale la vuelta al mundo.
Enrólate con Cutty Sark.

CUTTY SARK
SCOTS WHISKY

Casilda Rodriguez Art Director
Jeremy King Photographer
Enrique Astuy, Pedro Soler Copywriters
Francisco Carrillo Producer
Delvico Bates Agency
Varma (Cutty Sark) Client
Madrid, Spain

"A man's home is his castle."
—Sir Edward Coke

"If you want a great home,
first you need a great realtor."
—Adrienne Meltzer

Barbecue Starter.

Adrienne Meltzer & Associates, Inc.
Realtors
Great Estates Exclusive Affiliate
10 West Railroad Avenue, Tenafly, NJ
201-894-1900

Bob Crantz Art Director
Keith Bennett Designer
Chip Forelli Photographer
Tad DeWree Copywriter
DCA Advertising, Inc. Agency
Codorniu U.S.A. Client
New York, NY

Uncork an Occasion.

Vintage methode champenoise,
since 1872.
Imported by Codorniu U.S.A.,
Lake Success, New York.

Jeff York, Mark Piper Art Directors
Mike Lester Illustrator
J. Walter Thompson Agency
Quaker Oats Company Client
Chicago, IL

23

THE THOROUGHBREDS ARE BACK ON TRACK.

Which means at The Winner's Circle you can watch and bet on races televised live from Chicago's Sportsman's Park. Post time 1 pm, every Monday thru Saturday.

Thoroughbred racing will also be simulcast from Balmoral Park at 1 pm on Sundays.

Harness racing will be simulcast evenings from Maywood Park, Monday thru Saturday. Post time 8 pm.

Watch all the action on our big-screen TV's, enjoy lunch or dinner in our Derby Club, or just relax with drinks in our friendly lounge. **Admission is free.**

Any way you choose, it's a great way to see thoroughbred racing return to Chicago.

In Chicago, at 233 West Jackson (312) 427-2300 and 177 N. State (312) 419-8787, or in North Aurora, at 230 S. Lincolnway, where I-88 meets Highway 31. (708) 892-6200.

THE WINNER'S CIRCLE
HORSERACING • BAR • RESTAURANT

Carlos Segura Art Director/Designer
Doug Schiff Copywriter
Bayes Bess Vanderwarker Agency
The Winner's Circle Client
Chicago, IL

On Tuesday, August 29, for one hour the ABC Television Network will go black.

Tonight, ABC News will make history. Black history.
Tonight, for the first time on a major network, black correspondents, producers and researchers will collaborate on an extraordinary program about what it's like to be black in America.
Everyday people, entrepreneurs, black heroes, black history, drugs, education, the family.
Is everything black and white? Or are there shades of grey?

BLACK IN WHITE AMERICA
Tonight 10PM ⑦▫

ABCNEWS

Norman Schwartz Art Director
Ted Charron Copywriter
Charron, Schwartz & Partners, Inc. Agency
Robert Robbins Production
ABC Network News Client
New York, NY

To all the people who think the press goes too far sometimes, consider the alternative.

...details such as which ship was involved, where it was destined and where it was bound. It did concede in 1986 that the incident was classified as among its tw...

WASHINGTON (AP) — New details about the Navy's 1965 lo...

...andler of Greenpeace, said their research had established that many othe... have...

To learn more about the role of a Free Press and how it protects your rights, call the First Amendment Center at 1-800-542-1600.

If the press didn't tell us, who would?

A public service message of The Ad Council and The Society of Professional Journalists.

Ad Council

Barbara Simon Art Director
Virginia Stern Copywriter
Lowe & Partners Agency
Ad Council, SPJ Client
New York, NY

ROUND HILL
CHARDONNAY

Spring Wine Sale.
March 30–April 7

S U R D Y K S

The Liquor Store & Cheese Shop at East Hennepin and University Avenue

Paul Lang Art Director
Marvy Photographer
Greg Beaupre Copywriter
BBDO/Minneapolis Agency
Surdyk's Client
Minneapolis, MN

Chá de cadeira.

A Cia. de Móveis tem cadeiras para chás, almoços e jantares, salas de espera e de visita, pátios e varandas, cidade, campo e praia.
As cadeiras da Cia. de Móveis são bonitas, gostosas e tão confortáveis, que até chá de cadeira vira refresco numa delas.

Cia de Móveis

Rua Carlos Gomes, 740-A.
Estacionamento próprio para clientes.

Hiroko Sido Art Director
Oswaldo Mendes Copywriter
Mendes Publicidade Ltda. Agency
Cia de Moveis Client
Belem Para, Brazil

24

Gabi Wagner Art Director
CD Edmund Petri Creative Director
Gotz Schrage Photographer
Young & Rubicam Vienna Agency
Kodak Client
Vienna, Austria
"Dedicate Yourselves to the Colors"

Jeff Gandy Art Director
John McDermott Copywriter
Leslie Advertising Agency
Mitre Sports Client
Greenville, SC

Sherry Scharschmidt Art Director
Andrea Trotenberg Creative Director
Sports Illustrated/Walter Looss, Carl Skelak
   Photographers
Jeff Martin Copywriter
Bayer Bess Vanderwarker Agency
Quaker Oats Company Client
Chicago, IL

If only the Mets went down so easy.

Fluids. Minerals. Energy. Gatorade. For that deep down body thirst.

After devouring a tackle, a guard and a quarterback, what do you wash them down with?

Fluids. Minerals. Energy. Gatorade. For that deep down body thirst.

Joe Sciarrotta, Matt Canzano Art Directors
Doug Fraser Illustrator
Tenney Fairchild, Dave Merhard Copywriters
J. Walter Thompson Agency
Miller Breweing Company Client
Chicago, IL

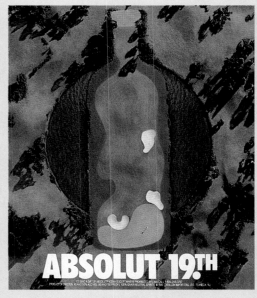

Steve Feldman, Tom McManus Art Directors
Steve Bronstein Photographer
Harry Woods, David Warren Copywriters
TBWA Advertising, Inc. Agency
Carillon Importers, Inc. Client
New York, NY

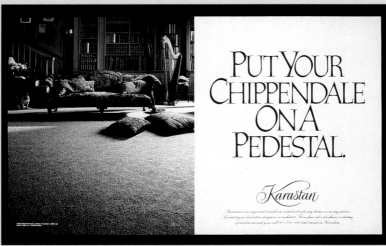

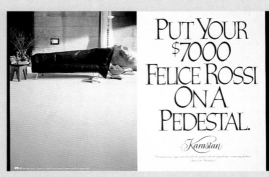

PUT YOUR CHIPPENDALE ON A PEDESTAL.

Karastan

PUT YOUR $7000 FELICE ROSSI ON A PEDESTAL.

Karastan

Steve Davis Art Director
Bruce Wolf Photographer
Suzanne Dowdee Producer
McKinney & Silver Agency
Karastan-Bigelow Client
Raleigh, NC

Wir finden, langweilige Möbel gibt es schon genug.

Wir finden, nichts geht über Multy-laterale Beziehungen.

Jurgen Weber Art Director
Paulo Greuel Photographer
H. Jurgen Schippers Copywriter
Wensauer DDB Needham, Ludwigsburg Agency
ligne roset Mobel GmbH Client
Ludwigsburg, West Germany "Look Back"

Colombo auf Ceylon ist nur eines von 76 Condor Urlaubszielen.

Ihr Hausarzt sagt, Sie sind fällig. Ihr Finanzamt sagt, Sie sind dran. Wo liegt das Problem, denken Sie, buchen Condor und tauchen erst mal unter.

Condor
Die Ferienflieger der Lufthansa

Die Malediven sind nur eines von 76 Condor Urlaubszielen.

Die Wohnung, die Sie mit Ihrer Freundin teilen, ist Ihnen zu eng. Das Großraumbüro geht Ihnen auf den Nerv. Sie fliegen mit Condor. Und plötzlich macht es Ihnen überhaupt nichts aus, Ihr schmales Handtuch zu teilen.

Condor
Die Ferienflieger der Lufthansa

Angelika Lang Art Director
Michael Ehrhart Photographer
Veronika Classen Copywriter
Michael Conrad & Leo Burnett Agency
Condor Flugdienst GmbH Client
Frankfurt, West Germany

Anna Lind-Lewin Art Director
Hakan Ludwigsson Photographer
Hakan Olofsson Copywriter
Ogilvy 2 Agency
KGF/General Foods Client
Stockholm, Sweden "Another Kind"

Richard Bates Art Director
Brian Searle-Tripp Creative Director
Tony Butler, Hamilton Budaza
  Illustrators/Typographers
Ogilvy & Mather, Rightford Seale-Tripp &
  Makin (Cape) Agency
Lion Match Company, Ltd. Client
Cape Town, South Africa

Tom Wambach Art Director
Pastore DePamphilis Rampone Photographer
Joel Meyerowitz Illustrator
Linda Howard Copywriter
North Castle Partners Agency
Tetley, Inc. Client
Stamford, CT

29

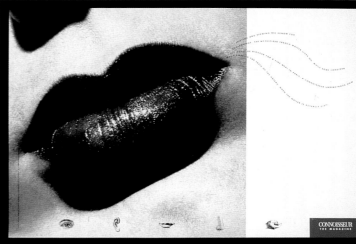

Tom Menillo Art Director
Tom Bonoaro Designer
Helmut Newton Photographer
Alison Gragnano Copywriter
Margeotes, Fertitta & Weiss Agency
CONNOISSEUR Client
New York, NY

Martha Healy Art Director
Alison DuMond Assistant Ad
Steven Klein Photographer
Photo Lettering Typographer
Ketchum, NY Agency
Coty, NY Client
New York, NY

Reggie Troncone Art Director/Creative Director
Albert Watson Photographer
Greengage Associates, Inc. Agency
Quality House of Graphics Production
Lily of France, Inc. Client
New York, NY

Marty Lipsitt, Gordon Bennett Art Directors
Jerry Cailor Photographer
Steven Landsberg Copywriter
Calet, Hirsch & Spector, Inc. Agency
Hunter Douglas, Inc. Client
New York, NY

For the new Peugeot ...
there are no bad roads !

Ernest J. Gottlieb, Robert T. Tang
Art Directors
Robert T. Tang Designer
Ronald Manulang Illustrator
Matari, Inc. Agency
Pt. Multi France Client
Jakarta, Indonesia

BEGITU NYAMANNYA PEUGEOT BARU INI...
KEMACETAN LALU LINTAS AKAN TERASA MENYENANGKAN

The new Suzuki DR.   Think of it as a 4-stroke on steroids.

The new Suzuki VX800.   When riding is the end, not the means.

Chad Farmer Art Director
Lee Kovel Creative Director
Aaron Jones Photographer
Bill Lindsey Copywriter
HDM Inc., Los Angeles Agency
American Suzuki Motor Corporation Client
Los Angeles, CA

TOYOTA CAME TO CANADA FOR SOME OF
THE BEST PARTS IN THE WORLD.

Richard Talbot Art Director
Larry Gordon Creative Director
Michael Rifelson Photographer
Robin Heisey Copywriter
Saatchi & Saatchi Compton Hayhurst Ltd.
Agency
Toyota Canada, Inc. Client
Toronto, Canada

TOYOTA CAME TO CANADA FOR ITS ENERGY RESERVES.

THE SCHED**U**LE.

The moving force behind Chicago's business.
UNITED AIRLINES

E**U**ROPE

Beginning with Nonstops
to Frankfurt and Paris.
The moving force behind Chicago's business.
UNITED AIRLINES

Marty Gustavsson Art Director/Designer
Bud Watts Executive Art Director
Leo Burnett U.S.A. Agency
United Airlines, Inc. Client
Arlington Heights, IL

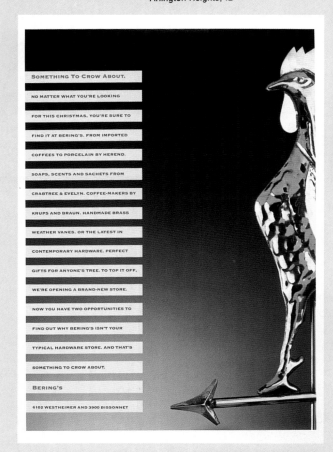

Sporten i Politiken går efter
spillet, ikke efter manden

POLITIKEN
-stof
til levende
tanker

Charles Hively Art Director
Craig Stewart Photographer
Laura McCarley Copywriter
The Hively Agency Agency
Bering's Hardware Client
Houston TX

Hele verden samlet ét sted
hver morgen

Dorte Zangenberg Art Director
Claus Lembourn Copywriter
Zangenberg & Lembourn/EWDB Agency
Politiken Client
Copenhagen, Denmark

SAMBUCA ROMANA

LIQUORE CLASSICO DI ROMA

Cynthia Rothbard Art Director
Phillip Dickson Photographer
Berenter Greenhouse & Webster Agency
The Paddington Corporation Client
New York, NY

33

Trade SINGLE UNIT

Griffin Stenger, Jerry Roach Art Directors
Linda Kaplan, Charlie Gennarelli
Creative Directors
Drake Spartman, Bob Waldner Copywriters
J. Walter Thompson Agency
Bell Atlantic Client
New York, NY

Building Savings: Con Edison's ApplePower Rebate Program

When it's time to decide how to light, cool and power buildings, there are many things to consider: reliability, equipment life, operating costs. High-efficiency equipment may meet your criteria, but it can strain your budget.

That's why we developed the Con Edison ApplePower Rebate Program—to reduce the cost of the equipment that reduces operating costs. With this program you can specify highly energy-efficient equipment at substantially lower prices (often even lower than standard equipment). This saves money now, and for years to come on Con Edison bills.

ApplePower helps you use high-efficiency equipment—electric, gas and steam air conditioning, lighting, electric motors and cool storage systems that produce cooling energy at night for daytime use—all at reduced costs.

Just fill out the attached coupon, or call the number below. We'll send you one of our brochures with specifics about the program and how you can qualify.

Call:
1-800-343-4646 ext. 700
(Monday through Friday, 9 a.m. to 5 p.m.)

Save money by saving energy.

Please send me more information about the AplePower Rebate Program. (Please print)

Name _____ Title _____
Company name _____ Address _____
City _____ State _____ ZIP _____ Phone ( ) _____
I am interested in: high-efficiency ☐ lighting ☐ electric motors ☐ electric air conditioning ☐ gas air conditioning ☐ steam air conditioning ☐ cool storage systems (produce cooling energy at night for daytime use)

Mail to: Con Edison, ApplePower Rebate Program, 298 Fifth Avenue, Box 700, N.Y., NY 10001

Con Edison ApplePower Rebate Program
THE ENERGY OF NEW YORK

Guy Mastrion Art Director
Bob Gaffney Creative Director
Kevin O'Callaghan Designer
Robert Moore Photographer
Saatchi & Saatchi Direct, NYC Agency
Consolidated Edison Client
New York, NY

In recent years it has become an all too frequent occurrence for professional photo retailer/distributors to open and close one after another. And while you may wonder how this could possibly affect your business as a professional photographer, imagine losing your backup support at a time when you need it the most.

That's why at Vistek we pay particular attention to how our present service will impact our future. When we commit to a manufacturer's product, we also commit to fully stocking and servicing the line. We ensure that it

is well represented in our rental department. And we provide backup should this equipment ever require repair while under warranty.

This is one reason why Vistek has remained

strong and enjoyed steady growth in an otherwise less than stable industry.

Another reason, and we believe the most important, is our people. Be it sales, rentals, service

or support staff, our team is responsible and dedicated to providing solutions. Whether it's of a technical nature or just general assistance, we're here to help. And if we can't help you, we'll find out who can. Because when it comes right down to it, securing our business for tomorrow really means taking care of your business today.

To see what we mean, visit 100 Queen St. E. in Toronto, Ont. M5C 1S6. Or call us at 365-1777 locally and 1-800-387-2076 toll free today. Or tomorrow. We'll still be here.

AT VISTEK, SELLING PROFESSIONAL PHOTOGRAPHIC PRODUCTS TODAY MEANS HAVING OUR SIGHTS FOCUSED CLEARLY ON TOMORROW.

 Vistek

Dale Henderson Art Director/Copywriter
Marie Poon Designer
George Simhoni Photographer
Henderson & Company Agency
Vistek Ltd. Client
Toronto, Ontario, Canada

34

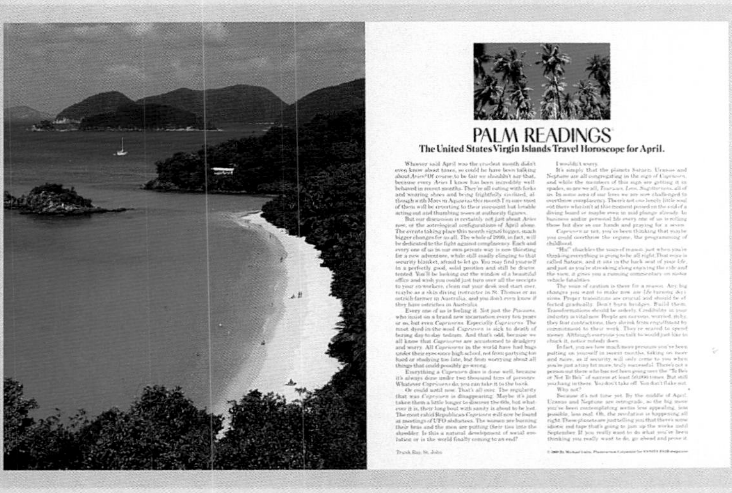
PALM READINGS
The United States Virgin Islands Travel Horoscope for April.

Penny Dorrance Art Director
Reggie Troncone Creative Director
Albert Watson Photographer
Greengage Associates, Inc. Agency
United States Virgin Islands (Division of Tourism) Client
New York, NY

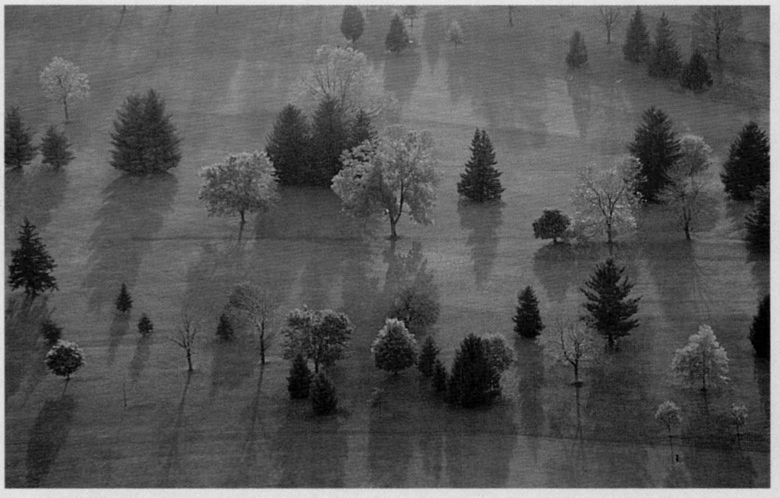

Joe Ivey Art Director
Gary Knutson Creative Director
Jay Maisel Designer
Howard Merrell and Partners, Inc. Agency
Ciba-Geigy Corporation Client
New York, NY

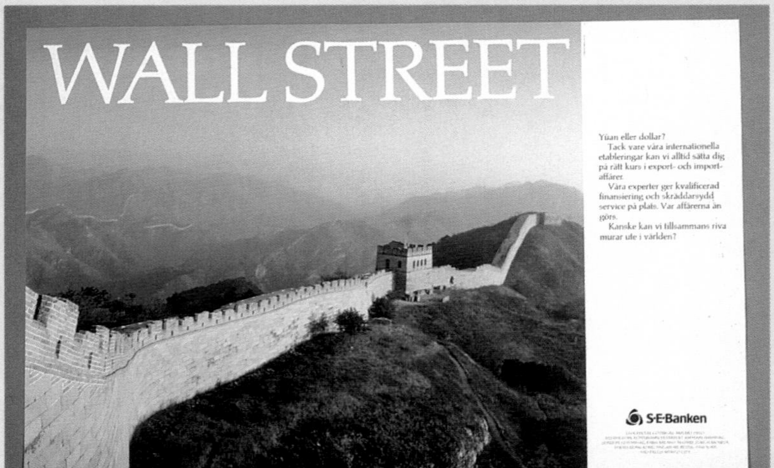
WALL STREET
Yüan eller dollar?
Tack vare våra internationella etableringar kan vi alltid sätta dig på rätt kurs i export- och importaffärer.
Våra experter ger kvalificerad finansiering och skräddarsydd service på plats. Var affärerna än görs.
Kanske kan vi tillsammans riva murar ute i världen?
S-E-Banken

Lorne Munthe de Wolfe Art Director
Per Ehrenstrahle Copywriter
Ehrenstrahle & Co. Agency
S-E-Banken Client
Stockholm, Sweden

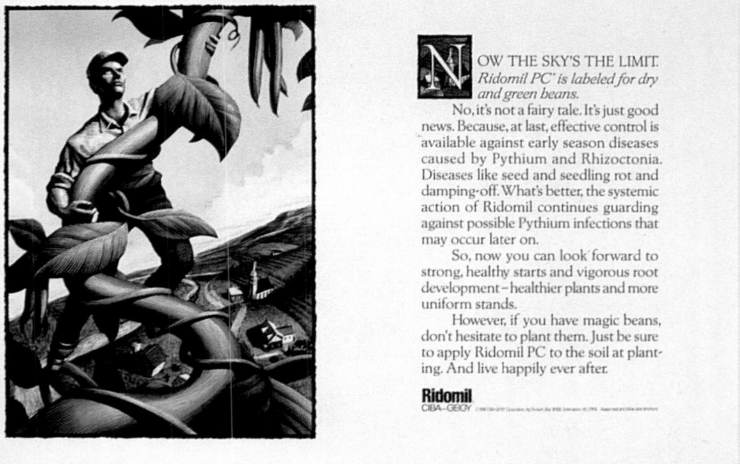
NOW THE SKY'S THE LIMIT.
Ridomil PC is labeled for dry and green beans.
No, it's not a fairy tale. It's just good news. Because, at last, effective control is available against early season diseases caused by Pythium and Rhizoctonia. Diseases like seed and seedling rot and damping-off. What's better, the systemic action of Ridomil continues guarding against possible Pythium infections that may occur later on.
So, now you can look forward to strong, healthy starts and vigorous root development–healthier plants and more uniform stands.
However, if you have magic beans, don't hesitate to plant them. Just be sure to apply Ridomil PC to the soil at planting. And live happily ever after.
Ridomil
CIBA-GEIGY

Darrel Fiesel Art Director
Millie Olson Creative Director
Mark Summers Illustrator
Darrel Fiesel Copywriter
Ketchum Advertising Agency
Ciba-Geigy Corporation Client
San Francisco, CA

John Klimo Art Director
Roz Rubenstein Creative Director
Olof Wahlund Photographer
Melissa Berman Copywriter
RR&J Advertising, Inc. Agency
John Paul Mitchell Systems Client
New York, NY

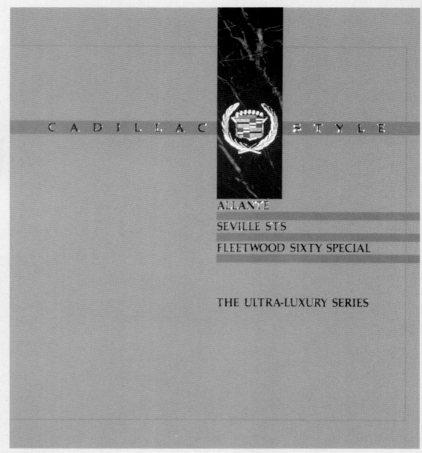

Jack Carmichael Art Director
John Klinger Creative Director
Lilly Marinelli Designer
Boulevard Studio Photographer
La Driere Studio Illustrator
DMB&B Agency
Cadillac Motor Car Division Client
Bloomfield Hills, MI

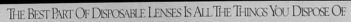

Michael Fountain Art Director/Designer
Aaron Jones Photographer
John Connelly Copywriter
I.C.E. Communications, Inc. Agency
Bausch and Lomb International Client
Rochester, NY

Goerge Pierson Art Director
Gary Dueno Designer
Jane Warrick-Owens Copywriter
Home Box Office, Inc. Design Firm/Client
New York, NY

Bob Meagher Art Director
Jim Erickson Photographer
Liz Paradise Copywriter
The Martin Agency Agency
FMC Corp. Client
Richmond, VA

Dick Prow Art Director
Richard Hamilton Smith Photographer
John Moline Copywriter
Rhea & Kaiser Advertising Agency
SOYBEAN DIGEST Magazine Client
St. Paul, MN

Jerry Sullivan Art Director
James Roof Photographer
Chat Chapman Copywriter
Sullivan Haas Coyle Agency
The Griffin Company Client
Atlanta, GA

Tom Smith Art Director/Designer
Nick Vedros, Stock Photographer
Michael Marino Copywriter
Wyse Advertising Agency
General Dynamics Client
Cleveland, OH

37

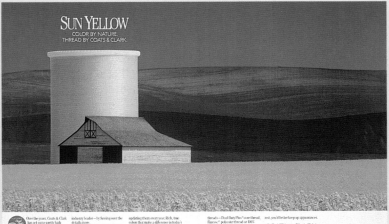

Jim Farmer Art Director/Designer
Brian Rodgers, Superstock Photographers
Carlos Jimenez Copywriter
Leslie Advertising Agency
Coats & Clark, Inc. Client
Greenville, SC

Ron Long Art Director
Don Rowley Illustrator
Don Finlayson Copywriter
Kamstra Communications, Inc. Agency
Harris Group Client
St. Paul, MN

Hugh Hough Art Director
George Jaccoma Creative Director
Terry Widener Illustrator
Martin Marshall Jaccoma Mitchell Agency
Panasonic Client
New York, NY

Stan Paulus Art Director
Sy Levin, Scott Maclean Copywriters
VanSant Dugdale Advertising Agency
Westinghouse Electronic Systems Group Client
Baltimore, MD

Christie Kelley Art Director
Tim Bieber Photographer
Jeff Moore Copywriter
Young & Rubicam Chicago Agency
Navistar International Corporation Client
Chicago, IL

Even an expert can't tell a Comforel pillow from down.

JoAnn Tansman Art Director
Chris Collins Photographer
Nina Sklansky Copywriter
BBDO Agency
DuPont de Nemours, Inc. Client
New York, NY

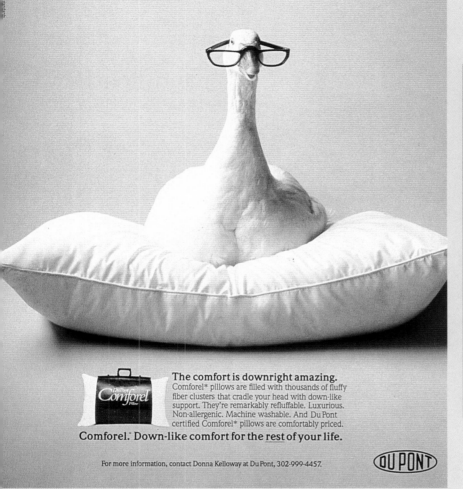

The comfort is downright amazing.

Comforel* pillows are filled with thousands of fluffy fiber clusters that cradle your head with down-like support. They're remarkably refluffable. Luxurious. Non-allergenic. Machine washable. And Du Pont certified Comforel* pillows are comfortably priced.

Comforel. Down-like comfort for the rest of your life.

For more information, contact Donna Kelloway at Du Pont, 302-999-4457.

DU PONT

This is the color of a very smart investment.

A lot of investments can make you money, but when things look uncertain, when inflation looms, few can protect your money like gold. That's why savvy investors keep 15% of their portfolios in gold. And the market place for gold is Comex, the most active metals market in the world. For further information, you can call (800) 333-2900. In New York, (212) 938-7921.

COMEX
GOLD · SILVER · COPPER · ALUMINUM

John Follis Art Director/Designer
Brian Kelley, John Follis Copywriters
Foollis & Verdi, NY Agency
The Commodities Exchange, Inc. Client
New York, NY

Nästa köp?

Den medelålders damen som köpte en blå kjol, vad vill hon ha nästa gång?

Den unga familjen som valde en ny stereo, vad satsar de på nästa gång?

Den äldre mannen som beställde en skinn-soffa, vad väljer han nästa gång?

Hur ser olika köpmönster ut? Vad kan du lära av dina kunders köp?

Din nyckel till ökad kunskap om kundernas beteende är butikskedjans eget kontokort.

Det profilerade kortet öppnar nya möjlig-heter för en offensiv säljplanering.

FinansSkandic är ledande i Sverige på kontokort och satsar aktivt på att bygga upp väl anpassade säljstödssystem för olika butiks-kedjor.

Vår roll är inte bara att svara för finansie-ring och administration av butikskedjans eget kort.

Vi hjälper också till att utveckla det egna kortet till din effektivaste säljkanal.

Kontakta FinansSkandic, Division Privat, om du vill veta mer.

Nästa köp?

Det vet du inom kort!

FinansSkandic
FinansSkandic AB, 10378 Stockholm.
Telefon 08-14 60 00.

Lorne Munthe de Wolfe Art Directors
Tommy Alvestav Copywriter
Ehrenstrahle & Co. Agency
FinansSkandic AB Client
Stockholm, Sweden

Until Barlow got ahold of it, it was just a great pocket knife.

Now it becomes a work of art. The knives are 100%
American made. The design motifs are pure Barlow.
Each design created from an original engraving by artist,
Stephen Barlow. Intricate detail. Meticulous hand finishing.
Distinctive Barlow beauty. BARLOW

Tom Chandler, Jim Barina Art Director
Bruno Photographer
Bob Mariani Copywriter
Mariani, Hurley & Chandler Agency
Barlow Designs Client
Providence, RI

Lee Barthelman Art Director
Charlie Hudson, Northlight Studio Photographer
Tom Koberna Copywriter
Haselow & Associates Agency
Fermenta ASC Corporation Client
Cleveland, OH

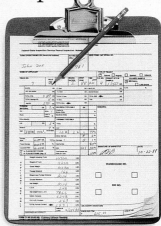

Your return from Bravo®
shows up where it counts.

It figures.

BRAVO AND PEANUTS. Use recommended cultural practices and a full-season Bravo spray program (6-7 applications). Bravo 720 test data from 29 trials in Alabama, Georgia and Florida show average yield over untreated check = 2123 lb/A. Individual yields and dollar return may vary depending on specific cultural practices and weather conditions. Fermenta ASC Corporation, 5966 Heisley Road, P.O. Box 8000, Mentor, Ohio 44061-8000. Always follow label directions carefully when using agricultural chemicals.

Bob Martin Art Director
Roger Bester Photographer
Dan Zenowich Copywriter
McKeefry and Co. Agency
Amerchol Corporation Client
Ozone Park, NY

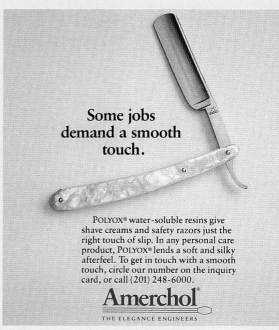

Some jobs
demand a smooth
touch.

POLYOX® water-soluble resins give
shave creams and safety razors just the
right touch of slip. In any personal care
product, POLYOX® lends a soft and silky
afterfeel. To get in touch with a smooth
touch, circle our number on the inquiry
card, or call (201) 248-6000.

Amerchol®
THE ELEGANCE ENGINEERS

40

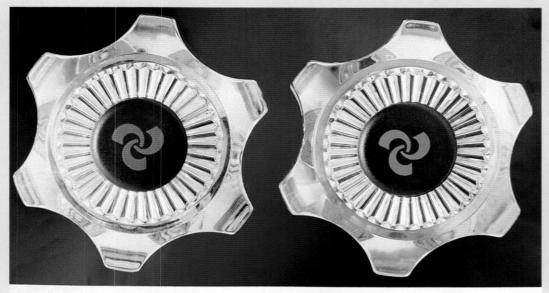

When you think of the number of times
we'll be turned on and off
it makes you go hot and cold.

Grant Harding Art Director
Owen Mundel Creative Director
Richard Mumford Copywriter
Mundels Agency
Cobra Watertech Client
Northcliff, South Africa

Adelaide Acerbi Art Director/Designer
Leo Torri Photographer
Studio Acerbi Agency
Driade Spa Client
Milan, Italy

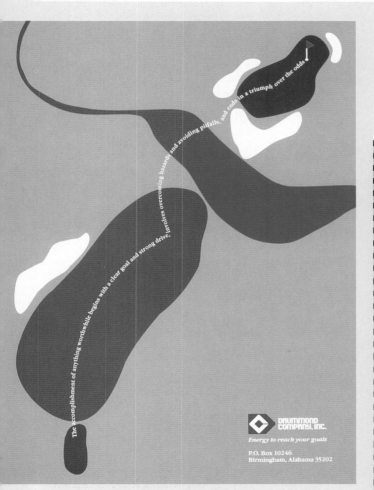

The accomplishment of anything worthwhile begins with a clear goal and strong drive; Involves overcoming hazards and avoiding pitfalls, and ends in a triumph over the odds

DRUMMOND COMPANY, INC.

Energy to reach your goals

P.O. Box 10246
Birmingham, Alabama 35202

Karen Schmoll Art Director
Robin Snow, Karen Schmoll Designers
Sankey 2 Agency
Precision Color Production
Drummond Company, Inc. Client
Birmingham, AL

41

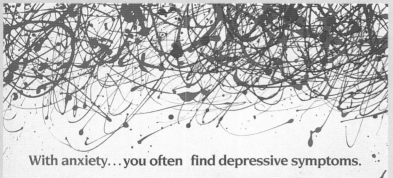

With anxiety...you often find depressive symptoms.

In a controlled trial of 976 outpatients with moderate to severe anxiety, over 70% also exhibited moderate to severe depressed mood. XANAX was significantly more effective than placebo in improving anxiety and the associated depressed mood.

XANAX is well tolerated. Side effects, if they occur, usually disappear with continued medication. Drowsiness and light-headedness are the most commonly reported adverse reactions.

The usual starting dosage of XANAX is 0.25 to 0.5 mg t.i.d.

Xanax
alprazolam Ⓒ

For anxiety with associated depressive symptoms.

Bill Reinwald Art Director
Quang Ho Illustrator
Peter Labadie Copywriter
Frank J. Corbett, Inc. Agency
The Upjohn Company Client
Chicago, IL

nissin
Cup O' Noodles.
Introduces Spicy Chicken Flavor.

TWIN-PACK

This exclusive flavor is chicken with a little zing. We've added red peppers, enhanced the broth, and added a few secret ingredients to an old favorite.

This is made for people who like a bit more *kick* in their cup.

Sachi Kuwahara
   Art Director/Designer/Photographer
Sawcheese Studio Design Firm
Nissin Foods USA Client
Santa Monica, CA

42

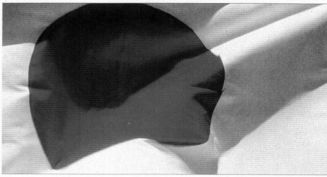

japan
A BILLBOARD SPOTLIGHT

The Japanese entertainment industry has inundated the world market. In 1989 Japan became the #1 Country for Compact Disc Sales and topped its own music sales record!

In this issue, Billboard features Japan's active development in these areas of the industry:
Compact Disc · Records · Tapes · DAT · Artist Tours · Promoters · Retail Marketplace · Home Entertainment Trends · Hardware/Software · Music Publishing

Your ad message in Billboard's annual spotlight on Japan will receive international exposure from Billboard's influential readership · 200,000 in over 100 countries!

For ad details call:
United States
Gene Smith · Associate Publisher
212-536-5001
Tokyo
Aki Kaneko · 03-498-4641
Bill Hersey · 03-498-4641

ISSUE DATE: June 2
AD CLOSE: May 8

Billboard

Angela Giusti Art Director
Elissa Tomasetti Promotion Manager
Sumya Ojakli Promotion Director
BPI Communications, BILLBOARD Magazine
   Client
New York, NY

Congratulations to all our nominated artists

Columbia. Changed with the spirit.

Josephine Didonato Art Director
Bonnie Timmons Illustrator
Joe DePascale Copywriter
CBS Records Client
New York, NY

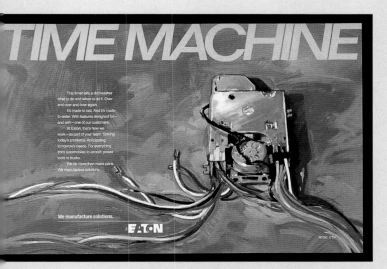

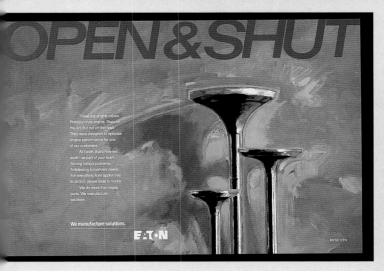

Trade Campaign

Ared Spendjian Art Director
Leonard Sorcher Copywriter
Brouillard Communications Agency
Eaton Corporation Client
New York, NY

MISTY HARBOR
ORIGINAL
RAINWEAR

Cathy Henszey Art Director
Karen Silveira Designer
Loren Hammer Photographer
Henszey & Albert Agency
Quality House of Graphics Production
Misty Harbor Client
New York, NY

Kelly Brown Brehm Art Director/Designer
Paul Pelak, Robert Little Photographers
Arnold Advertising Corp. Agency
Izod Lacoste Golf & Tennis Client
Reading, PA

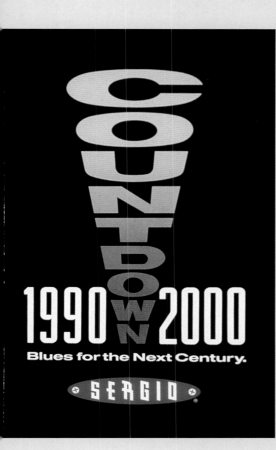

Marc Gobe Art Director/Photographer/Designer
Lee-Anne Shapiro Illustrator/Designer
Michael Shapiro Copywriter
Cato Gobe & Associates Design Firm
Englishtown Sportswear, Ltd. Client
New York, NY

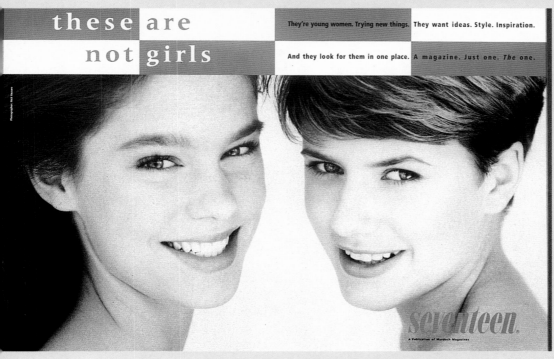

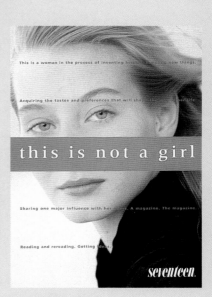

May Liu Art Director
Alan Bodine, May Liu Creative Directors
Nick Vaccaro, Barry Hollywood Photographers
Inadvertant Agency
SEVENTEEN Magazine Client
New York, NY

Paul Curtin Art Director
Leslie Dressel, Bill Hovard Designers
Michal Venera Photographer
Curtin Emerson Ransick Agency
Paul Curtin Design Design Firm
Samsung Semiconductor Client
San Francisco, CA

A SLOW FIFO, IS NO FIFO.

WOOLLY MAMMOTH   FIN-BACKED DIMETRODON   DODO BIRD   SLOW FIFO

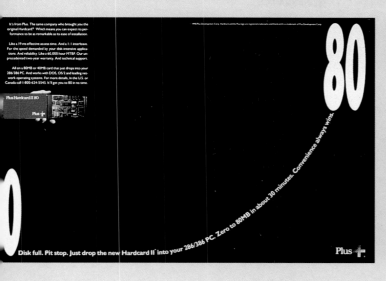

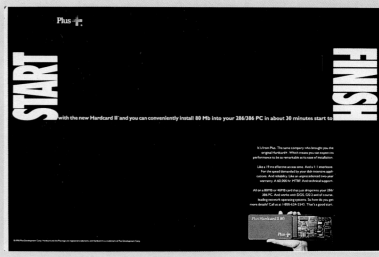

Ken Woodard Art Director
Lynda Pearson Creative Director
Steve Underwood Photographer
Ketchum Advertising Agency
Plus Development Corporation Client
San Francisco, CA

THE MOST POWERFUL REASON FOR STARTING EARLY IS ALSO THE MOST NATURAL.

YOUR WEED AND GRASS CONTROL CAN BE JUST AS EASY.

Richard Shiro Art Director
Carla Stedwell, Millie Olson Creative Directors
Steve Underwood Photographer
Ketchum Advertising Agency
Ciba-Geigy Corporation Client
San Francisco, CA

You can't tell a lot just by looking.

Dean Narahara Art Director
Mark Green Photographer
Laurie Ripplinger Copywriter
Taylor Brown Smith & Perrault Agency
Chevron Chemical Client
Houston, TX

How to tell a good resin   from a bad one.

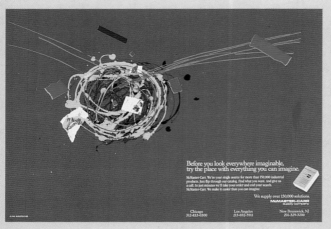

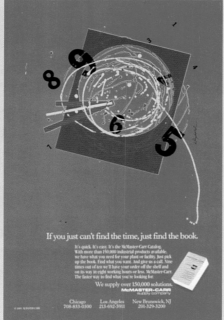

Before you look everywhere imaginable, try the place with everything you can imagine.

If you just can't find the time, just find the book.

Before you find it hard, find it easy.

We supply over 150,000 solutions.

Tom Fath Art Director
Linda Masterson Creative Director
Pat Dypold Illustrator
Ketchum/Mandabach & Sims Agency
McMaster Carr Client
Chicago, IL

This is what you pay for our peripherals.

This is what you get.

The highest quality always comes with the highest price tag. Right?
Wrong. Everex peripherals are different. Why? Because Everex is different.

Say we design a product that's high performance, reliable, chock-full of nifty bells and whistles. Say it's even compatible with all the leading industry standards.

Any other company would consider it an outstanding job. We consider it a job half done.

It's all part of Everex's philosophy. Always innovate. Never compromise. You'll see it all the way across our PC-compatible line — the longest line of peripherals

offered by any company.
So whether you're interested in tape backup systems, modems, graphics boards or memory/multi-function boards, call 1-800-821-0806

for the name of your nearest Everex Reseller.
Chances are, you'll get more product than you need. For less money than you'd expect.

EVEREX

This is what you pay for our super VGA.

This is what you get.

The Everex Viewpoint 16-bit super VGA. It's supported by one of the widest arrays of application drivers available. It's one of

the first to provide 1024 x 768 resolution. And it's expandable to 512K.
But it's designed for a budget that isn't expandable. To find out more, call

1-800-821-0806 for the name of your nearest Everex Reseller.
Chances are, you'll get more graphics than you need. For less money than you'd expect.

EVEREX

This is what you pay for our tape backup.

This is what you get.

Rob Hollenbeck Art Director
Ernie Friedlander Photographer
Michael Ward Copywriter
TFB/BBDO Agency
Everex Systems, Inc. Client
Palo Alto, CA

Even if you didn't know their price, chances are you'd still choose Everex tape backup systems. They're so easy to use, most novices won't even need the

manual. Yet they still offer everything the most sophisticated user could desire, from diagnostic software to automatic schedulers.
To find out more, call

1-800-821-0806 for the name of your nearest Everex Reseller.
Chances are, you'll get more backup than you need. For less money than you'd expect.

EVEREX

48

FOREIGN EXCHANGE. There's a world of evolving technology at International Paper's command. And we funnel it wherever it can make for better products for our customers. Since we acquired France's second-largest paper company, Aussedat Rey, we're sharing with them methods we've perfected for making alkaline papers that stay white for decades. And they're sharing non-impact printing know-how with us. Technology transferred between our Arizona Chemical subsidiary and its Swedish counterpart Bergvik Kemi is creating improved ingredients for products from printer's ink to chewing gum. And advanced graphics techniques developed by our people in Korea add point-of-purchase appeal to food packaging in California. When ideas fly, business takes off. **INTERNATIONAL ⓐ PAPER.** Use our imagination.

MOST COPIED ORIGINAL. International Paper is by far the world's leader in copier paper. Our people at Hammermill pioneered its development. And because our research and development experts work directly with major copier manufacturers, our paper technology moves at just as fast a pace as copier technology. We, for example, were the very first to offer to business a line of papers designed especially for desktop publishing. Today, our papers are not only state-of-the-art, they're tested for quality 38 times. That's why they run through your copiers so beautifully, reliably and fast. Copy after clean, crisp copy. And that's why our leadership in copier paper has never been duplicated. **INTERNATIONAL ⓐ PAPER.** Use our imagination.

ORIENT EXPRESS. We found a very effective way to compete with Japan: sell them something. And so last year alone, we increased sales of International Paper products in Japan and throughout the Orient by an astonishing 45%. The fact is, International Paper is one of America's largest exporters—5,000 shipments of everything from paper pulp to containerboard to timber each year to ports of call on every continent. With the result that more than $1,000,000,000 from some 72 countries Over There is winding up Over Here. The balance of trade actually tipping *our* way for a change. Just imagine. **INTERNATIONAL ⓐ PAPER.** Use our imagination.

Ruthanna Richert Art Director
Mike Quon Illustrator
Terry Scullin Copywriter
BBDO Agency
International Paper Client
New York, NY

Mark Hayosh & Sam Minnella Art Director
Marc A. Williams, Joseph A. Puhy
   Creative Directors
McNamara Associates & Skidmore/Sahratian
   Illustrators
Young & Rubicam, Inc. Agency
Goodyear Tire & Rubber Company Client
Detroit, MI

Unheard of reliability.

WIN phones have a mean time between failure of 6 years. And the industry's best out-of-box reliability.

Which proves the best-made phones aren't necessarily the best-known.

WIN
Communications Corporation
A NIAC COMPANY

Unheard of flexibility.

WIN systems are user-programmable. And they can work behind Centrex.

So you don't have to adapt to us. We adapt to you.

WIN
Communications Corporation
A NIAC COMPANY

The best phone systems you never heard of.

Chances are, you've never heard of WIN. And that's unfortunate.

Because telecommunications experts – and our customers – will tell you the ½ million phones we've sold under the names Marathon and POETS are probably the most dependable, user-friendly key systems ever made.

Here's something else you should know. Recently we became part of Nissho Iwai, an $80 billion global corporation. And we now have the resources we need to get the attention our products deserve.

So why not spend some time with a WIN dealer, exploring the great unknown? Call 1-800-950-UWIN.

WIN
Communications Corporation
A NIAC COMPANY

Art Zimmermann Art Director
Charles Orrico Photographer
Jack Schultheis Copywriter
Kopf Zimmermann Schultheis Agency
Win Communications Corp. Client
Melville, NY

W.S. 195 FT.
57 FT.
225 FT.
12°
T 10

A man with jumbo clients.

When your clients include the world's largest airframe manufacturer, you *better* know about planes. And Jaime Mendez does.

Before joining The Home, and entering the insurance business a dozen years ago, Jaime was in the Air Force.

Today, he's Assistant Vice President of the Major Accounts Property Unit in our San Francisco office.

And when he isn't underwriting jumbo jets, he's underwriting jumbo banks, high-tech firms and hotels. All, Fortune 1000 companies.

These days, The Home is concentrating on *larger, more complex risks* like these. And to do so, we're building a whole new Home around people like Jaime.

Talented, experienced people, who know their business from the ground up.

The Home underwrites Commercial Lines, Major Accounts, Specialty Lines and upscale Personal Lines.

Home Insurance
A subsidiary of AMBASE CORPORATION

THE HOME TODAY

She earned her stripes in pipes.

When we made Jan Noll the head of our Jackson, Mississippi branch, it didn't catch anybody by surprise, exactly.

True, she'd need to be a schoolteacher (in Latin and English, no less), she'd proven herself exceptionally good with people.

Indeed, Jan acquired a small army of admiring colleagues during her 15 years at The Home. And meantime, she managed to underwrite everything from pipelines to the world's largest catfish processor.

At The Home, we're building our entire business around people like Jan Noll. Whether they're Home veterans or newly recruited, they have talents and experience well beyond the ordinary.

You see, we've made a decision to concentrate on larger, more complex risks. To provide consistent, reliable coverage on such risks, for you and your policyholders.

And the only way we can guarantee you coverage like that is to have people like Jan.

The Home underwrites Commercial Lines, Major Accounts, Specialty Lines and upscale Personal Lines.

Home Insurance
A subsidiary of AMBASE CORPORATION

Mel Rustom Art Director/Designer
Marty Umans Photographer
Barry Biederman Copywriter
Biederman, Kelly & Shaffer Agency
The Home Insurance Company Client
New York, NY

WE DON'T JUST SELL YOU A PUMP AND KISS YOU GOODBYE

Many pump companies do exactly that. They love 'em and leave 'em. But that's not the way Flygt does business. You're important to us. We make it our business to be sure you get what you paid for...and more.

Our application engineers will work with you to help select the submersible pump or mixer that's just right for your application. With Flygt there's no guess work. Because Flygt submersibles offer a wider range of horsepower, capacity and heads than you can get from all other manufacturers combined.

And we'll give you something else that you can't get from the other guys... assurance that wherever you are, your submersible pump will get factory authorized service when it's needed. Flygt's nationwide network of authorized factory repair and service centers, each stocked with genuine Flygt spare parts, are only a phone call away. Our truck mounted shop-on-wheels is available coast to coast to provide on-site emergency service.

Flygt is the only submersible pump manufacturer to provide regional training schools, each staffed with field seasoned professionals, to train your personnel to properly service and maintain your investment. Our own in house video production studio supplements this program with periodic video taped service and maintenance tips.

Quality products, quality service and quality training. All available anywhere in the U.S.A....right now. And all backed by almost 50 years of on-line experience.

If you want the best, then why not specify the best...specify Flygt submersible pumps and mixers. Contact your local Flygt representative or Flygt Corporation, Norwalk, CT 06856.

ITT Flygt
ITT Fluid Technology Corporation

FLYGT

WE DON'T JUST SELL YOU A PUMP AND WISH YOU LUCK

A lot of companies are like that. They sell you a piece of equipment and then you're on your own. Flygt doesn't operate that way. You're important to us. We make it our business to be sure you get what you paid for...and more.

Our application engineers will work with you to help you select the submersible pump or mixer that's just right for your application. With Flygt there's no guess work. Because Flygt submersibles offer a wider range of horsepower, capacity and heads than you can get from all other manufacturers combined.

And we'll give you something else that you can't get from the other guys... assurance that wherever you are, your submersible pump will get factory authorized service when it's needed. Flygt's nationwide network of factory authorized repair and service centers, each stocked with genuine Flygt spare parts, are only a phone call away. Our truck mounted shop-on-wheels is available coast to coast to provide on-site emergency service.

Flygt is the only submersible pump manufacturer to provide regional training schools, each staffed with field-seasoned professionals, to train your personnel to properly service and maintain your investment. Our own in-house video production studio supplements this program with periodic video taped service and maintenance tips.

Quality products, quality service and quality training. All available anywhere in the U.S.A....right now. And all backed by almost 50 years of on-line experience.

If you want the best, then why not specify the best...specify Flygt submersible pumps and mixers. Contact your local Flygt representative or Flygt Corporation, Norwalk, CT 06856.

ITT Flygt
ITT Fluid Technology Corporation

FLYGT

Rick St. Vincent Art Director
Edward Powell Copywriter
St. Vincent, Milone & O'Sullivan Agency
ITT Flygt Corporation Client
New York, NY

SCANET HELPS YOU BRIDGE THE GENERATION GAP.

[body copy]

WHY AN INTELLIGENT NETWORK MIGHT NOT BE SUCH A DUMB IDEA.

SCANET
BY
DATACO

SCANET HAS 85% OF THE INDUSTRY TALKING.

SCANET
BY
DATACO

Mogens Sorensen Art Director
Walter van Lotringen Illustrator
Bergsoe 3 Agency
Dataco A/S Client
Klampenborg, Denmark

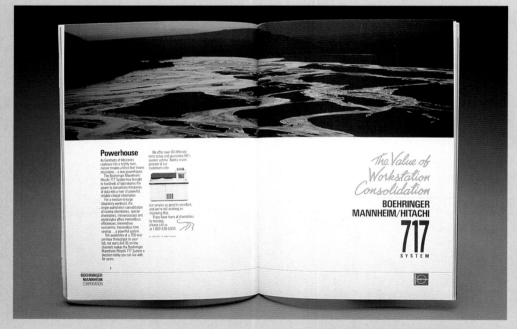

Ann Sugar Art Director
Kay Kilgore Copywriter
Kevin Shaha Account Supervisor
Abelson-Taylor, Inc. Agency
Boehringer Mannheim Corporation Client
Chicago, IL

ROCK AROUND THE CLOCK.

When you get started on a big new excavation project, you naturally want your drilling equipment to operate shift after shift without costly breakdowns. But it's at least equally important for the machines to get a lot of work done in a short time, and finish the job quickly. Preferably ahead of time, which after all is money.

The deciding factor is how well the system of hardware and software functions, as an organic whole. Seen in this perspective, what seemed to be the cheapest solution may well turn out to be a very expensive mistake.

With Atlas Copco you get the maximum return on your investment. Knowing your industry well, we can apply our philosophy on methods and productivity to your problems, and come up with the optimum total solution. With Atlas Copco you can earn more per hour.

ATLAS COPCO MCT AB, S-101 84 STOCKHOLM. TOTAL ROCK DRILLING TECHNOLOGY

Atlas Copco

Goran Thell Art Director
Per Ehrenstrahle Copywriter
Ehrenstrahle & Co. Agency
Atlas Copco Client
Stockholm, Sweden

SAYONARA.

WORTH THE OBSESSION.

YOU CAN BANK ON US.

Robert Billings Art Director
Ron Burkhardt Creative Director
Bob Haigh Copywriter
Pete Turner Photographer
Burkhardt & Christy, NY Agency
BMW of North America, Motorcycles Client
New York, NY

Pity there is no award for badness. Even in the torturous Paris-Dakar Rally, famed for taking no prisoners, one rider and one machine are simply declared the winners.

Which, somehow, doesn't begin to describe the horrific honors of being shaked, baked and sandblasted for twenty-one days over 7000 miles of unremitting rock, desert and goat paths.

The guts and the glory, however, do begin to describe the BMW Paris-Dakar and the BMW R100GS, direct descendants of the recent winners of Paris-Dakar Rallies.

Inarguably they're adventure bikes with integrity to the core. Select components, in fact, are individually X-rayed to analyze their stress values.

Artisans handweld critical junctures in the frame and with feeling, not slam-bam force, they install screws and nuts that are cadmium plated to resist corrosion.

Moreover, each BMW is inspected an average of once every seventy-two seconds. And the people who craft it are proud enough to sign their work twenty-six times.

So once you fill the Paris-Dakar's huge, 9¼ gallon fuel tank, for example, you'll have the confidence to connect the dots on a map any way you see fit.

After all, the largest, fastest machines in their class, the R100GS and the Paris-Dakar, with their 980cc flat twin engines, not only humble an assortment of grueling non-roads, they're equally at home on the interstate.

Speaking of sudden surprises in the earth's contours, BMW's Paralever, patented worldwide, does for each motorcycle's suspension what roots do for trees. The tires are held firmly to virtually any surface.

Unless, of course, you choose the liberating effects of fifty-six foot-pounds of torque which are available at a mere 3,750 rpm's.

Which may partly be why Cycle World observes that the Paris-Dakar is "Wild, wonderful and a little bit wicked," and remarks of the R100GS, "...its uses are limited only by the imagination of its rider."

So talk to your authorized BMW motorcycle dealer. In California, he'll have the R100GS only. But here as elsewhere, he'll always have advice, options and details such as the three-year, unlimited-mileage, limited warranty* and the BMW Motorcycle Roadside Assistance Plan.

And though you could wind up caked with dust from two continents, you could also wind up with a motorcycle that's as bad as its got to be.

BAD TO THE BONE.

WORTH THE OBSESSION.

53

Posters

Oil painting by Paul Pascarella, Taos, NM

Andy Baltimore Art Director
Jacki McCarthy Designer
Paul Pascarella Illustrator
GRP Records Design Firm/Production/Client
New York, NY

Macintosh. The shortest distance from inspiration to reality.

Jan Davis Art Director/Designer
Michael Furman Photographer
Apple Computer Creative Services Agency
Apple Computers Client
Philadelphia, PA

Mike Conboy Art Director
Larry Conely Group Creative Director
Dick Reed Photographer
Wunderman Worldwide Agency
Hill's Pet Products Client
Detroit, MI

1990 INTERNATIONAL TRANS-ANTARCTICA EXPEDITION

OTIS

Gene Mayer Art Director/Designer
Wayne Eastep Photographer
Gene Mayer Associates, Inc. Design Firm
Otis Elevator Company Client
New Haven, CT

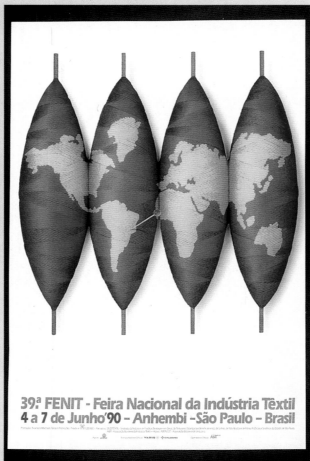

Kat Tragos Art Director
Desmond Hall Copywriter
Young & Rubicam New York Agency
Jamaica Tourist Board Client
New York, NY

Beatriz Faria Santos Art Director
Marcos A. Cezar Photographer
ALMAP/BBDO Communications Ltd. Agency
Alcantara Machado Fairs/Promotion Client
San Paolo, SP, Brazil

Kazuyuki Mori Art Director/Designer
Kunihiro Togawa Photographer
Orikomi Co. Agency
NTT Client
Nagoya, Japan

Paul Davis Art Director/Designer
Paul Davis Studio Design Firm
New York Shakespeare Festival Client
New York, NY

Yusaku Nakanishi Art Director/Designer
Noboru Aoki Photographer
Degree, inc. Design Firm
Loft Umeda Seibu Client
Osaka, Japan

Nelu Wolfensohn Art Director/Illustration
Danielle Surprenant Designer
Graphisme Lavalin Design Firm
Orchestre Metropolitain de Montreal Client
Montreal, Quebec, Canada

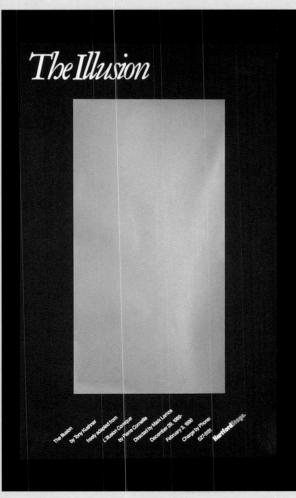

William Wondriska Art Director/Designer
William Wondriska Associates, Inc. Design Firm
The Hartford Stage Company Client
Farmington, CT

Jerry Press Art Director
Yukako Okudaira Designer
Judith Wadia Illustrator
Port Authority of New York and New Jersey
    Agency/Client
New York, NY

"SO WHAT"

Nimm's leicht.
Mit einer Dames bist
Du nie allein.

Charly Frei Art Director
Edmund Petri Creative Director
Uli Burtin Photographer
Young & Rubicam Vienna Agency
Austria Tabakwerke "Dames" Client
Vienna, Austria
"So What - Take It Easy, with a Dames
    You're Never Alone"

Lanny Sommese Art Director/Designer/Illustrator
Sommese Design Design Firm
Penn State Department of Architecture Client
State College, PA

Keisuke-Nagatomo Art Director
Shigeki-Kato Designer
Seitaro-Kuroda Illustrator
Kz Co., Ltd. Design Firm
FM-802 Co., Ltd. Client
Tokyo, Japan

John Sayles Art Director/Designer/Illustrator
Todd Hotchkiss Copywriter
Sayles Graphic Design, Inc. Design Firm
Iowa Architects Council Client
Des Moines, IA

The Art Group Art Direction
Pamela Hanson Photographer
The Art Group Design Firm
Hamiltons Client
New York, NY

Mark Fuller Art Director
Jim Erickson Photographer
Kerry Feuerman Copywriter
Suzanne Paul Agency
Wrangler Jeans Client
Richmond, VA

Paul Sahre, Kent Smith Designers
Paul Sahre Typography
School of Art, Kent State University Client
Kent, OH

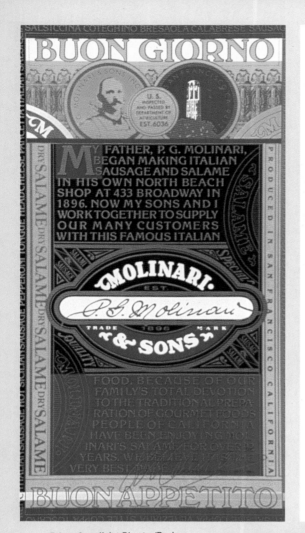

John **Lionti** Art Director
John **Kleber** Illustrator
Liggett-Stashower Agency
The Cleveland International Film Festival
Cleveland, OH

Primo Angeli Art Director/Designer
Mark Jones Illustrator
Primo Angeli, Inc. Design Firm
Molinari & Sons Client
San Francisco, CA

60

Milton Glaser Art Director/Designer
Milton Glaser, Inc. Design Firm
French Government Client
New York, NY

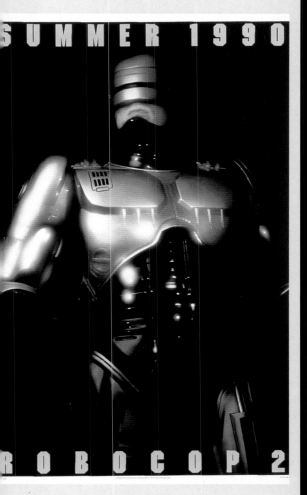

SUMMER 1990

ROBOCOP 2

Brian D. Fox, Mary Trainor Art Directors
William Hawkes Photographer
Luis Sola Title Design
B.D. Fox & Friends, Inc. Agency
Orion Pictures Corp/Tina Tanen Client
Santa Monica, CA

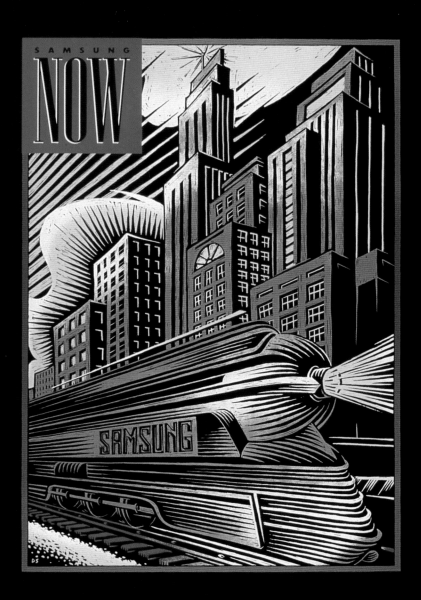

Paul Curtin Art Director
Ignatius Tanzil Designer
Dave Stevenson Illustrator
Curtin Emerson Ransick Agency
Paul Curtin Design Design Firm
Samsung Semiconductor Client
San Francisco, CA

Primo Angeli Art Director/Designer
Mark Jones, Eric Kubly
    Computer Illustration and Lettering
Primo Angeli, Inc. Design Firm
Qantas Airways/
    Australia Week in San Francisco Client
San Francisco, CA

61

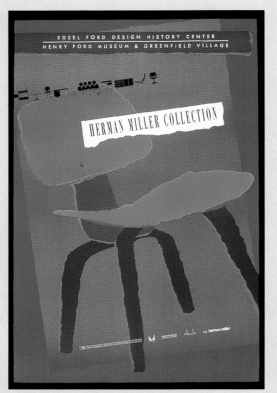

Kerry Burg, Doug Keyes Art Directors
Doug Keyes Designer
Michael Dougan Illustrator
NBBJ Design Firm
The Empty Space Theatre Client
Seattle, WA

Linda Powell Art Director/Designer
Technical Marketing, Inc. Illustration
Henry Ford Museum Client
Zeeland, MI

Chad Farmer Art Director/Designer
Lee Koyel Creative Director
Nancy Santullo Photographer
HDM Inc. Los Angeles Agency
Nissin Foods Client
Los Angeles, CA

Cheryl L. Oppenheim
    Art Director/Designer/Illustrator
Winnie Klotz Photographer
Meg Galea, David Eng Producers
Metropolitan Opera Guild Design
    Design Firm/Client
New York, NY

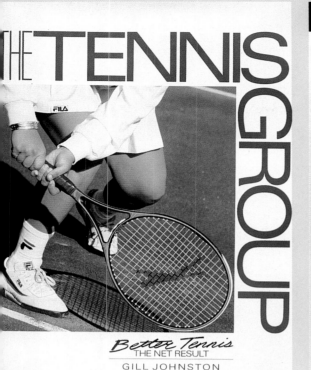

John D. Adams Art Director/Designer
Robbie Roberts Photographer
John Crussen Copywriter
Adams & Associates, Ltd. Client
Toronto, Ontario, Canada

Jeffrey Keyton Art Director
Stacy Drummond, Steve Byram Designers
Andrew Moore Photographer
MTV Networks Creative Services Agency
MTV Music Television Client
New York, NY

Keizo Matsui Art Director
Yuko Araki Designer
Nob Fukuda Photographer
Keizo Matsui Associates Agency
Suntory Limited Client
Osaka, Japan

Dorte Zangenberg Art Director
Claus Lembourn Copywriter
Zangenberg & Lembourn EWDB Agency
Politiken Client
Copenhagen, Denmark

Annual Reports

Leandro Arroyo Art Director
Enrique del Rio Designer
Robert Latorre Photographer
Julio Mendez Illustrator
Gerencia Informacion Grafica-VISA Design Firm
Fomento Proa, S.A. de C.V. Client
Monterrey, N.L., Mexico

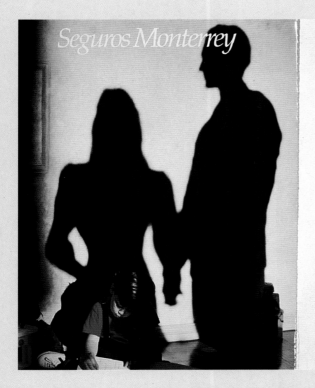

En el año de 1989, las primas totales emitidas en Seguros Monterrey fueron de 619 mil millones de pesos, cifra superior en un 25% en términos reales a la obtenida en 1988, habiendo superado ampliamente las metas establecidas.

Lo anterior, en un ambiente económico donde la industria aseguradora creció sólo el 12%. Así, nuestros esfuerzos nos permitieron incrementar nuestra participación en el mercado total en 1.2 puntos porcentuales, el mayor crecimiento en participación de todas las compañías aseguradoras en México. Con lo anterior, nuestra participación del mercado total durante 1989 fue de 10.9%.

Nuevamente se logró una cifra importante en el seguro de vida individual, al haber emitido 231,075 pólizas, amparando una suma asegurada de 14.3 billones de pesos, cifra mayor en un 36% en términos reales a la puesta en vigor en 1988. Confirmando nuestro liderazgo en el mercado, obtuvimos una participación de 23.8% en este ramo, habiendo continuado la gran aceptación de nuestros productos y la excelente distribución de los mismos por la fuerza de ventas. Las primas iniciales del ramo de vida, vendidas durante 1989, fueron de 170 mil millones de pesos, 2% mayores en términos reales que las de 1988, y el total de primas del ramo de vida ascendió a 322 mil millones de pesos, lo que representa un crecimiento de 19%, también en términos reales. En estas cifras se reflejan los productos de grupo y colectivo. La suma asegurada promedio por póliza en el ramo de vida individual en 1989, fue de 61.9 millones de pesos, que representa un crecimiento real del 46% sobre la del año anterior.

MILES DE MILLONES DE PESOS   –5–   Seguros Monterrey

64

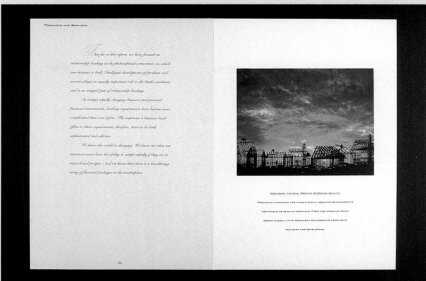

Gary Baker Art Director/Designer
Baker Design Associates Design Firm
First Los Angeles Bank Client
Santa Monica, CA

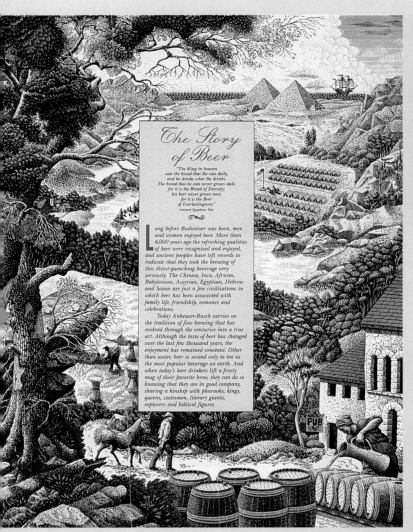

Gerhard Ade Art Director
Pam Picken Designer
Dan Mainzer Photographer
Ade Skunta and Company Agency
GenCorp Inc. Client
Cleveland, OH

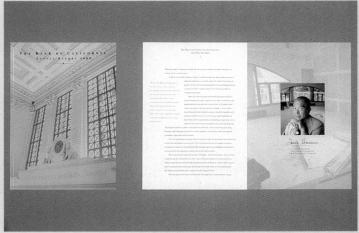

Paul Roy Harmon Art Director
Pam Hawkins, Paul Roy Harmon Designers
Mike Strauss Photographer
Michael Halbert Illustrator
Busch Creative Service Design Firm
Anheuser-Busch Companies Client
St. Louis, MO

David Broom Art Director
Jeff Rutherford, David Broom Designers
Tom Zimberoff Photographer
Broom & Broom, Inc. Design Firm
The Bank of California Client
San Francisco, CA

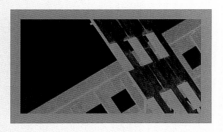

Jim Berté Art Director/Designer
Maxine Gomberg Photographer
Robert Miles Runyan & Associates
  Agency/Design Firm
Electro Rent Corporation Client
Playa del Rey, CA

James A. Stygar Art Director/Designer
Jim Erickson Photographer
Stygar Group, Inc. Design Firm
Cadmus Communications Corporation Client
Richmond, VA

The Houston Food Bank 1989 Annual Report

"I happened to have a pickup truck..."

"They come in and the first thing they do is look in the refrigerator. They're amazed that there's food, and they say, 'But, can I have some, too?'"

Ward Pennebaker, Jeffrey McKay Art Directors
Jeffrey McKay Designer
Beryl Striewski Photographer
Pennebaker Design Design Firm
The Food Bank Client
Houston, TX

Leslie A. Segal Art Director
Victor Rivera Designer
Jim Barber, Harry Benson Photographers
Corporate Annual Report, Inc. Design Firm
Reebok International, Ltd. Client
New York, NY

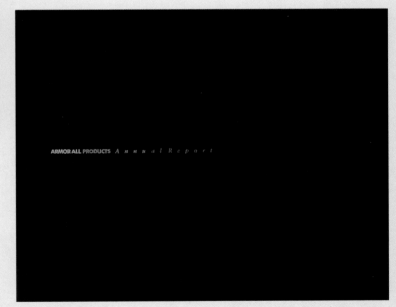

Bryan L. Peterson Art Director/Designer
Jim Simms Photographer
Peterson & Company Design Firm
Centex Corporation Client
Dallas, TX

Michael M. Dula, Larry Pao Art Directors
Larry Pao Designer
Jeffrey Zwart Photographer
Larry Pao Design, Inc. Design Firm
Armor All Products Corporation Client
Costa Mesa, CA

Frank Oswald, Randy Smith Art Directors
Randy Smith Designer/Illustrator
John Still Photographer
Weisz Yang Dunkelberger Design Firm
Centre Reinsurance Corporation Client
Westport, CT

Roslyn Eskind Art Director
Peter Scott Designer
Douglas Forster Photographer
Eskind Waddell Design Firm
Malartic Hygrade Gold Mines (Canada), Ltd.
 Client
Toronto, Ontario, Canada

Carl Seltzer Art Director
Ann Klimasaka Designer
Steve Williams Photographer
Carl Seltzer Design Office Design Firm
Great Western Financial Corporation Client
Newport Beach, CA

Daniel Darst Art Director
Tracy Hubbard, Renee Borsari Designers
Optima Group, Inc. Design Firm
Sotheby's Client
Milford, CT

Albert Ross, Robert Bothell Art Directors
Robert Bothell Designer
Cheryl Rossum Photographer
SGI Graphics, Inc. Design Firm
ITT Corporation Client
Stamford, CT

Martin Miller Art Director
Nancy Lyon Designer
John Olson Photographer
Miller & Pagani, Inc. Design Firm
American Exploration Company Clien.
New York, NY

Martin Miller Art Director
Nancy Lyon Designer
Miller & Pagani, Inc. Design Firm
King World Productions, Inc. Client
New York, NY

Mike Melia Art Director
Mike Melia, Jordan Louie, Mark Steingruber
    Designers
David Guggenheim Photographer
Melia Design Group Design Firm
T2 Medical, Incorporated Client
Atlanta, GE

Jordan Barrett Art Director
Maggy Cuesta, Jordan Barrett Designers
Chris Spollen, Curtis Parker Illustrators
Jordan Barrett & Associates Design Firm
Capital Bancorp Client
Miami, FL

Geoffrey Frost, Ray Behar Art Directors
Ray Behar Designer
Kan Photography Photographer
Strategic Design Center Design Firm
Foote Cone & Belding Communications, Inc.
Client
New York, NY

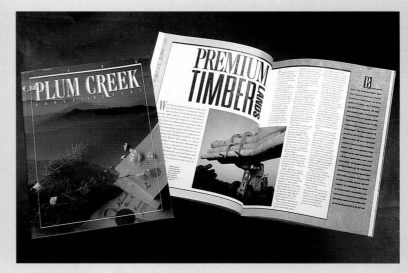

Leslie A. Segal Art Director
Patrina Marino Designer
Gary Galdstone, Jeff Smith Photographers
Corporate Annual Reports, Inc. Design Firm
Olin Corporation Client
New York, NY

Jani Drewfs Art Director
Paula Cox, Jani Drewfs, Denise Weir Designers
Kevin Latona Photographer
Hornall Anderson Design Works Design Firm
Plum Creek Timber Company, L.P. Client
Seattle, WA

71

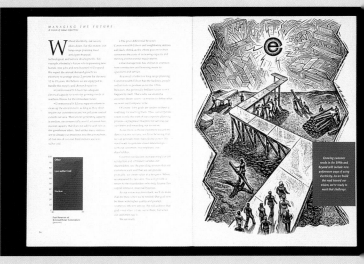

Douglas Oliver Art Director/Designer
Bill Varie Photographer
Margaret Burchett Copywriter
Moravaoliverberte Design Firm
W.M. Keck Foundation Client
Santa Monica, CA

Ron Kovach Art Director
Angela Chpin, Lois Grimm Designers
David Wagenaar Photographer
**Mobium Corporation for Design
    and Communication** Design Firm
Commonwealth Edison Company Client
Chicago, IL

Paula Savage, Kenny Ragland Art Directors
Kenny Ragland Designer
Arthur Meyerson Photographer
Savage Design Group Design Firm
Battle Mountain Gold Company Client
Houston, TX

Louis Gagnon Art Director/Designer
Jean Blais Photographer
Nolin Larosee et Associes, Inc. Design Firm
Sidbec-Dosco, Inc. Client
Montreal, Quebec, Canada

Stan Reed Art Director
Dan Donovan Designer
Joe Paskus Photographer
Reed Design Associates, Inc. Agency
Telephone & Data Systems, Inc. Client
Madison, WI

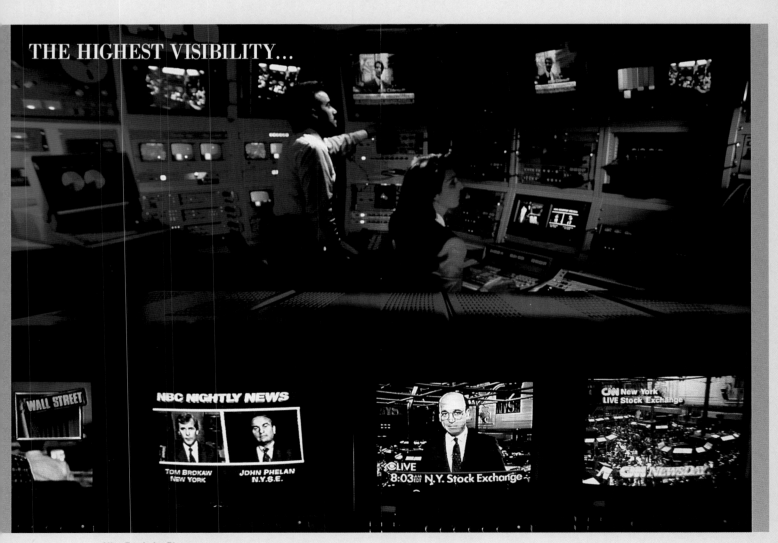

THE HIGHEST VISIBILITY...

Alisa Zamir Art Director
Cecile Hu Designer
Major Photography Photographer
Taylor & Ives, Inc. Design Firm
New York Stock Exchange, Inc. Client
New York, NY

1988

Challenge

The Challenge of the Enterprise

MONY
FINANCIAL SERVICES

HELPING INSURE
A STRONGER AMERICA

AMBAC

Bob Newman Art Director/Designer
Greg Heisler Photographer
Doug Fraser, Warren Gebert, Zita Asbaghi,
   Paul Selwyn Illustrators
Newman Design Associates, Inc. Design Firm
MONY Financial Services Corp. Client
Guilford, CT

William R. Tobias Art Director
Julia Georgiadis, William R. Tobias Designers
Anthony Edgeworth, Neil Selkirk Photographers
Willaim R. Tobias Design, Inc. Design Firm
AMBAC Indemnity Corporation Client
New York, NY

Bob Pellegrini Art Director
Peter Wong Designer
Ovak Arslanian Photographer
Pellegrini & Associates Design Firm
Texaco, Inc. Client
New York, NY

Diana de Lucia, Patricia Kovig Art Directors
Patricia Kovic Designer
Bard Martin Photographer
Luciano Toma Illustrator
Noonan, Russo Communications Agency
Diana de Lucia Design Design Firm
Marrow-Tech, Inc. Client
New York, NY

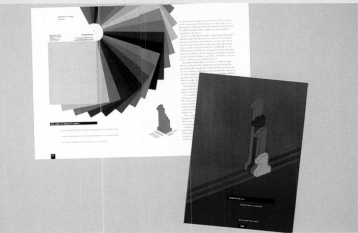

Jennifer Morla Art Director
Jennifer Morla, Marianne Mitten Designers
Tom Tracy Photographer
Guy Billout Illustrator
Morla Design Design Firm
San Francisco International Airport Client
San Francisco, CA

Tor Pettersen, Colleen Crim Art Directors
Colleen Crim, Claire Barnett Designers
Paul Bradforth Photographer
Tor Pettersen & Partners Design Firm
Evode Group PLC Client
London, England

Roger Cook, Don Shanosky
   Art Directors/Designers
Arthur Beck, D.W. Mellor Photographers
Cook and Shanosky Associates, Inc.
   Design Firm
The Black & Decker Corporation Client
Princeton, NJ

Jason Calfo, Michael Aron
   Art Directors/Designers
Barbara Kasten, Harry Callahan, Brian Lanker
   Photographers
Lou Dorfsman Consultant/Illustrator
Calfo, Aron, Inc. Design Firm
International Center of Photography Client
New York, NY

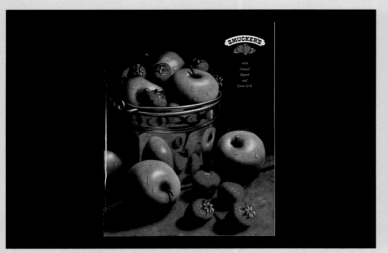

Kim Zarney Art Director
Kathryn Kleinman Photographer
Amy Nathan Food Stylist
The Board Room Design Group Design Firm
The J.M. Smucker Company Client
Cleveland, OH

Len Fury, Tom Ridinger Art Directors
Tom Ridinger Designer
Elliot Erwitt Photographer
Corporate Annual Reports, Inc. Design Firm
SCOR U.S. Corporation Client
New York, NY

Ron Monti Art Director/Designer
Jeremy Green Photographer
Glenn Wells, Ron Monti Illustrators
Ron Monti Designs Design Firm
Morris Goldseker Foundation of Maryland Client
Baltimore, MD

Douglas Wolfe Art Director
Robert Prow Designer
Greg Booth, Tim Bieber Photographers
Richard A. Goldberg Illustrator
Hawthorne, Wolfe, Inc. Design Firm
Southwestern Bell Corporation Client
St. Louis, MO

Ron Jefferies Art Director
Susan Garland, Kenton Lotz Designers
Jim Sims Photographer
The Jefferies Association Design Firm
Baker Hughes Inc. Client
Los Angeles, CA

Kent Hunter Art Director
Saeri Yoo Park Designer/Illustrator
Frankfurt Gips Balkind Design Firm
Associated Press Client
New York, NY

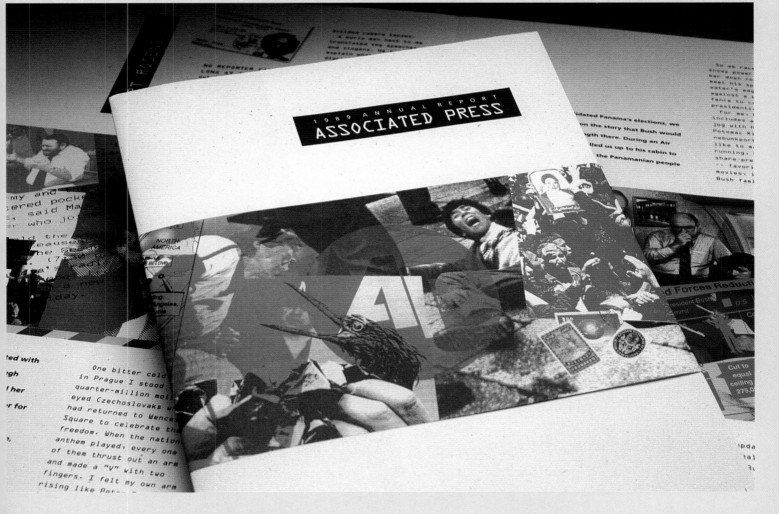

Jim Stanton Art Director/Illustrator
Steven Begleiter, Diane Padys Photographers
Hill and Knowlton, Inc. Agency
The Great Atlantic & Pacific Tea Company, Inc.
  Client
New York, NY

Kan Tai-Keung, Yu Chi-Kong Art Directors
Eddy Yu Chi-Kong Designer
Leong Ka-tai Photographer
Kan Tai-Keung Design & Associates, Ltd.
  Design Firm
Kowloon-Canton Railway Corporation Client
Hong Kong

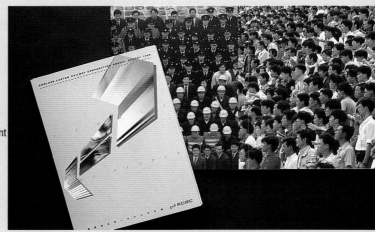

Bill Cahan Art Director
Talin Gureghian Designer
Nikolay Zurek Photographer
Cahan & Associates Agency/Design Firm
GATX Leasing Corporation Client
San Francisco, CA

David Bloch Art Director/Designer
Essay Photography:William Taufic Photographer
Cathie Bleck Illustrator
Bloch Graulich Whelan, Inc. Design Firm
Republic New York Corporation Client
New York, NY

James Cross Art Director
John Clark Designer
Greg Booth Photographer
Cross Associates Design Firm
NCR Corporation Client
Los Angeles, CA

Cherly Lewin Art Director
Raymond Meier, Josh Haskin Photographers
Annie Berkelman Copywriter
Lewin Design Assoc. Design Firm
Tiffany & Company Client
New York, NY

Kerry Leimer Art Director/Designer
Darrell Peterson Photographer
Leimer Cross Design Design Firm
GNW Financial Corporation Client
Seattle, WA

Nelu Wolfensohn Art Director
Danielle Surprenant Designer/Ilustrator
Graphisme Lavalin Design Firm
Lavalin Industries Client
Montreal, Quebec, Canada

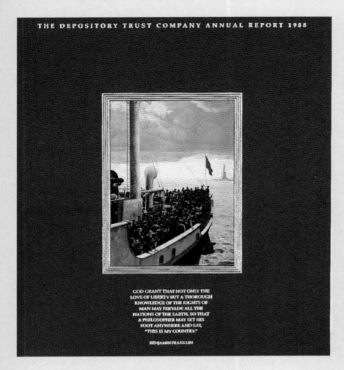

GOD GRANT THAT NOT ONLY THE
LOVE OF LIBERTY BUT A THOROUGH
KNOWLEDGE OF THE RIGHTS OF
MAN MAY PERVADE ALL THE
NATIONS OF THE EARTH, SO THAT
A PHILOSOPHER MAY SET HIS
FOOT ANYWHERE AND SAY,
"THIS IS MY COUNTRY."

BENJAMIN FRANKLIN

Richard Dorzio, Eileen Hedy Schultz
Art Directors
Eileen Hedy Schultz Designer
Michael Hirst, John Olson Photographers
Dean Ellis Illustrator
In-house Design Firm
The Depository Trust Company Client
New York, NY

ⒶⒼⓄⓊⓇⓄⓃ

ⓅⒽⒶⓇⓂⒶⒸⒺⓊⓉⒾⒸⒶⓁⓈ ⒾⓃⒸ

ⒶⓃⓃⓊⒶⓁ

ⓇⒺⓅⓄⓇⓉ

Ⓛ⑨⑧⑨

Douglas Joseph, Rik Besser Art Directors
Rik Besser Designer
Jeff Zaruba Photographer
Besser Joseph Partners Design Firm
Agovron Pharmaceuticals, Inc. Client
Santa Monica, CA

1989 Annual Report

OGDEN

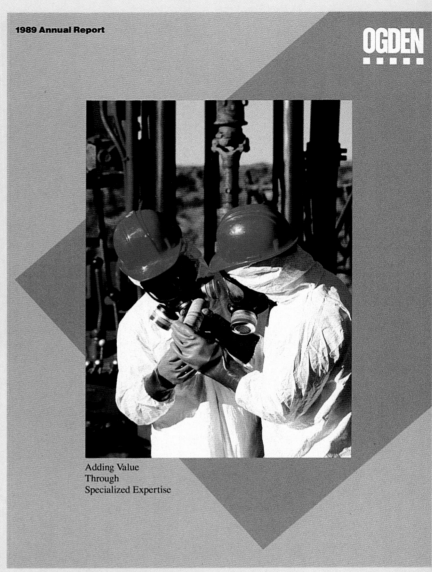

Adding Value
Through
Specialized Expertise

Richard Danne Art Director
Phil Goldberg, Katherine Megrue,
Richard Dunne Designers
Robert Colton Photographer
Richard Danne & Associates, Inc. Design Firm
Ogden Corporation Client
New York, NY

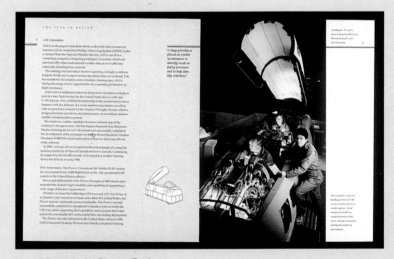

Naomi Burstein Art Director/Designer
Bob Day Photographer
Judy Alter Illustrator
Burstein/Max Associates, Inc. Design Firm
United Industrial Corporation Client
New York, NY

80

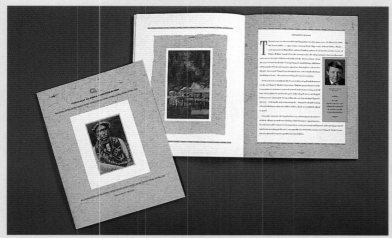

Terri Lynn Burmester Art Director
George Susich Designer
Bradley Communications, Inc. Agency
Chugach Alaska Corporation Client
Anchorage, AK

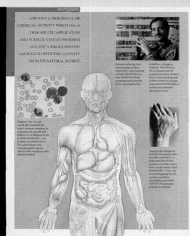

Hoi L. Chu Art Director
Ben Perez Designer
Tobey Sanford Photographer
H.L. Chu & Company, Ltd. Design Firm
Genetics Institute, Inc. Client
New York, NY

Marco de Plano Art Director
Lorena Suri, Julia Roederer Designers
Ty Hyon, Paul Kopelow, Ken Haas
    Photographers
De Plano Design, Inc. Agency
Church & Dwight Company, Inc. Client
New York, NY

Robert Adam Art Director
Ralph James Russini, Robert Adam Designers
Harry Giglio, Mark Perrott Photographers
Adam, Filippo & Associates Design Firm
National Steel Corporation Client
Pittsburgh, PA

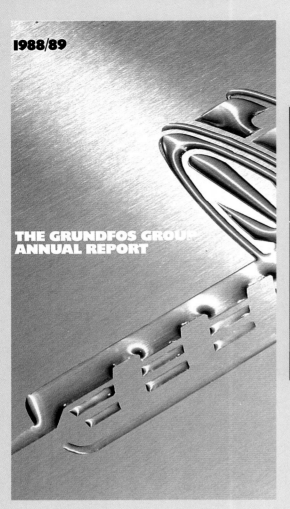

1988/89

THE GRUNDFOS GROUP
ANNUAL REPORT

Malcolm Foster Art Director
Bob Holder Copywriter
Bergsoe 3 Agency
Grundfos A/S Client
Klampenborg, Denmark

Hershell George Art Director/Designer
Dick Frank Photographer
Hershell George Graphics Design Firm
Shorewood Packaging Corporation Client
New York, NY

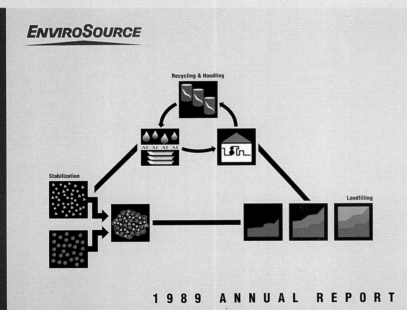

ENVIROSOURCE

Recycling & Handling

Stabilization

Landfilling

1989 ANNUAL REPORT

Brenda L. Mason, Robert L. Meyer Art Directors
Scott Clark, Brenda L. Mason Designers
Brenda L. Mason Illustrator
Gloria Baker Photographer
Robert Meyer Design, Inc. Design Firm
EnviroSource, Inc. Client
Stamford, CT

San Francisco
School Volunteers
1988-89 Report

Abby Herget Designer
Burson-Marsteller Agency
Bianchi Graphics Production
San Francisco School Volunteers Client
San Francisco, CA

Maggie McElvein Art Director/Designer
Gannett Company, Inc. Agency/Client
Arlington, VA

"The problem of humanizing the office environment by changing the look and feel of office furniture does not really get at the whole problem. How offices and office furniture can change at a single person's discretion is an equally important question."

Currently working on projects for Herman Miller's office business, Geoff Hollington is pushing, as a good designer will, our assumptions about the problem and the scope of the solution. That step in the process of creating a lasting design always comes first.

Who's designing our future?

1989 Annual Report
Herman Miller, Inc. and Subsidiaries

Stephen Frykolm Art Director
Derrick Johnson, Stephen Frykholm Designers
Ken Soderbeck Photographer
Herman Miller, Inc. Client
Zeeland, MI

CHICAGO MERCANTILE EXCHANGE®
Annual Report

1988: Market Dynamics Realign

Steve Liska Art Director
Lisa Ouchi-Yamamoto, Steve Liska Designer
Alan E. Cober Illustrator
Liska and Associates, Inc. Design Firm
Chicago Mercantile Exchange Client
Chicago, IL

Aubrey Balkind, Kent Hunter Art Directors
Kent Hunter, Riki Sethiadi Designers
Scott Morgan, Geof Kern, Chris Sanders
  Photographers
Frankfurt Gips Balkind Design Firm
Time Warner, Inc. Client
New York, NY

Time Warner Inc. 1989 Annual Report

WHY?

83

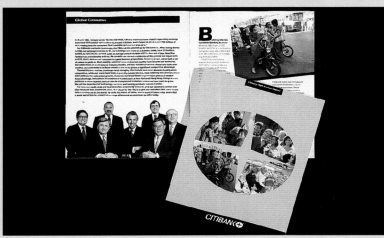

Bruce L. Crocker Art Director/Designer
Bill Gallery, David Witbeck Photographers
Shigeo Fukuda Illustrator
Crocker Inc., Boston Design Firm
Harvard Community Health Plan Client
Boston, MA

Jack Odette Art Director/Designer
Citibank Communication Design Design Firm
Citicorp/Citibank Client
New York, NY

Jurek Wajdowicz Art Director
Lisa LaRochelle, Jurek Wajdowicz Designers
Emerson, Wajdowicz Studios, Inc. Design Firm
Freedom House Client
New York, NY

Fritz Haase, Friedrich Meckseper Art Directors
Jens Noldner Photographer
Friedrich Meckseper Copywriter
Atelier Haase & Knels Design Firm
Verlag Galerie Peerlings, Krefeld Client
Bremen, West Germany

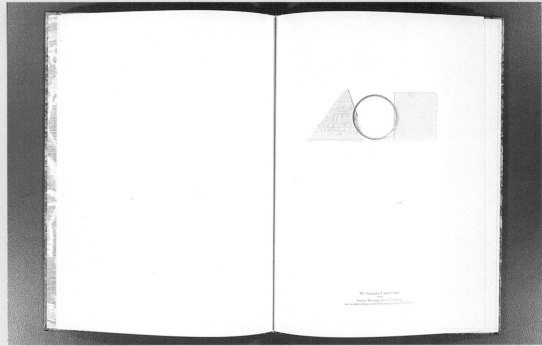

We begin and end with people.

Matsushita Graphic Communication Systems, Inc.

Norio Tamaki Art Director/Designer
Hisashi Kawaguchi, Katsuhiko Tokumaru
    Photographers
CDP Japan Agency
**Matsushita Graphic Communication
    Systems, Inc.** Client
Tokyo, Japan

Barry Shepard, Karin Burklein Arnold,
    Steve Ditko Art Directors
Karin Burklein Arnold, Miles Abernethy
    Designers
Rick Rusing Photographer
Carol Hughes Illustrator
SHR Design Communications Design Firm
Audi of America, Inc. Client
Scottsdale, AZ

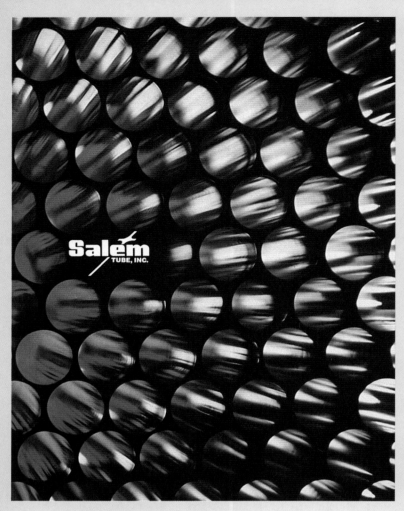

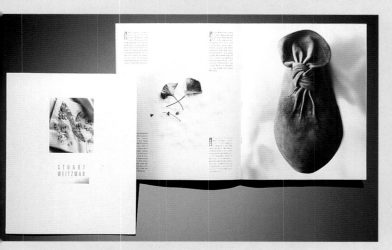

Diana Howard Art Director/Designer
Raymond Meier Photographer
Diana Howard, Inc. Agency
Stewart Weitzman Client
New York, NY

William Snyder, Beth Story Art Directors
Beth Story Designer
William Snyder Design, Inc. Agency
Exxon Chemical Company Client
New York, NY

Karen A. Skunta Art Director/Designer
Barney Taxel Photographer
Ade Skunta and Company Agency
Vitantonio Manufacturing Company Client
Cleveland, OH

Jack Odette Art Director
Nadine Robbins, Mike Focar Designers
Citibank Communications Design Design Firm
Citibank Client
New York, NY

Bob Neufeld Art Director/Designer
Peter Loppacher, Jim Barber, Neil Selkirk
    Photographers
Shearson Lehman Agency/Design Firm
Shearson Lehman Hutton Client
New York, NY

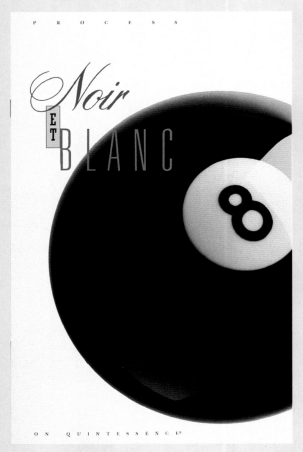

PROCESS

Noir
ET BLANC

ON QUINTESSENCE®

Steve Liska Art Director
Anne Schedler Designer
Liska and Associates, Inc. Design Firm
Potlatch Corporation Client
Chicago, IL

Cheryl Heller Art Director/Designer
Bruce Wulf Photographer
Wells, Rich, Greene, Inc. Agency
S.D. Warren Paper Company Client
New York, NY

Adelaide Acerbi Art Director/Designer
Leo Torri Photographer
Studio Acerbi Agency
Supergres Industria Ceramiche
Albert Ferretti Interiors Client
Milan, Italy

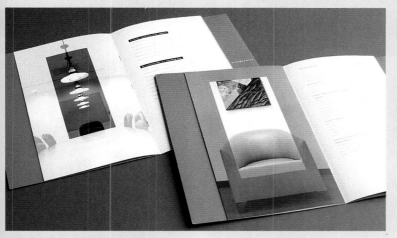

James Cross Art Director
Joseph Jacquez, Lee-Ping Cho Designers
Rick Ueda Photographer
Cross Associates Design Firm
Micronomics Client
Los Angeles, CA

Karin Smatt Creative Director
Smatt Florence, Inc. Agency
Hirshl & Adler Galleries Client
New York, NY

Ken Cook Art Director/Illustrator
Kurt Jennings, Ken Cook Designers
Bright & Associates Design Firm
Royal Caribbean Client
New York, NY

Luann Bice Art Director/Designer
Louis Bencze and client-supplied Photographer
Hornall Anderson Design Works Design Firm
M.A. Segale, Inc. Client
Seattle, WA

Michael Salisbury Art Director/Illustrator
Ben Guevara, Pam Hamilton, Mike Salisbury
   Designers
Mike Funk Photographer
Salisbury Communications Agency/Design Firm
Gotcha Sportswear Client
Torrance, CA

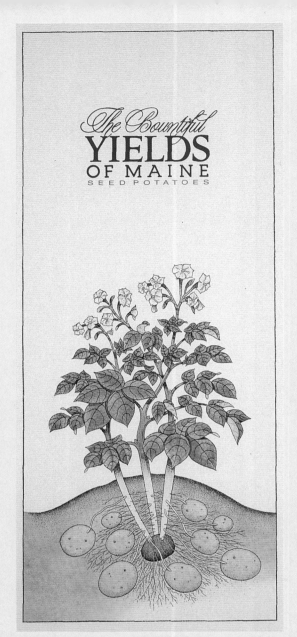

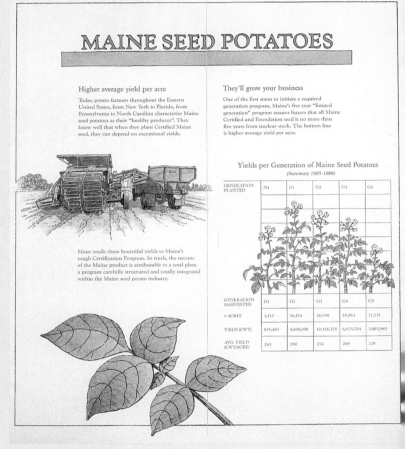

Judy Scribner Art Director/Designer
Connie Tucker Photographer
Marcel LaRue Illustrator
Ad-Media, Inc. Agency/Design Firm
Maine Potato Board Client
Augusta, ME

MAINE SEED POTATOES

Higher average yield per acre

Today, potato farmers throughout the Eastern United States, from New York to Florida, from Pennsylvania to North Carolina characterize Maine seed potatoes as their "healthy producer". They know well that when they plant Certified Maine seed, they can depend on exceptional yields.

They'll grow your business

One of the first states to initiate a required generation program, Maine's five year "limited generation" program assures buyers that all Maine Certified and Foundation seed is no more than five years from nuclear stock. The bottom line is higher average yield per acre.

Many credit these bountiful yields to Maine's tough Certification Program. In truth, the success of the Maine product is attributable to a total plan; a program carefully structured and totally integrated within the Maine seed potato industry.

Yields per Generation of Maine Seed Potatoes
(Summary 1985-1988)

GENERATION PLANTED	N4	G1	G2	G3	G4
GENERATION HARVESTED	G1	G2	G3	G4	G5
# ACRES	3,115	16,174	36,938	25,963	17,731
YIELD (CWT)	819,483	4,698,098	10,118,329	6,975,704	3,883,983
AVG. YIELD (CWT/ACRE)	263	290	274	269	219

Douglas D. Eymer Art Director/Illustrator
Peter Miller Copywriter
Eymer Design Design Firm
AGFA, Compugraphic Division Client
Waltham, MA

Mary Shanahan Art Director/Designer
Pamela Hanson Photographer
Mary Shanahan Design Firm
Josephs Client
New York, NY

Clas Lindman Art Director/Designer
Lindman Advertising, Inc. Agency
Swedish Tourist Board Client
New York, NY

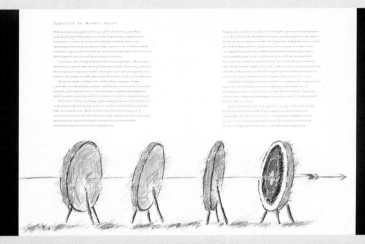

Tor Pettersen Art Director
Nicholas Kendall, Jeff Davis Designers
Zafer Baran Illustrator
Biss Lancaster Agency
Tor Pettersen & Partners Design Firm
SCAPA Group PLC Client
London, England

Port Miolla Association Art Direction/Designer
Stephanie Witham Illustrator
Marketing Corporation of America Agency
Port Miolla Association Design Firm
Levi's Client
South Norwalk, CT

Robert Adam Art Director
Barbara S. Peak, Ralph James Russini
   Designers
Harry Giglio Photographer
Adam, Filippo & Associates Design Firm
Robert Carter & Associates, Inc. Client
Pittsburgh, PA

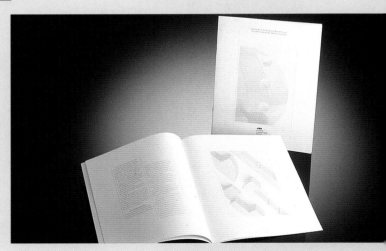

Jim Lingenfelter Art Director
Eric Saulitis Designer
Kamstra Communications, Inc. Agency
Ergodyne Corporation Client
St. Paul, MN

James A. Stygar Art Director/Designer
Stygar Group, Inc. Design Firm
American Wood Council Client
Richmond, VA

Julia Chong Tam Art Director/Designer
Robert Ragsdale Photographer
Julia Tam Design Design Firm
Diamond Bullet Merchandising, Inc. Client
Palos Verdes, CA

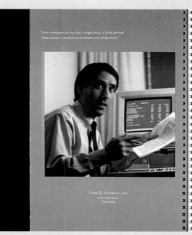

Paul Waner Art Director
Mark Schrader Designer
Dana Duke Photographer
Donaldson, Lufkin & Jenrette Agency
Wood, Struthers & Winthrop Client
New York, NY

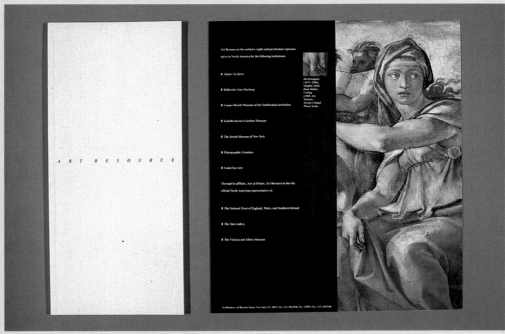

John Caldwell Art Director
Carl Muller Designer
Joe Carlson Photographer
John Caldwell Design Design Firm
Capri Lighting Client
South Pasadena, CA

Daniel Darst Art Director
Anne Endrusick, Renee Borsari Designers
Optima Group, Inc. Design Firm
Art Resource Client
Milford, CT

Peggy Redfern Art Director/Designer
Eric Henderson Photographer
Cole Henderson Drake, Inc. Agency
The Ritz-Carlton Hotel Company Client
Atlanta, GA

Shari Finger Art Director/Designer
Stuart Bakal-Schwartzberg Photographer
Burson-Marsteller Agency
Johnson & Johnson Client
New York, NY

Keith D. Gold Art Director/Creative Director
Stacey Harper Designer
McClean & Friends Illustrator
Gold & Associates Agency/Design Firm
Kight's Copy Center Client
Ponte Vedra Beach, FL

Annette Simon Art Director
Brian Lanker Photographer
Robert Cunningham Illustrator
McKinney & Silver Agency
Norwegian Cruise Line Client
Raleigh, NC

99

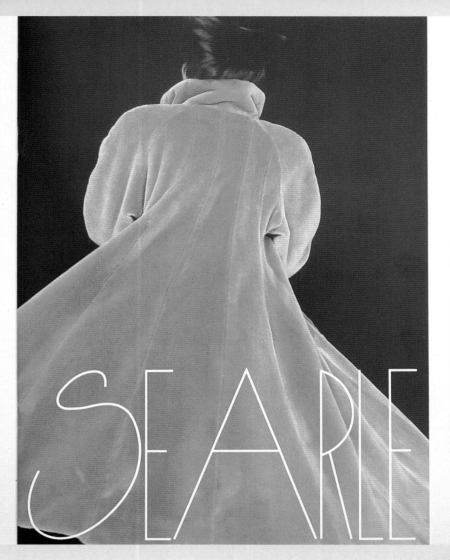

Roy Weinstein Art Director
Louise Kozminski Designer
Eddy Kohli Photographer
Studio Designs NY Agency
Searle Blatt Clothes Client
New York, NY

George Coan, Richard Burns Art Directors
Richard Burns, George Coan Designers
Seymore Mednick Photographer
Leslie Longaker Illustrator
Studio 3 Design Firm
The Vanguard Group, Inc. Client
Philadelphia, PA

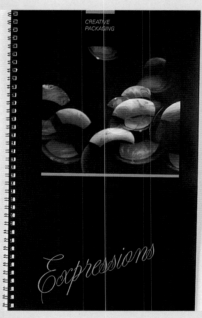

Janet Fried Art Director/Designer
George Kamper Photographer
ICE Communications Agency
Geo. Kamper Productions, Ltd. Design Firm
Bausch & Lomb International Client
Rochester, NY

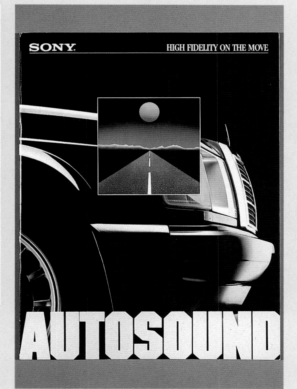

John W. Channell Art Director
George Segnini, Kenny Hall Designers
Bill Ash, Nick Basilion Photographers
Ron Bertuzzi Illustrator
Group One Concept, Inc. Design Firm
Sony Corporation of America Client
New York, NY

Robert Pearlman Art Director/Designer
Anthony Bannister, Phil McCowen,
    Michael Main, Michael Kahn Photographers
United States Agency for International
    Development (USAID) Agency
Robert Pearlmen & Partners Design Firm
Republic of Botswana Client
Darien, CT

Barry Slavin Art Director
Doug Besser Designer
Dennis Manarchy Photographer
Kurtzman/Slavin/Linda Agency/Design Firm
Central Park Athletic Club Client
Northfield, IL

Marie deVera Seiden, Sam Minnella
  Art Directors
Marc A. Williams, Joseph A. Puhy
  Creative Directors
Ken Stidwill, Paul Primeau, Alan Kaplan
  Photographers
Marvin Mattelson Illustrator
Young & Rubicam, Inc. Agency
Lincoln-Mercury Division Client
Detroit, MI

Steve Liska Art Director
Robert Prow Designer
Dave Shipley Copywriter
Liska and Associates, Inc. Design Firm
NEC Technologies, Inc. Client
Chicago, IL

Fred J. DeVito Art Director
Charles Bumgardner Creative Director
Kevin McGuinness, Elizabeth King Designers
Fred J. DeVito, Inc. Agency
Bergdorf Goodman Client
New York, NY

Risto Hankaniemi Art Director
Markku Lahdesmaki Photographer
Reijo Taajaranta Copywriter
Campaign Oy Design Firm
Riku & Maarit Client
Helsinki, Finland

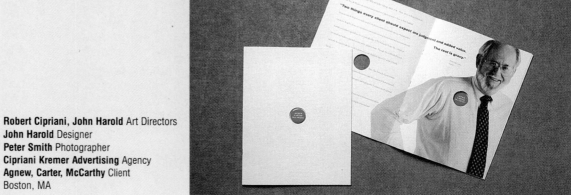

Robert Cipriani, John Harold Art Directors
John Harold Designer
Peter Smith Photographer
Cipriani Kremer Advertising Agency
Agnew, Carter, McCarthy Client
Boston, MA

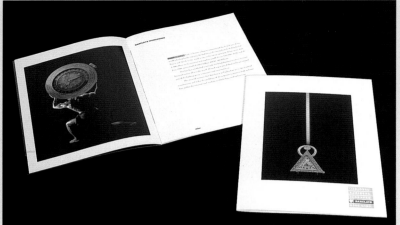

Peter Wong Ming Faye Art Director/Designer
Chiuzac, Ltd. Photographer
Peter Wong Design & Associates, Ltd.
　　Design Firm
Barclays Bank PLC Client
Hong Kong

Dale Henderson Art Director
Marie Poon, Dale Henderson Designers
Gill Alkin Photographer
Henderson & Company Design Firm
Stratasystems Canada, Inc. Client
Toronto, Ontario, Canada

Molly K. Murphy Art Director/Designer
Tom Graboski Associates, Inc. Design Firm
Kron u.s.a. Client
Coconut Grove, FL

Jeffrey Keyton Art Director
Stacy Drummond, Steve Byram Designers
MTV Networks Creative Services Design Firm
MTV Music Television Client
New York, NY

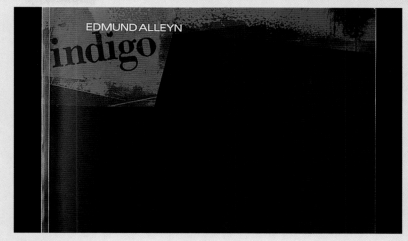

Nelu Wolfensohn Art Director
Lise Charbonneau-Gravel Designer
Charlotte Rosshandler Photographer
Graphisme Lavalin Design Firm
La Galerie d'Art Lavalin Client
Montreal, Quebec, Canada

Jose Serrano Art Director
Tracy Sabin Designer/Illustrator
Knoth & Meads Agency
Sabin Design Design Firm
McMillin Communities Client
San Diego, CA

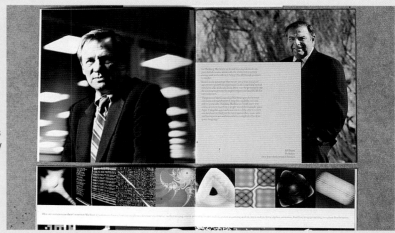

Robert Cipriani Art Director/Designer
John Goodman, Al Fisher Photographers
Cipriani Kremer Advertising, Inc. Agency
Thinking Machines Corporation Client
Boston, MA

Louis F.D. Kelley Art Director
Anne Andreae Designer
Louis Kelley Associates Agency
Kenner Printing Company Client
New Canaan, CT

James O'Mara Art Director/Photographer
James O'Mara, Emmanual St. Juste Designers
Mr. Jax Agency/Client
O'Mara & Ryan Ltd. Design Firm W.
Vancouver, British Columbia, Canada

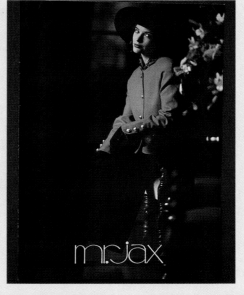

SUNBEAMS and SUNBURN

Loretta Leiva, Marion Jay Art Directors
John Sposato Designer/Illustrator
Anne Cifu Editor
John Sposato Design & Illustration Design Firm
Estee Lauder Client
New York, NY

Clifford Selbert Art Director
Lynn Riddle Designer
Susie Cushner Photographer
Clifford Selbert Design, Inc. Design Firm
Icon Acoustics, Inc. Client
Cambridge, MA

Or do we watch BBC, ITV and BSB?

Or do we watch BBC, ITV, BSB and Sky?

John Pearson-Taylor Art Director
Neal Wilson Photographer
Genesis Design Design Firm
Videotron Cable Communications Client
London, England

Roger Cook, Don Shanosky
  Art Directors/Designers
Arthur Beck, Richard Frank Photographers
Cook and Shanosky Associates, Inc.
  Design Firm
Mead Paper Client
Princeton, NJ

Michael Stetson Art Director
Jill Loewenthal Designer
Frank English Photographer
Metro-North Commuter Railroad Client
New York, NY

Nancy Leung Art Director
Karen Lim, Nancy Leung Designers
Olympia & York, Design &
    Communications Department Design Firm
CityCentre, Edmonton Client
Toronto, Ontario, Canada

Eva Stefenson, Holly Jaffe Art Directors
Rita Winnis Designer
Steven Wallace Photographer
Creative Resources Design Firm
Liz Claiborne, Inc. Client
New York, NY

John Van Dyke Designer
Terry Heffernan Photographer
Heffernan Films Design Firm
Mead Client
San Francisco, CA

Jean Mccartney Art Director/Designer
Steven Randazzo Photographer
In-house Agency
West Point Pepperell, Inc. Design Firm/Client
New York, NY

James Moore Art Director/Designer
Elise M. Geibel Copywriter
Graphic Arts Productions Design Firm
Cushman & Wakefield Client
New York, NY

David Edelstein, Lanny French, Rick Jost,
 Eric Haggard Art Directors
Edelstein Associates Advertising, Inc. Agency
Generra Sportswear Client
Seattle, WA

Susan Nappi Art Director
Carl Corey Photographer
Hollister & Company Agency
Reebok International, Ltd. Client
Wellesley, MA

Sibylle Haase, Fritz Haase Art Directors
Fritz Haase Photographer
Sibylle Haase Illustrator
Atelier Haase & Knels Design Firm/Client
Bremen, West Germany

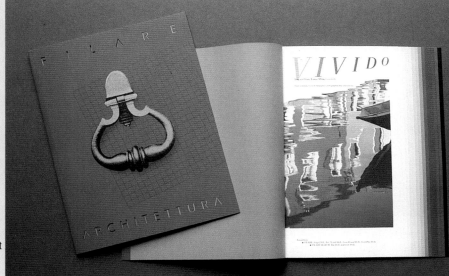

James Cross Art Director
Eric Atherton Designer
Cross Associates Design Firm
Simpson Paper Company Client
Los Angeles, CA

Vasken Kalayjian, Tetsuya Matsuura
  Art Directors
Ron Dube, Vásken Kalayjian Designers
Louis A. Nazario Photographer
Glazer and Kalayjian, Inc. Design Firm
Con Edison Client
New York, NY

Jann Church Art Director
Shelly Beck, Jann Church Designers
Clifford Lester Photographer
Jann Church Partners Adv. & Graphic Design
  Agency/Design Firm
Environmental Systems Research Institute
  Client
Newport Beach, CA

Steven Sandstrom Art Director/Designer
C.B. Harding Photographer
Sandstrom Design Design Firm
AVIA Group International Client
Portland, OR

Donald P. Grodt Art Director
Marc Cohen Photographer
Marinelli Communications, Inc. Agency
Frederick Wildman & Sons, Ltd. Client
New York, NY

Karin Smatt Art Director
Albert Watson Photographer
Smatt Florence, Inc. Agency
Nan Duskin Client
New York, NY

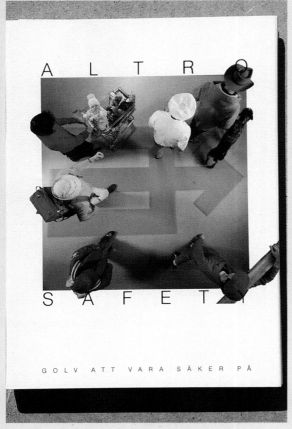

Lars Ransheim Art Director/Designer
Lotta Strahlen Ad Assistant
Peter Jorgensen Photographer
Lars Ransheim Advertising Agency Agency
Altro Nordic AB Client
Falsterbo, Sweden

Klaus Laubmayer Art Director/Photographer
Rosalina Leung Graphic Design
Michele Pietra Stylist
Editorial Service NY Agency
Mirage/Elliot & Kastle, Inc. Client
New York, NY

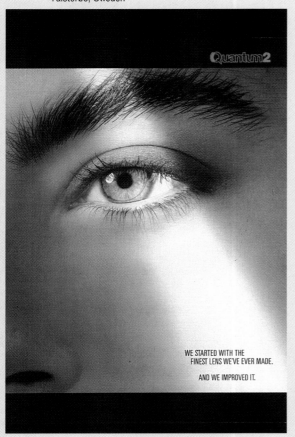

Evelyn Evagash Designer
Karen Leeds Photographer
Mary Driscoll Production
Evagash Design Associates Agency
Risdon Corporation Client
Newtown, CT

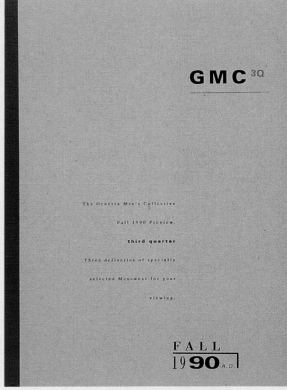

David Edelstein, Lanny French, D. Thom Bissett
Art Directors
Howard Petrella Photographer
Edelstein Associates Advertising, Inc. Agency
Generra Sportswear Client
Seattle, WA

Resource and Referral Service

KLANG-VISIONEN

"TO HEAR WITH EYES..."

Bob Warkulwiz, Mike Rogalski, Bill Smith Art Directors
Bill Smith, Jr. Designer
Mark Riedy, Greg Dearth Illustrators
Warkulwiz Design Associates Design Firm
Citibank Client
Philadelphia, PA

Chris Garland Art Director/Designer
J. Grant Brittain, Henry Groskinsky,
 Jim Matusik, Norman Rothschild,
 Mark Segal Photographers
Wardrop Murtaugh Temple, Inc. Agency
Consolidated Papers, Inc. Client
Los Angeles, CA

Lorenz Meyboden, Regina Spiekermann Art Directors
Atelier Haase & Knels Design Firm
Medias Res Client
Bremen, West Germany

Mogens Sorensen Art Director
Walter van Lotringen Illustrator
Bill Riley Copywriter
Bergsoe 3 Agency
Danish Ministry of Foreign Affairs Client
Klampenborg, Denmark

Be on top of Europe in 1992

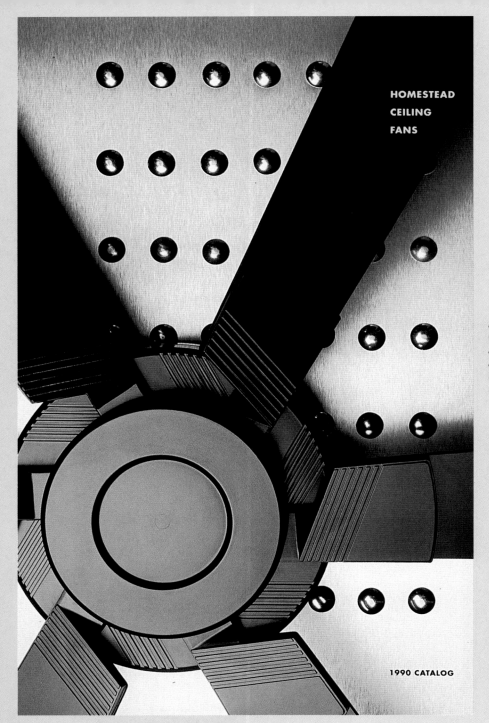

HOMESTEAD
CEILING
FANS

1990 CATALOG

John Caldwell Art Director
Gina Bessire Designer
Joe Carlson Photographer
John Caldwell Design Design Firm
Homestead Ceiling Fans Client
South Pasadena, CA

Jack Carmichael, Linda Meek Art Directors
John Klinger Creative Director
Linda Meek Designer
Northlight Studio Photographer
McNamara Studio Illustration
DMB&B Agency
Cadillac Motor Car Division Client
Bloomfield Hills, MI

114

Louis Goldberg, Kathy Keen Art Directors
Melissa Keenan, Kathy Keen, Louis Goldberg
  Designers
Hill and Knowlton, Inc. Design Firm
Kellogg Company Client
Chicago, IL

Adelaide Acerbe Art Director/Designer
Studio Acerbi Agency
Driade Spa Client
Milan, Italy

Margie Adkins Art Director/Designer
Arthur Meyerson Photographer
Trafton Printing, Inc. Client
Ft. Worth, TX

115

House Organs

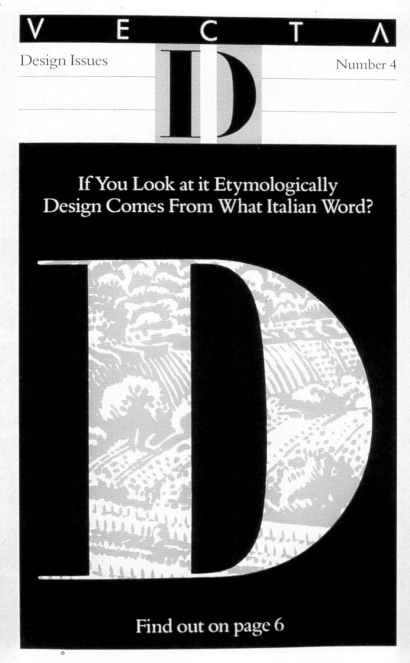

Milton Glaser Art Director/Illustration
George Beylenan Creative Director
Suzanne Zumpano, Alix Corn Designers
Milton Glaser, Inc. Design Firm
VECTA Client
New York, NY

LOCKHEED

HORIZONS

Issue 28

Carl Seltzer Art Director
Michelle Wolins Designer
Russ Underwood Photographer
Carl Seltzer Design Office Design Firm
Lockheed Corporation Client
Newport Beach, CA

117

Mike Melia Art Director
Jordan Louie, Mark Steingruber, Mike Melia
 Designers
Melia Design Group Design Firm
AT&T of Puerto Rico Client
Atlanta, GA

Wolfgang Mueller, Peter Stolvoort Art Directors
Peter Stolvoort Designer
Mueller & Wister, Inc. Agency/Design Firm
Wyeth-Ayerst Laboratories Client
Norristown, PA

Rogert Cook, Don Shanosky Art Directors
Don Shanosky, Roger Cook, Robert Fankle
 Designers
Mary Lynn Blasutta Illustrator
Cook and Shanosky Associates, Inc.
 Design Firm
Squibb Corporation Client
Princeton, NJ

Scott Ray, Jan Wilson Art Directors/Designers
Peter Lacker Photographer
James McGoon Illustrator
Peterson & Company Design Firm
Frito-Lay, Inc. Client
Dallas, TX

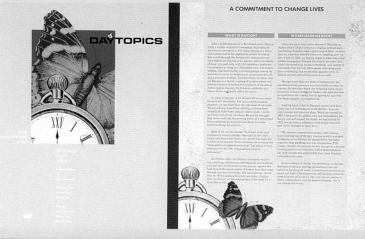

Ken Cook Art Director
Jill Savini, Ken Cook Designers
John Pirman, Philippe Weisbecker Illustrators
Bright & Associates Design Firm
AT&T Client
New York, NY

Ellen Fleury Art Director
Laurie Leifer Creative Director
Michael Buonauro, Paula Moscato, Bob Gatullo
  Photographers
Heliz Communications Agency
Fleury Design Design Firm
Daytop Village, Inc. Client
Huntington Station, NY

Tom Taylor Art Director/Designer
Chuck Egerton, Alan Haywood,
  Marc Pokempner Photographers
Norm Kohn, Kenny Higdon Illustrators
Ranson Taylor Walsh Agency
Northern Telecom, Inc. Client
Reston, VA

Michael Arola Art Director
Robin Campbell, Michael Arola Designers
Sean Thonson, Gastone Jung, David Le Bon,
  James Haefner Photographers
AC&R Advertising, Inc. Agency
Pirelli Armstrong Tire Corporation Client
Irvine, CA

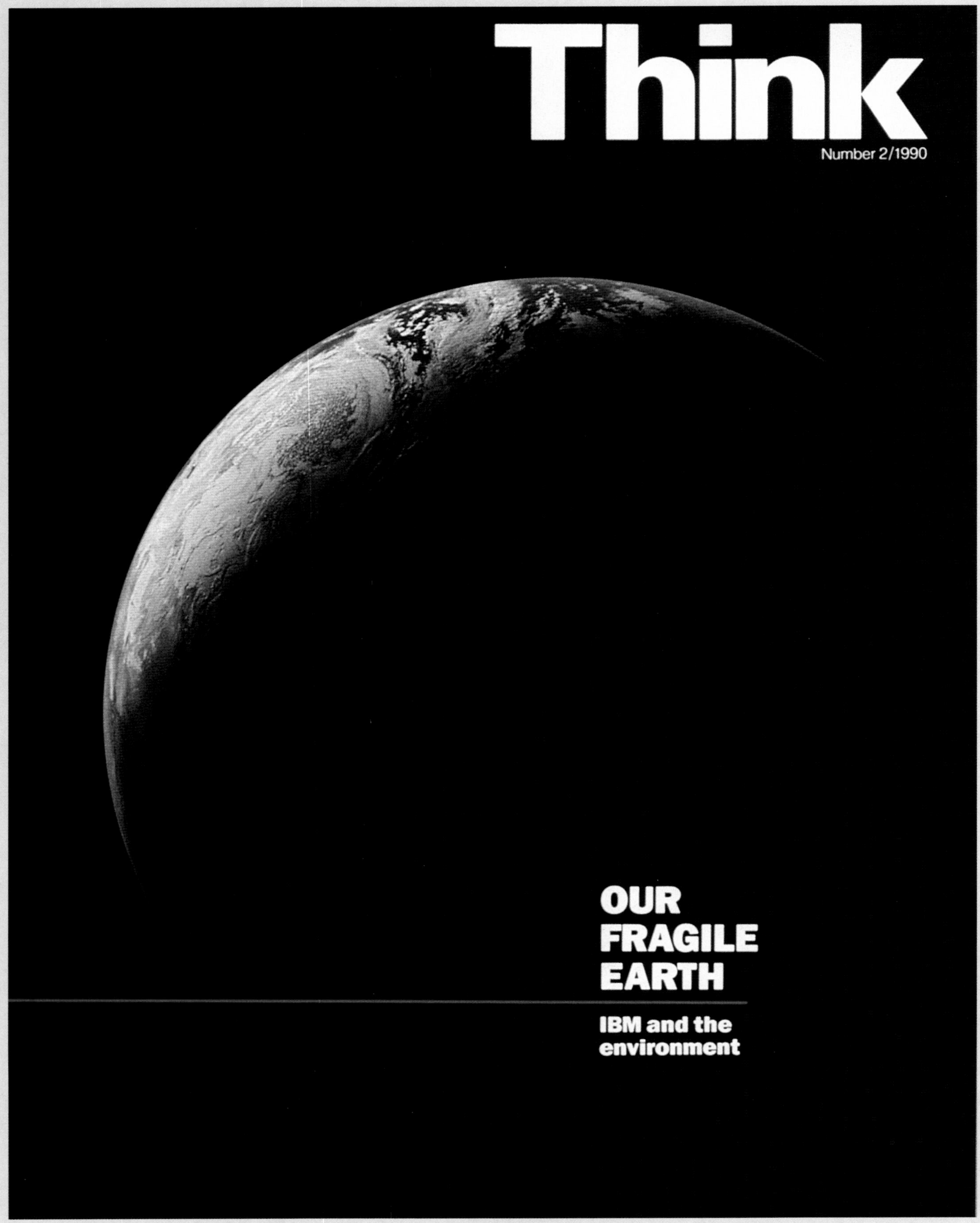

Think

Number 2/1990

OUR
FRAGILE
EARTH

**IBM and the
environment**

One touch of nature makes the whole world kin.
WILLIAM SHAKESPEARE

Respect for the planet

The IBM company has always taken its environmental responsibilities seriously. And we always will. Our continuing resolve is to conduct our business in the safest way possible and to use our technology to help preserve the Earth's fragile ecosystem.

We must ensure that our employees are protected in the workplace, and that their families, friends and neighbors live in communities free of environmental problems caused by our operations. If something does go wrong, we must do what we have always done: dig in and set it right.

Beyond this, I believe that an international company like our own has a special opportunity—and obligation—to use its resources for the benefit of humanity. IBM's main offerings, computer systems, can be an invaluable tool for environmental scientists and planners in assembling data, analyzing trends— even exploring alternative courses of action.

One of IBM's Basic Beliefs is respect for the individual. By being an environmentally responsible company, we are expanding that belief: We are practicing respect for the planet— and for the people who inhabit it.

JOHN F AKERS
CHAIRMAN OF THE BOARD

Ron Couture Art Director
Newsvision Design Firm
THINK Magazine-IBM Corporation Client
Mount Kisco, NY

Acknowledgments

Many people, not all of them named elsewhere in this report, contributed to its preparation. Special thanks are due the following: Joy Steltzner of Corporate Executive Communications; Barbara Burnett of Corporate Environmental Programs; Stephen Quigley and John Back, who are *Think*'s European and Far East correspondents; freelance writers Bob Hawkins and Pat Frischmann; researcher Judith Posner; Ryoko Miyahara of IBM Asia/Pacific Group Communications; and Kyoko Higashi of IBM Japan Employee Communications

SPECIAL CREDITS

Page 17: reprinted by special permission. All rights reserved. H S Bloom Page 19: "Touch" by Walt Jackson from *The Contemporary World Poets* Translated by Robert Fry by permission of Donald Junkins. Edna. Page 20: "The Blue Mountain Clay Road. The Enemy" by Ammon Michael's Translated by Mark Strand. Page 22: from *Mechanism* from *Gosling Films An Anthology of Contemporary Latin American Poetry* © 1942, 1947 by New Directions Publishing Corp. Translated by William Kent Davis. Reprinted by permission of New Directions Publishing Corp. Page 24: from "The Wild Swans at Coole" by William Butler Yeats in *Variety Macmillan Publishing Company* renewed 1947 by Bertha George Yeats. Page 26: from "May Day" from *The Collected Poems* by Sara Teasdale © 1920 by The Macmillan Company copyright renewed 1948 by Mamie T Wheless. Reprinted with permission of Macmillan Publishing Company. Page 28: from "Evening of a Flower" from *Leaves Poetry Quartet* ... by Barbara Howes. © 1966 by Barbara Howes. Page 30: "Autumn" by *Momomondo from An Anthology of Japanese* Court Poetry translated by Daniel H in English. © 1961 by the President and Fellows of Harvard College. Page 34: from "Stones" by Robert Frost from *The Poetry of Robert Frost* © 1916, 1969 by Holt Rinehart and Winston. © 1944 by Robert Frost Reprinted by permission of Henry Holt and Company Inc. Page 36: from "The First Week at Last" by Robert Frost by permission of the poet.

Ralph Hollins

"In the last five years," says Ralph Hollins, "numbers of the red-backed sandpiper stopping at Portsmouth on their migration to the Arctic have declined by 40 percent."

The reason, according to Hollins, a computer performance specialist who retired from IBM United Kingdom in 1988, is population pressure.

Born and raised in the country, Hollins became interested in wildlife at an early age, but it wasn't until his own children were grown that he had time to take it seriously.

As a member of the Hampshire Ornithological Society, he helps monitor seabird populations on the South Hampshire coast. He also devotes 50 hours a year to counting common hedgerow birds as part of a national census. "Bird counting provides the factual basis for arguing conservation issues," he says.

Hollins' contribution to environmental protection continues to grow. As a member of the Hampshire and Isle of Wight Naturalist Trust, he has a say in regional conservation issues.

A hotel group is proposing to recover and build on a disused part of the old Portsmouth harbor. "There's nothing wrong with that," Hollins says, "but they also plan to dam up an adjacent waterway that joins the Langstone and Portsmouth harbors and make an artificial lake, because they say their clients won't want to see mud from their windows when the tide goes out."

Hollins has a dual motivation for his interest in wildlife. "It's exciting finding new species, and I'm also trying to use my retirement to help influence land use decisions so they respect wildlife."

Reggie White

Reggie White is a professional environmentalist. An engineer and former manager of the East Fishkill, N.Y., plant's environmental analysis laboratory, White was a natural choice when the supervisor of his hometown of Poughkeepsie needed people to serve on a resource recovery plant oversight committee.

"I've been a member of the committee for 10 years," says White, whose duties have included evaluating the environmental impact of proposed sites for the plant, searching out possible landfill locations, and inventorying the town's natural resources.

White says the committee meets monthly as a rule, but over the years the time required increased incrementally whenever there was a knotty issue on the agenda.

"We're always trying to do new things," he says of the recycling advisory group.

When one tugs at a single thing in nature, he finds it attached to the rest of the world.
JOHN MUIR
UNITED STATES

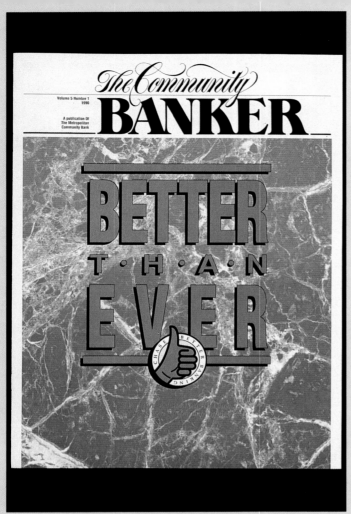

Joe Notovitz Art Director
Gil Livne Designer
Notovitz Design, Inc. Design Firm
Chase Manhattan Bank Client
New York, NY

Wayne Bressler Art Director
Gary Van Dis Creative Director
MB Cunniff Asst. Art Director
Karen Bruere Managing Editor
The NEW YORKER Magazine, Inc. Agency/Client
New York, NY

Barbara Fina Art Director/Designer
Nicholas Wilton Illustrator
Fina Design Communications Design Firm
Pershing Client
New York, NY

Bill Smith, Jr. Art Director
Kirsten Engstrom, Bill Smith, Jr. Designers
Warkulwiz Design Associates Design Firm
Provident National Bank Client
Philadephia, PA

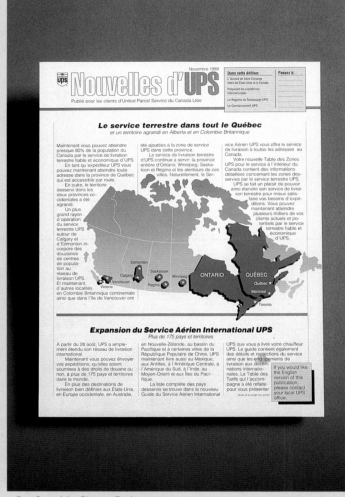

Robert Cooney Designer
R.A. Cooney, Inc. Design Firm
Marine Office of America/Continental Insurance
   Client
New York, NY

Dan Cassel Art Director/Designer
Bob Withstandley Illustrator
Geneva Morrell Copywriter
Dan Cassel Group, Inc. Design Firm
United Parcel Service Client
Stamford, CT

John Brown Art Director
Terri Renigar, Joan Rutledge Designers
In-house Photographer
Jan Lukens Illustrator
In-house Design Firm
R.J. Reynolds Tobacco Co., Public Relations
   Client
Winston-Salem, NC

Bob Pellegrini Art Director
Liz Small-Hildebrandt Designer
Ouak Arslanian Photographer
Pellegrini & Associates Design Firm
Texaco, Inc. Client
New York, NY

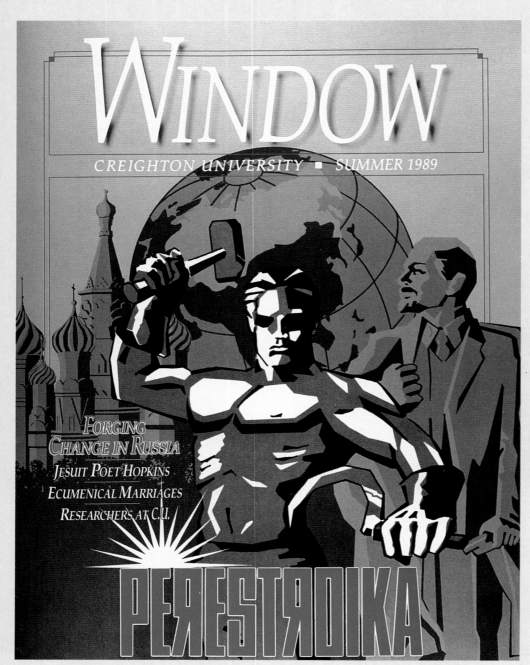

Ray Dotzler Art Director
**Jana M. Martin, Robert U. Guthrie,
Pamela A. Vaughn** Editors
Dotzler Creative Arts Design Firm
Creighton University Client
Omaha, NE

Cliff Johnson Art Director/Designer
Jerry Burns, Roger Grigg Photographers
Raphael Boguslav, Mike Lester Illustrators
Clifford Johnson Design Design Firm
Equifax, Inc. Client
Roswell, GA

John Staresinic **Art Director**
Donna Reveler Designer
Michael Small Photographer
Acart Graphic Services, Inc. Agency/Design Firm
**Professional Association of Foreign
    Service Officers** Client
Ottawa, Ontario, Canada

David Broom Art Director
Kimiko Murakami Chan, David Broom Designers
Broom & Broom, Inc. Design Firm
Chevron Corporation Client
San Francisco, CA

Carl Seltzer Art Director
Ann Kumasaka Designer
Eric Schulzinger Photographer
Carl Seltzer Design Office Design Firm
Lockheed Corporation Client
Newport Beach, CA

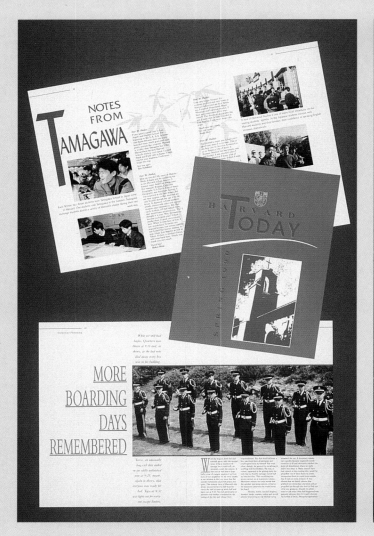

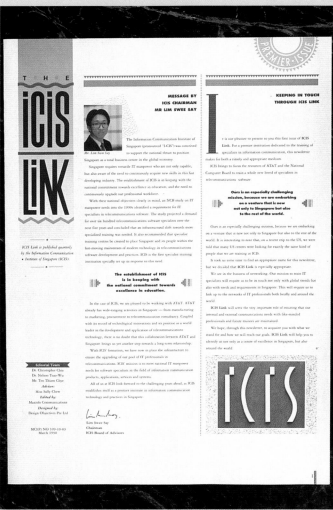

Carl Menifee Wilson Art Director
Steve Shaw Copywriter
Carl M. Information Design Design Firm
Harvard School Client
Pasadena, CA

Ronnie S.C. Tan Art Director
Darrell Bay Hui Kam, Ronnie S.C. Tan Designers
Design Objectives Pte. Ltd. Design Firm
Information Communication Institute
   of Singapore Client
Singapore

Gene Mayer Art Director
Karin Krochmal Designer
Steve Karchin Illustrator
Gene Mayer Associates, Inc. Design Firm
Otis Elevator Company Client
New Haven, CT

John W. Channell Art Director
George Segnini, John W. Channell Designer
Simon Metz Photographer
Group One Concepts, Inc. Design Firm
Performance Network, Inc. Client
New York, NY

Magazine Covers

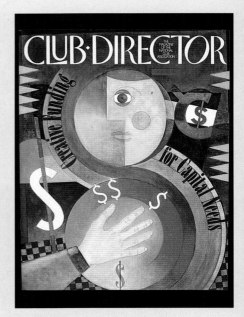

Florian Bachleda Art Director
Buckmaster Photographer
Lisa Kennedy Editor
Edna Suarez Photo Editor
THE VILLAGE VOICE Client
New York, NY

Kathy Kelley Art Director/Designer
Kevin O. Mooney Photographer
CHICAGO Magazine Client
Chicago, IL

Jack Lefkowitz Art Director/Designer
Robert Wasilowski Illustrator
Jack Lefkowitz, Inc. Design Firm
National Club Association Client
Leesburg, VA

Ronnie S.C. Tau Art Director/Designer
Darrel Bay Hui Kam Design Illustrator
Design Objectives Pte. Ltd. Design Firm
Diners Publishing Pte. Ltd. Production
Overseas Chinese Banking Corporation Client
Singapore

Lisa Powers Art Director/Designer
Robert Neubecker Illustrator
RESTAURANT BUSINESS
Bill Communications Client
New York, NY

Patricia Bradbury, Jon Houston, Ron Meyerson
Art Director
Daniel Pelavin Illustrator
NEWSWEEK Client
New York, NY

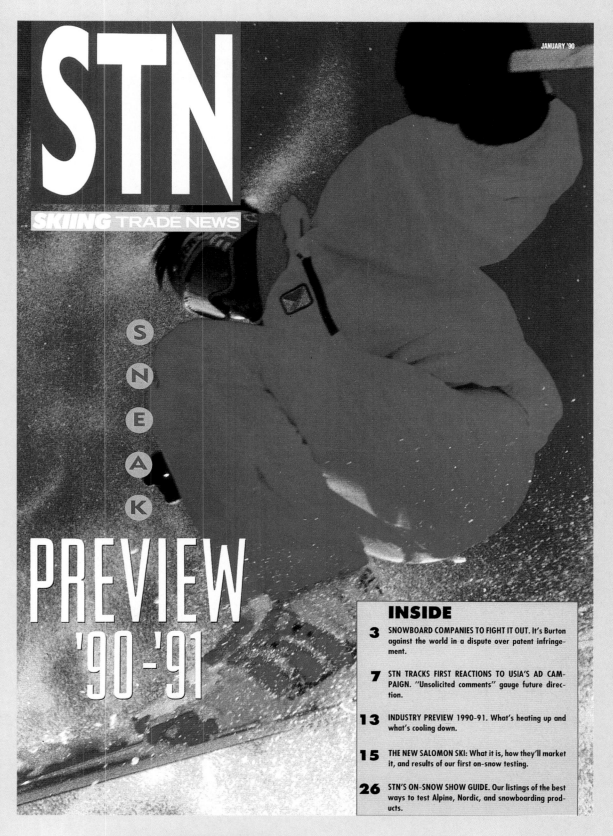

STN
SKIING TRADE NEWS

S
N
E
A
K

PREVIEW
'90-'91

Ann Bennett Art Director/Designer
Allan Laidman Photographer
SKIING TRADE NEWS-Times Mirror Magazines
  Client
New York, NY

JANUARY 1, 1990 $2.50

MAN OF THE DECADE
TIME

Mikhail
Gorbachev

01

724404 1

Rudolph C. Hoglund Art Director
Hans Jorg Limbach Sculptor
Roberto Brosan Photographer
TIME Magazine Client
New York, NY

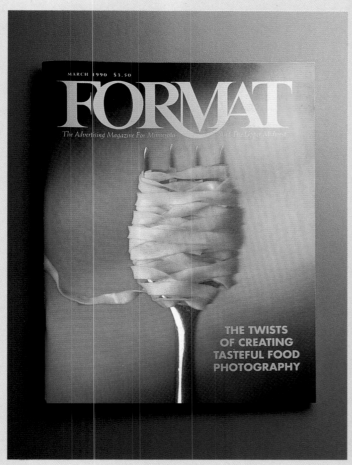

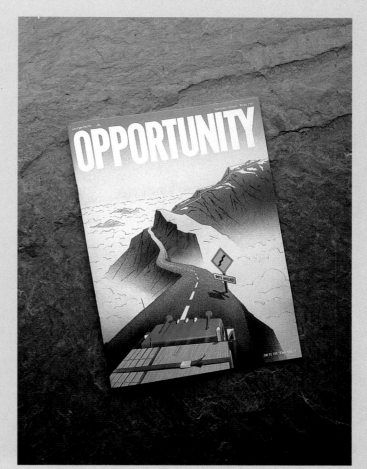

Jim Marvy Art Director
MARVY/Kozo Photographer
FORMAT Magazine Client
Hopkins, MN

Mike Melia, Mark Steingruber Art Directors
Mark Steingruber Designer
Min-Jae Hong Illustrator
Melia Design Group Design Firm
OPPORTUNITY/Georgia-Pacific Corporation
    Client
Atlanta, GA

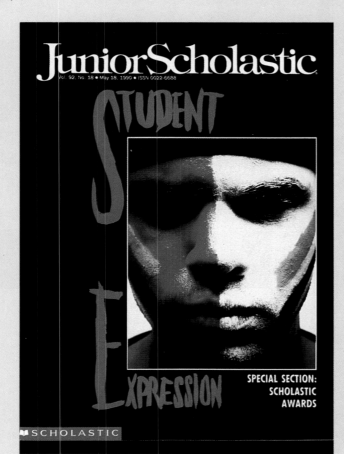

Ellen Jacob Art Director
Glenn Davis Designer
Anthony Lu Illustrator
Scholastic, Inc. Client
New York, NY

Andrew P. Kner Art Director
Paul Davis Illustrator
Paul Davis Studio Design Firm
PRINT Magazine Client
New York, NY

Karl W. Henschel Art Director
W. Liebchen Designer
Gerd Thiel Photographer
Studio Sign Agency/Design Firm
KPMG Frankfurt Client
Frankfurt, West Germany

Karl W. Henschel Art Director
Gerol W. Thiel Photographer
Studio Sign Agency/Design Firm
GWP WIRTSCHAFTSWOCHE Client
Frankfurt, West Germany

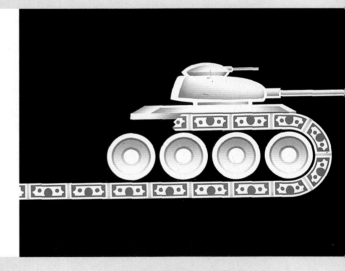

Judy Garlan Art Director/Designer
Nick Gaetano Illustrator
THE ATLANTIC Client
South Orange, NJ

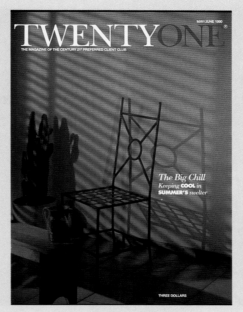

Sandra Ellis Langan Art Director/Designer
Cathy Gendron Illustrator
The Quarton Group-Publishers Agency
The Professional Golfers Association
   of America Client
Troy, MI

Lori Twietmeyer Art Director/Designer
Jasnine Menlove Photographer
The Quarton Group-Publishers Agency
Century 21 Real Estate Client
Troy, MI

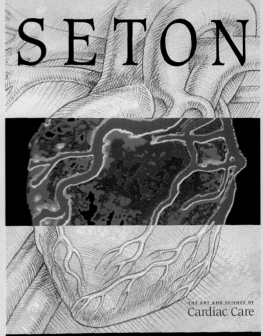

Abby Herget, Kevin Akers Art Directors
Kevin Akers Designer
Gordon Edwardes Photographer
Vince Perez, Ward Schuaker Illustrators
Burson-Marsteller Agency
Seton Medical Center Client
San Francisco, CA

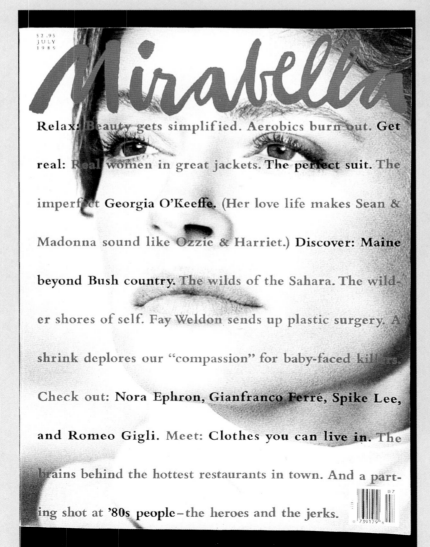

Karen Lee Grant Art Director
Andrzej Janerka, Karen Lee Grant Designers
Richard Gorman Photographer
MIRABELLA Client
New York, NY

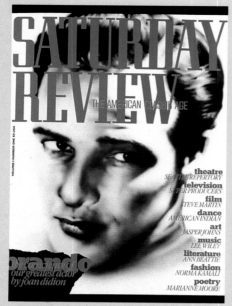

Michael Salisbury Art Director/Designer
Vernita Rae Illustrator
Salisbury Communications Agency/Design Firm
General Media Client
Torrance, CA

Tom Lewis, Jim Sims
    Art Directors/Designers/Illustrators
Lewis Clark & Graham Agency/Design Firm
The Junior League of Atlanta, Inc. Client
Atlanta, GA

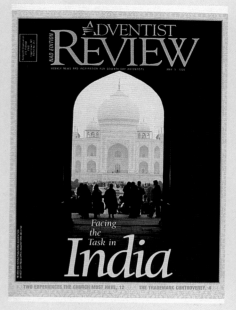

Steve Hall, Bryan Gray Art Directors
Bryan Gray Designer/Photographer
Review & Herald Pub'l Assoc. Agency
ADVENTIST REVIEW Client
Hagerstown, MD

Hall Kelley Art Director/Designer
Terry Hoff Illustrator
Hall Kelley Organization, Inc. Design Firm
Cadence Design Systems, Inc. Client
Sunnyvale, CA

Paul Davis Art Director/Illustrator
Jeanine Esposito Designer
Paul Davis Studio Design Firm
WIGWAG Magazine Company, Inc. Client
New York, NY

Carol Mills Art Director/Designer
Peter Ogilvie Photographer
Mills Associates, Inc. Design Firm
Communications Venture Group, Ltd. Client
New York, NY

Industrial Launderer November 1989

BAR CODING GARMENTS

Jack Lefkowitz Art Director/Designer
Robert Wasilowski, Pam Lefkowitz Illustrators
Jack Lefkowitz, Inc. Design Firm
INDUSTRIAL LAUNDERER Client
Leesburg, VA

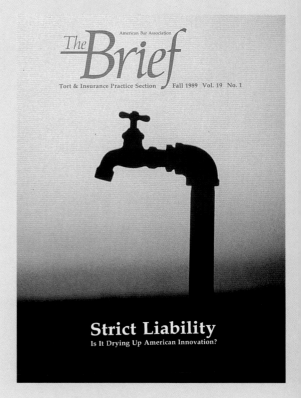

The *Brief*

American Bar Association

Tort & Insurance Practice Section   Fall 1989   Vol. 19   No. 1

Strict Liability
Is It Drying Up American Innovation?

Robert P. Wooley Art Director
Donna Tashjian Creative Director
Mary Anne Kulchawik Design Assistant
Christopher Kean Photographer
Jack J. Podell Director, ABA Press
THE BRIEF-American Bar Association Press
   Client
Chicago, IL

Michael Waitsman Art Director
W.B.Park Designer/Illustrator
Christopher T. Lutz Editor-in-Chief
LITIGATION-The American Bar Association
   Client
Winter Park, FL

ISSUE NO. 188
Contemporary African artists
like Souleymane   Keita of
Senegal reflect   the continent's
rich and varied   art scene

Thaddeus A. Miksinski,Jr. Art Director/Designer
Souleymane Keita Illustrator
United States Information Agency Agency
TOPIC Magazine Client
Washington, D.C.

Harold A. Perry Art Director
Joe Anderson, Harold A. Perry Designers
Jim Richards Photographer
MOTOR Magazine Client
Garden City, NY 11530

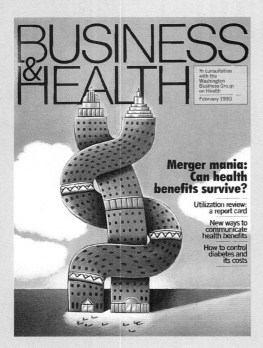

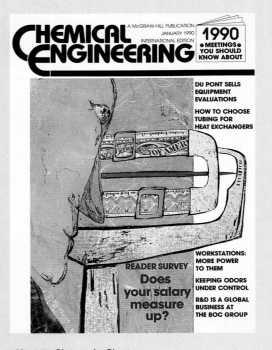

Carol Waters Art Director
Terry Widener Illustrator
Medical Economics Co., Inc. Design Firm
BUSINESS & HEALTH Client
Oradell, NJ

Maureen Gleason Art Director
Marlene Jaeger Assistant Art Director
Gamma One Photographer
Frances Jetter Illustrator
CHEMICAL ENGINEERING Client
New York, NY

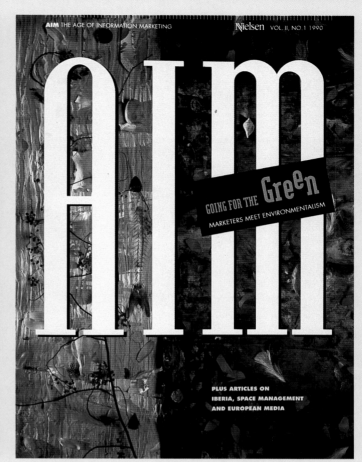

Peter Wong Ming Faye Art Director/Designer
Anthony McHugh Photographer
Peter Wong Design & Associates, Ltd.
 Design Firm
Epicure, Ltd. Client
Hong Kong

Kent Hunter Art Director
Kin Yuen Designer
Hans Neleman Photographer
Paul Leith, J. Otto Siebold, Rob Colvin
 Illustrators
Frankfurt Gips Balkind Design Firm
A.C. Nielsen Client
New York, NY

Jerold Smokler Art Director
Phillip Dixon Photographer
HARPER'S BAZAAR
The Hearst Corporation Client
New York, NY

Fo Wilson Art Director/Designer
Tom Christopher Illustrator
PSYCHOLOGY TODAY Client
Long Island City, NY

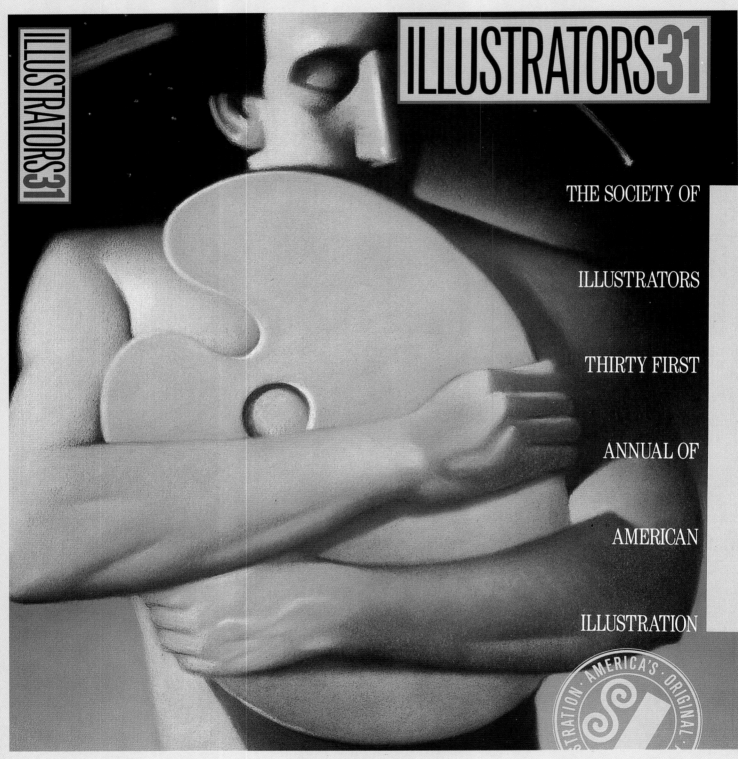

Paul Gamarello Designer
Gary Kelley Illustrator
Madison Square Press Publisher
Eye Tooth Design Design Firm
Society of Illustrators Client
New York, NY

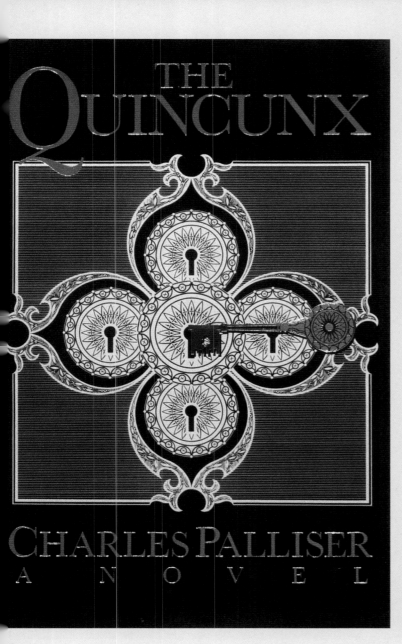

THE QUINCUNX

CHARLES PALLISER
A NOVEL

James Harris Art Director
Andrew M. Newman Designer
Joanne Trovato Illustrator
Andrew M. Newman Graphic Design, Inc.
  Design Firm
Ballantine Books Client
New York, NY

James S. Johnston Art Director
Ann Walston Designer/Letterer
Johns Hopkins University Press Client
Baltimore, MD

MASQUERADE
AND OTHER STORIES BY
ROBERT WALSER

WALSER ∙ MASQUERADE AND OTHER STORIES ∙ JOHNS HOPKINS

TRANSLATED BY SUSAN BERNOFSKY
FOREWORD BY WILLIAM H. GASS

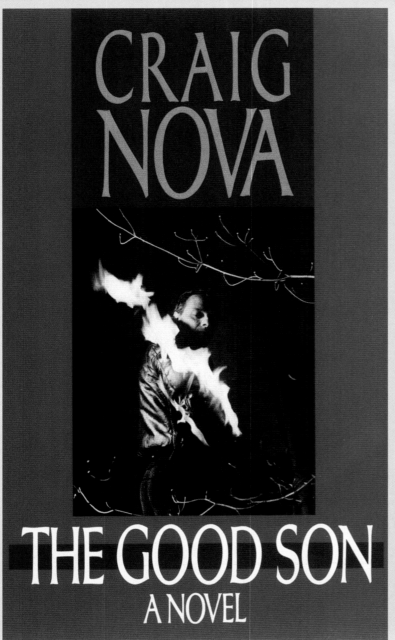

CRAIG NOVA

THE GOOD SON
A NOVEL

Victor Weaver Art Director/Designer
Suzanne Opton Photographer
Dell Publishing Client
New York, NY

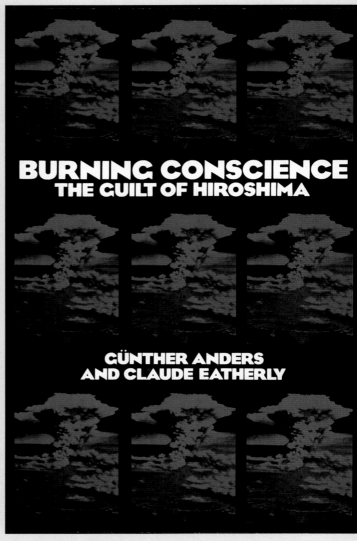

BURNING CONSCIENCE
THE GUILT OF HIROSHIMA

GÜNTHER ANDERS
AND CLAUDE EATHERLY

SOME FREAKS

DAVID MAMET

MORE FROM THE AUTHOR OF WRITING IN RESTAURANTS

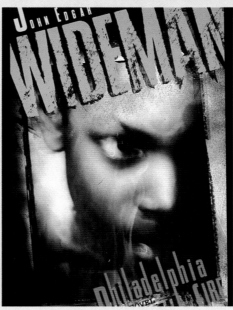

Neil Stuart Art Director/Designer
David Sutan Illustrator
Penguin USA Client
New York, NY

Susan Newman Art Director
Jeffrey J. Fauille Designer
Faville Graphics Design Firm
Paragon House Publishing Company, Inc. Client
New York, NY

Raquel Jaramillo Art Director/Designer
Diana Klein Photographer
Henry Holt and Company Client
New York, NY

140

Kevin Bailey Art Director/Designer/Illustrator
Steven Sessions, Inc. Agency/Design Firm
Battle Publications Client
Houston, TX

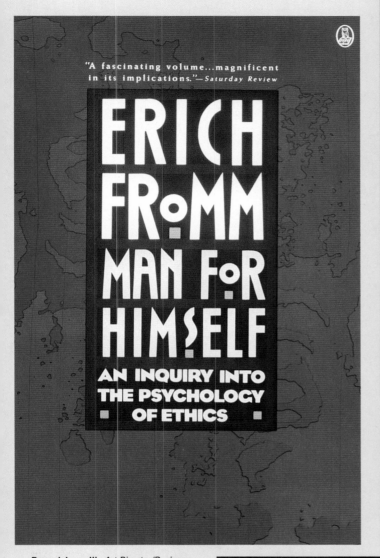

FACE THE SOLUTION

IT ONLY TAKES A MOMENT
BY TOM BATTLE

Raquel Jaramillo Art Director/Designer
Henry Holt and Company Client
New York, NY

Darci D. Mehall Art Director/Designer
Houghton Mifflin Company Client
Boston, MA

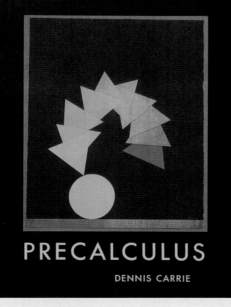

PRECALCULUS
DENNIS CARRIE

BLICKWECHSEL

VANSANT

SWAFFAR   ARENS   SHATTUCK   GÄTTENS

Sandra Gonzalez Art Director/Designer
Houghton Mifflin Company Client
Boston, MA

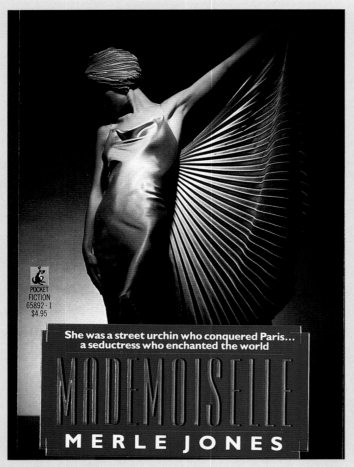

She was a street urchin who conquered Paris...
a seductress who enchanted the world

MADEMOISELLE
MERLE JONES

Bruce Hall Art Director
Onofrio Paccione, Bruce Hall Designers
Onofrio Paccione Photographer
Pocket Books, Inc. Client
New York, NY

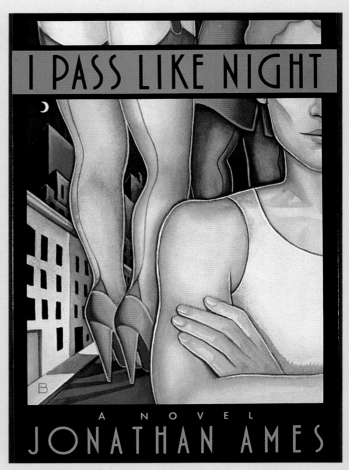

I PASS LIKE NIGHT
A NOVEL
JONATHAN AMES

Cheryl Asherman Art Director
Bascove Designer/Illustrator
Wm. Morrow Client
New York, NY

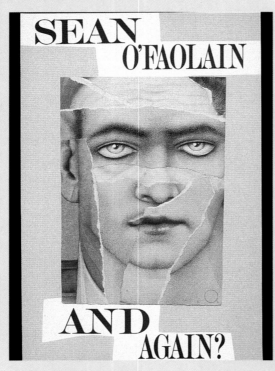

SEAN O'FAOLAIN
AND AGAIN?

Stephen Brower Art Director/Designer
Mel Odom Illustrator
Carol Publishing Group Client
New York, NY

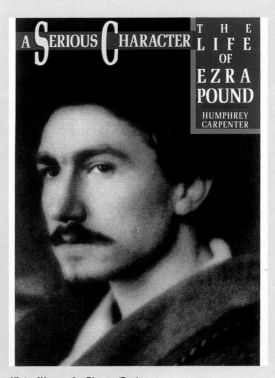

A SERIOUS CHARACTER
THE LIFE OF EZRA POUND
HUMPHREY CARPENTER

Victor Weaver Art Director/Designer
Christine Rodin Illustrator
Dell Publishing Client
New York, NY

142

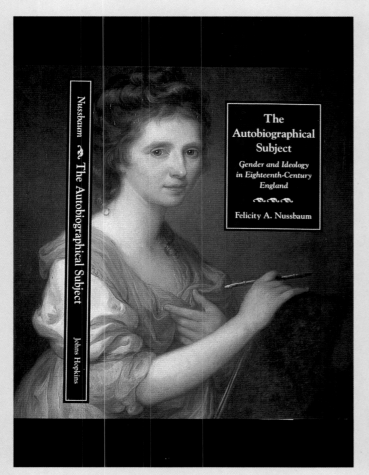

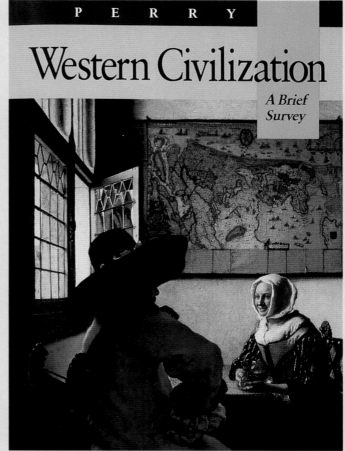

Linda Manly Wade Art Director/Designer
John Lavoie Art Editor
Houghton Mifflin Company Client
Boston, MA

James S. Johnston Art Director
Ann Walston Designer
Johns Hopkins University Press Client
Baltimore, MD

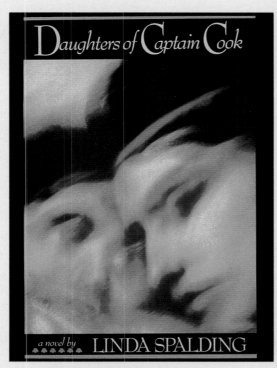

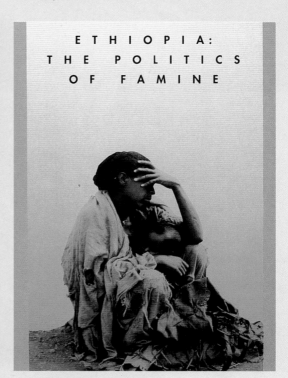

Stephen Brower Art Director/Designer
Michael Ondaatje Photographer
Carol Publishing Group Client
New York, NY

Jurek Wajdowicz Art Director/Designer
Emerson, Wajdowicz Studios, Inc. Design Firm
Freedom House Client
New York, NY

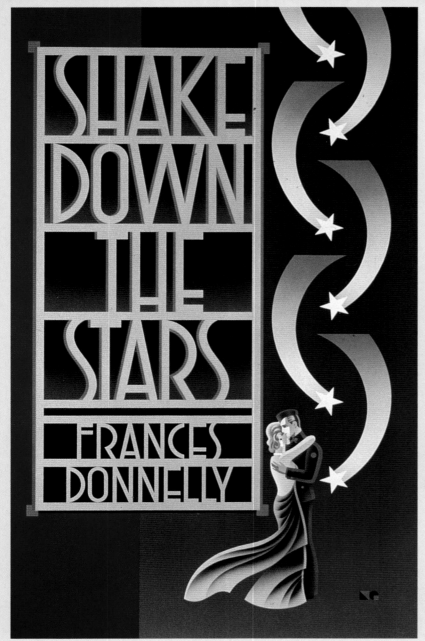

George Paturzo Art Director
Nick Gaetano Designer/Illustrator
St. Martin's Press Client
South Orange, NJ

Neil Stuart Art Director/Desig
Randee St. Nichols Photogra
Penguin USA Client
New York, NY

Morris Taub Art Director
Bob Conge Designer/Illustrator
Conge Design Design Firm
New American Library Client
New York, NY

Stephen Brower Art Director/Designer
James McCarron Illustrator
Carol Publishing Group Client
New York, NY

144

Gerold Counihan Art Director
Andrew M. Newman Designer
Andrew M. Newman Graphic Design, Inc.
    Design Firm
Delacorte Press Client
New York, NY

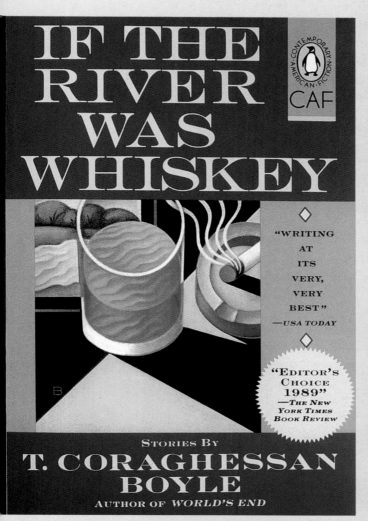

Melissa Jacoby Art Director/Designer
Bascove Illustrator
Penquin USA Client
New York, NY

Stephen Brower Art Director/Designer/Illustrator
Ron Zinn Lettering
Carol Publishing Group Client
New York, NY

Teresa Delgado Art Director
Circa '86 Inc. Designer
Michael G. Merle Photographer
Harper & Row Publishers, Inc.,
    College Division Client
New York, NY

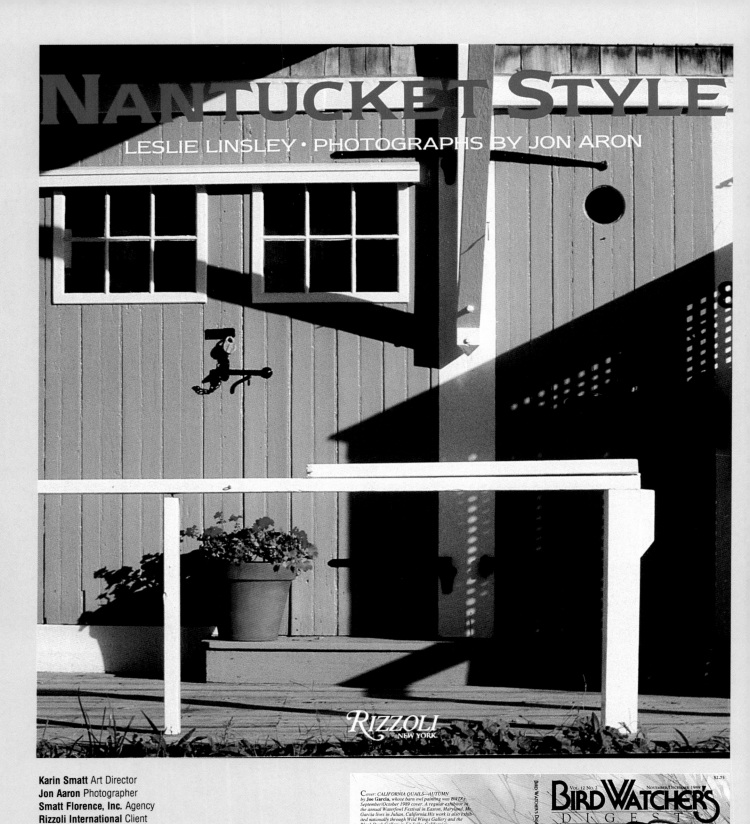

NANTUCKET STYLE

LESLIE LINSLEY • PHOTOGRAPHS BY JON ARON

RIZZOLI
NEW YORK

Karin Smatt Art Director
Jon Aaron Photographer
Smatt Florence, Inc. Agency
Rizzoli International Client
New York, NY

Robert Ayers, John Johanek Art Directors
John Johanek Designer
Joe Garcia Illustrator
Publication Design, Inc. Design Firm
BIRD WATCHER'S DIGEST Client
Allentown, PA

Cover: CALIFORNIA QUAILS—AUTUMN by Joe Garcia, whose barn owl painting was BWD's September/October 1989 cover. A regular exhibitor in the annual Waterfowl Festival in Easton, Maryland, Mr. Garcia lives in Julian, California. His work is also exhibited nationally through Wild Wings Gallery and the Black Duck Gallery in La Jolla, California. (To order a limited edition print of this painting, please see page 93.)

VOL. 12 No. 2   NOVEMBER/DECEMBER 1989 $2.75

BIRD WATCHER'S DIGEST

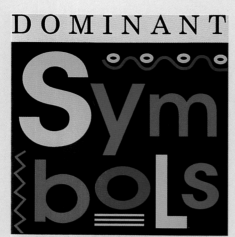

DOMINANT
Sym bols
in Popular Culture
Ray B. Browne, Marshall W. Fishwick
Kevin O. Browne

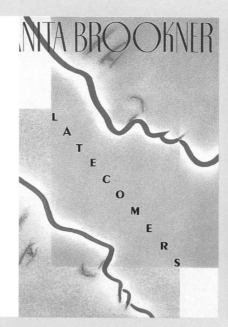

Laura Darnell Dumm Art Director/Designer
Dumm Art Design Firm
Bowling Green University Client
Cleveland, OH

Louis Fili Art Director/Designer
Barbara Nessim Illustrator
Pantheon Books Client
New York, NY

Raquel Jaramillo Art Director/Designer
Photoworld Photographer
Henry Holt and Company Client
New York, NY

Slavney

Perspectives on "Hysteria"

Perspectives on "Hysteria"

Phillip R. Slavney, M.D.

Johns Hopkins

Linda Dickinson Art Director/Designer
Robert Harbison Photographer
Allyn and Bacon Client
Needham, MA

James S. Johnston Art Director
Glen Burris Designer/Letterer
Johns Hopkins University Press Client
Baltimore, MD

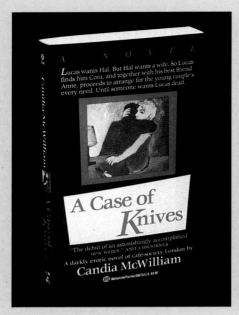

Donald E. Munson Art Director
Barbara Leff Designer
Max Schuman Illustrator
Ballantine, Fawcett, Ivy Books Client
New York, NY

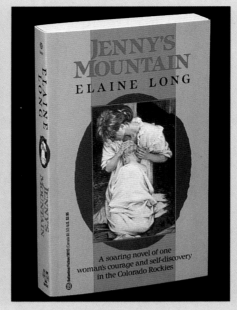

Donald E. Munson Art Director
Kathleen Lynch Designer
Walter Rane Illustrator
Ballantine, Fawcett, Ivy Books Client
New York, NY

Ruth Ross Art Director
Brad Foltz Designer
Sandra Dionisi Illustrator
Ballantine, Fawcett, Ivy Books Client
New York, NY

Mark Anderson, Earl Gee Art Directors
Earl Gee Designer/Illustrator
Geoffrey Nelson Photographer
Mark Anderson Design Design Firm
Z Typography Client
San Francisco, CA

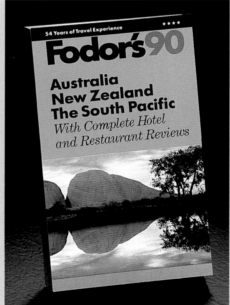

Fabrizio La Rocca Art Director
Vignelli Associates Designer
Karl Tanner Illustrator
Vignelli Associates Design Firm
Fodor's Travel Publications Client
New York, NY

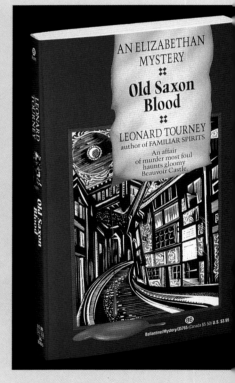

Donald E. Munson Art Director/Designer
Richard Aquan, Stephen Alcorn Illustrators
Ballantine, Fawcett, Ivy Books Client
New York, NY

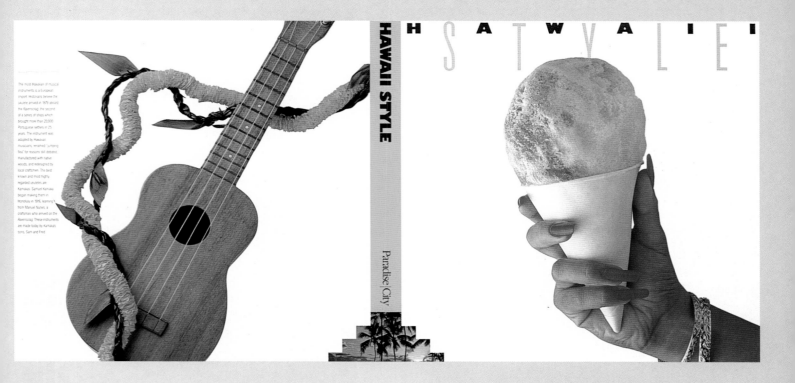

HAWAII STYLE

Paradise City

Kunio Hayashi Art Director
Joy S. Matsuura, Kunio Hayashi Designers
Dana Edmunds Photographer
Media Five Limited Design Firm
Paradise City Client
Honolulu, Hawaii

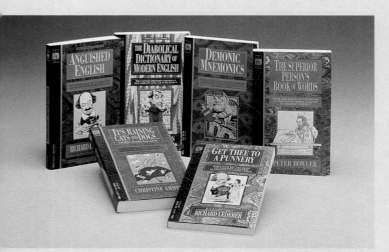

Tree Trapanese, Peggy Leonard, David Un,
   Barbara Van Buskirk Art Directors
John Courtney, Bill Thompson, Cathy Bobak,
   Dennis Corrigan Illustrators
Lorraine Castellano Typography
Designed To Print & Associates Design Firm
Dell Publishing Client
New York, NY

Paul Waner Art Director
Jennifer Fullmer-Constable Designer
James Yang Illustrator
Donaldson, Lufkin & Jenrette Graphics Dept.
   Agency
Donaldson, Lufkin & Jenrette Client
New York, NY

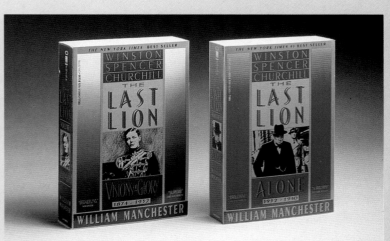

David Un, Peggy Leonard, Tree Trapanese,
   Gerald Counihan Art Directors
Peggy Leonard Designer
Lorraine Castellano Typography
Designed To Print & Associates Design Firm
Dell Publishing Client
New York, NY

149

Record Covers

Stephen Van Handel Art Director/Designer
Van Handel Design Design Firm
Point Of View Records Client
Long Beach, CA

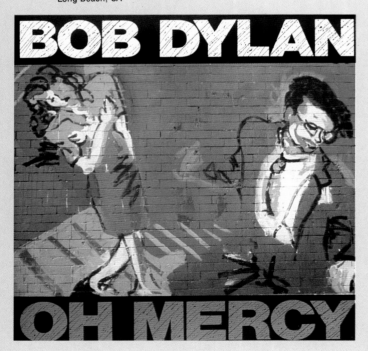

Christopher Austopchuk Art Director/Designer
Trotsky Illustrator
In-house Design Firm
CBS Records Client
New York, NY

Allen Weinberg Art Director/Designer
William King Photo Illustration
Sue Mingus Photographer
In-house Design Firm
CBS Records, Inc. Client
New York, NY

Carol Chen, John Warwicken Art Directors
Chris Musto Designer
Vivid/Id Design Firm
CBS Records Client
New York, NY

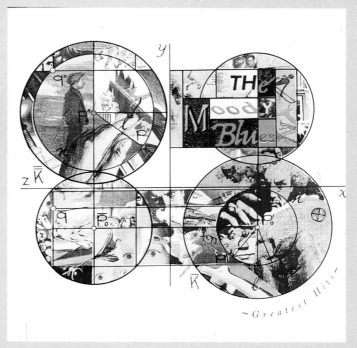

Michael Bays, Margery Greenspan Art Directors
Margery Greenspan Designer/Illustrator
Diana Klein Illustrato
In-house Design Firm
Polygram Records, Inc. Client
New York, NY

Margery Greenspan Art Director
Michael Klotz Designer/Illustrator
In-house Design Firm
Polygram Records, Inc. Client
New York, NY

Michael Bays Art Director
Michael Klotz Designer/Illustrator
In-house Design Firm
Polygram Records, Inc. Client
New York, NY

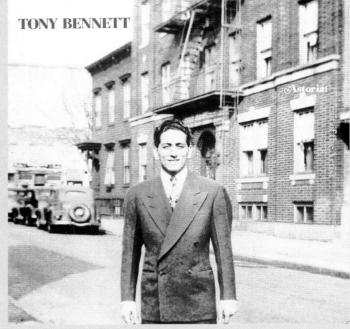

Jeffrey J. Faville Art Director/Designer
Buckmaster Photographer
Faville Graphics Design Firm
Next Plateau Records, Inc. Client
New York, NY

Josephine Didonato Art Director
In-house Design Firm
Polygram Records, Inc. Client
New York, NY

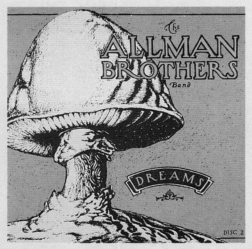

Chris Thompson Art Director
David Lau Designer
In-house Design Firm
Polygram Records, Inc. Client
New York, NY

Michael Bays Art Director
Michael Klotz Designer/Illustrator
In-house Design Firm
Polygram Records, Inc. Client
New York, NY

Marie Rodrigue Art Director
Chantale Audet Designer
StockShot-Four-By-Five Photographer
Verge LeBel Communication, Inc. Design Firm
V'la L'Bon Vent Client
Quebec, Quebec, Canada

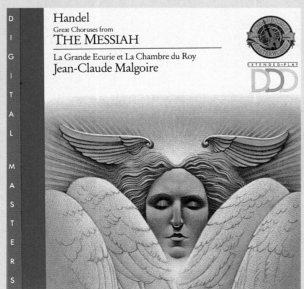

Allen Weinberg Art Director/Designer
Bill Nelson Illustrator
In-house Design Firm
CBS Records, Inc. Client
New York, NY

David Houghton Art Director
Graham Henderson Photographer
Open Circle Design Design Firm
BMG Music Canada, Inc. Client
Oakville, Ontario, Canada

Gunnar Swanson Art Director/Designer/
Photographer/Illustrator
Gunnar Swanson Design Office Design Firm
Metaphor Records Client
Venice, CA

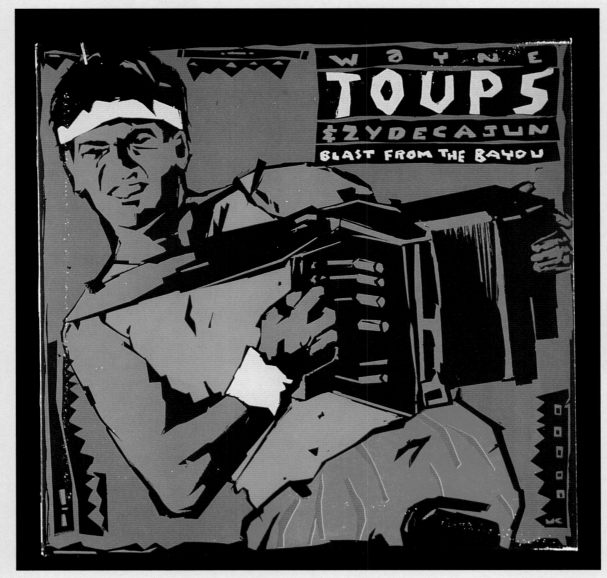

Chris Thompson Art Director
Michael Klotz Designer/Illustrator
In-house Design Firm
Polygram Records, Inc. Client
New York, NY

James O'Mara
   Art Director/Designer/Photographer
Ray Fulber Hand Lettering and Illustration
S.L. Feldman & Associates Agency
O'Mara & Ryan, Ltd. Design Firm
Duke Street Records Client
W. Vancouver, British Columia, Canada

Jim Mokarry Art Director/Designer
J.R. Rost Photographer
Jim Mokarry Design Design Firm
Jing Client
Brooklyn, NY

Arnold Simon Art Director/Designer/Illustrator
Arnold Simon Design Design Firm
Yasmin & Lou Duo-Guitarists Client
Ft. Lauderdale, FL

Y A S M I N & L O U
D U O · G U I T A R I S T S

Albert Kay Associates, Inc.
Concert Artists Management
58 West 58th St., New York, NY 10019-2510

Art and Design: Arnold Simon

Robert Felsenstein Art Director/Designer
Barbara Haum Photographer
In-house Design Firm
Epic Records, Inc. Client
New York, NY

Andy Baltimore Art Director
Jacki McCarthy Designer
Jeff Sedlik Photographer
GRP Records Design Firm/Client
New York, NY

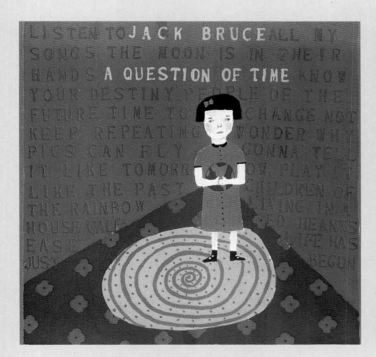

Christopher Austopchuk Art Director/Designer
Laura Levine Illustrator
In-house Design Firm
CBS Records Client
New York, NY

Michael Bays, Patti Drosins Art Directors
Sheryl Lutz-Brown Designer
Caroline Greyshock Photographer
In-house Design Firm
Polygram Records, Inc. Client
New York, NY

Package Design

Josh Freeman Art Director
Dan Cook, Greg Clarke Designers
Laura Smith Illustrator
Josh Freeman/Associates Design Firm
Seika/Artdink Client
Los Angeles, CA

Walter F. Cerny Art Director/Designer
VSG Corp. Agency/Design Firm/Client
Tamarac, FL

Paul Curtin Art Director
Ignatius Tanzil, Peter Locke
    Designers/Illustrators
Paul Curtin Design Design Firm
Cocolat Client
San Francisco, CA

John Sayles Art Director/Designer/Illustrator
ACME Printing Company Production
Norwest Bank Iowa, N.A. Client
Des Moines, IA

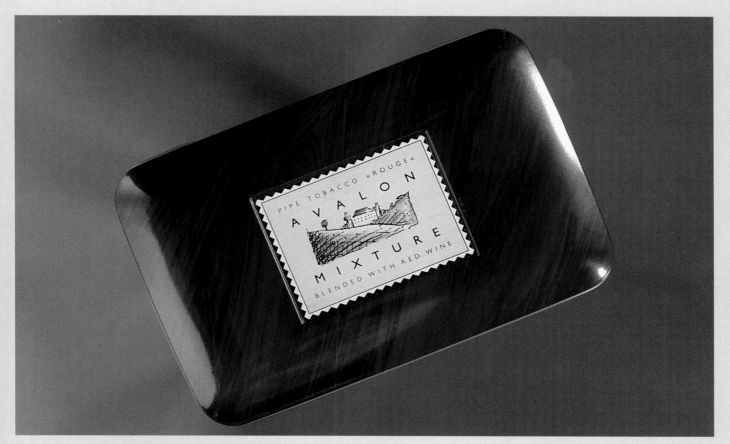

Harald Schweers, Fritz Haase Art Directors
Andreas Wilhelm, Holger Sinn, Maurice Morell
    Designers
Atelier Haase & Knels Design Firm
Stanwell Vertriebs GmbH Client
Bremen, West Germany

157

Courtney Reeser Art Director/Designer
Donata Maggipinto Copywriter
SBG Partners Design Firm
Williams-Sonoma Client
San Francisco, CA

Courtney Reeser Art Director
Mark Bergman Designer
Steve Calarco Photographer
SBG Partners Design Firm
Fenwick, Inc. Client
San Francisco, CA

Ronald Wong Creative Director
Catherine Stano, Dominick Alessandros,
   Gary Stilovich Designers
The Schechter Group Design Firm
Pepsi Cola USA Client
New York, NY

158

Denis Keller Art Director/Designer
Design Board Behaeghel & Partners
  Design Firm
Johnson Wax GmbH Client
Brussels, Belgium

Cindy Berglund Art Director/Designer
Roger Lundquist, Jerry Beglund Illustrators
Cindy Berglund Illustration & Design
  Design Firm
FMG, Tsumura International, Inc. Client
Arden Hills, MN

Henrik Schroder Art Director
Hanne Sogliera Designer
Hammerschmidt Photography Photographer
Weber & Sorensen Rekl. Bur. A/S Agency
Glygore Limfjord A/S Client
Aarhus, Denmark

Keith D. Gold Art Director/Creative Director
Carol Levy, Keith D. Gold Designers
Gold & Associates Agency/Design Firm
Mozart Marketing Inc./California Pacific Inc.
  Client
Ponte Vedra, FL

159

Ken Womack Art Director/Designer
Alan Babb Production
Rives Smith Baldwin Carlberg Agency
Kentucky Fried Chicken Client
Houston, TX

Ron Pike Art Director/Designer
Jack Stockman Illustrator
Noble & Associates Agency
McCain Citrus, Inc. Client
Chicago, IL

Tim Girvin Art Director/Illustrator
Stephen Pannone Designer
Tim Girvin Design, Inc. Design Firm
Wall Data Client
Seattle, WA

160

Paul Curtin Art Director
Ignatius Tanzil, Peter Locke
    Designers/Illustrators
David Campbell Photographer
Paul Curtin Design Design Firm
Hercules Computer Technology Client
San Francisco, CA

Paul Curtin Art Director
Peter Locke Designer/Photographer/Illustrator
Paul Curtin Design Design Firm
Lapis Technologies, Inc. Client
San Francisco, CA

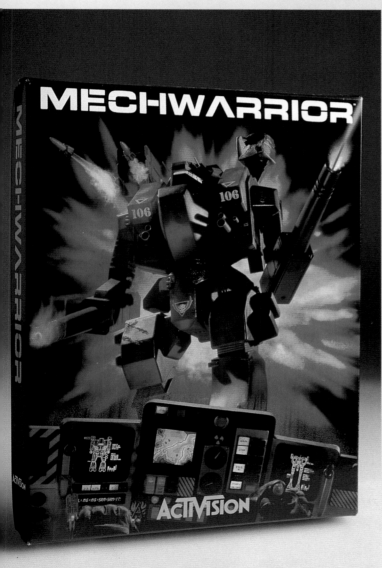

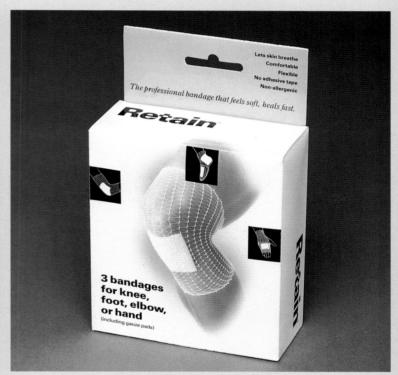

Marty Neumeier Art Director
Christopher Chu, Marty Neumeier Designers
Jeanne Carley Photographer
Neumeier Design Team Design Firm
Western Medical, Ltd. Client
Atherton, CA

Bob Schonfisch Art Director
Larry Keenan Photographer
Steve Sanders Model Maker
John A.S. Skeel Producer
Jon Zax Pyrotechnics
Mediagenic Client
San Francisco, CA

Bonnie Moore Corwin Art Director
William Lunderman V.P./Creative Services
Revlon, Inc., Beauty Care Division Client
New York, NY

Sandra Williams Art Director
Mauro Caputo Designer/Illustrator
Bill Lutz Group Studio
Colonia, Inc. Client
New York, NY

T.J. Musios Art Director
Andre Smith Designer
Robert Jordan Photographer
In-house Design Firm
Avon Products, Inc. Client
New York, NY

Marty Neumeier Art Director
Christopher Chu, Marty Neumeier Designers
Curtis Wong, Christopher Chu Illustrators
Neumeier Design Team Design Firm
Claris Corporation Client
Atherton, CA

Bonnie Moore Corwin Art Director
William Lunderman V.P./Creative Services
Revlon, Inc., Beauty Care Division Client
New York, NY

Steven Sessions Art Director
Kevin Bailey, Steven Sessions Designers
Steven Sessions, Inc. Agency/Design Firm
Parker-Herbex Hair Care Products Client
Houston, TX

Cathy Henszey, Karen Silveira Art Directors
Karen Silveira Designer
Henszey & Albert Agency
Carmelo Pomodoro Client
New York, NY

Bonnie Moore Corwin Art Director
Judith Burger Designer
William Lunderman V.P./Creative Services
Revlon, Inc., Beauty Care Division Client
New York, NY

Carol Denison Art Director/Designer
Michael Surles, Carol Denison Illustrators
Denison Design Associates Design Firm
Montpellier Vineyards Client
Sausalito, CA

Primo Angeli Art Director
Doug Hardenburgh Designer
Primo Angeli, Inc. Design Firm
Pete's Brewing Company Client
San Francisco, CA

Ralph Abreu, Kim Mitchell Art Directors
Abreu/Mitchell Advertising Agency
Hargrave Vineyard Client
Speonk, NY

Ralph Abreu, Kim Mitchell Art Directors
Lauren Jarrett Illustrator
Abreu/Mitchell Advertising Agency
Hargrave Vineyard Client
Speonk, NY

David Broom Art Director
Kimiko Murakami Chan Designer
Pham Van My Illustrator
Broom & Broom, Inc. Design Firm
Christian Brothers Client
San Francisco, CA

Fred Mittleman Art Director/Designer
Mittleman/Robinson, Inc. Design Firm
Paddington Corp. Client
New York, NY

Daniel J. Bond Art Director/Designer
Neil Gerstman Photographer
Daniel J. Bond, Paula Sullivan Illustrators
Daniel J. Bond Design Firm
Swank, Inc. Client
New York, NY

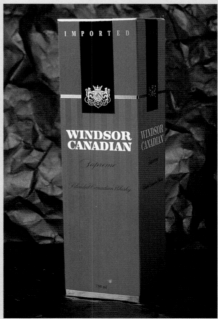

Michael Salisbury Art Director
Terry Lamb, Michael Salisbury Designers
Pam Hamilton, Terry Lamb, Pat Linse
  Illustrators
Salisbury Communications Agency/Design Firm
Kirin Brewery Client
Torrance, CA

Peter DiDonato Art Director
Patty Weller-Bressler Designer
DiDonato Associates Design Firm
Jim Beam Brands, Co. Client
Chicago, IL

Susan Edelmann Art Director/Designer
Roger Redford Illustrator
Mark Oliver, Inc. Agency
Kalyra Winery Client
Santa Barbara, CA

Barbara Vick Art Director/Designer
Katherine Salentine Illustrator
SBG Partners Design Firm
Fleischmann's Vinegar Client
San Francisco, CA

Stephen Ford Art Director
Pamela DeCesare Designer
David Bishop Photographer
Teague Agency/Design Firm
Fallow Deer Assoc. Client
New York, NY

Muts Yasumura Art Director
Richard Hsiung Designer
CYB Yasumura Design Firm
Kraft/General Foods, Inc. Client
New York, NY

Jack Anderson Art Director
Mary Hermes, David Bates, Jack Anderson
 Designers
Jack Anderson, Mary Hermes Illustrators
Hornall Anderson Design Works Design Firm
Consolidated Restaurants Client
Seattle, WA

Keith Puccinelli Art Director/Designer/Illustrator
Rockwell Printing Printer
Puccinelli Design Design Firm
Biscotti Cookie Company Client
Santa Barbara, CA

Paul A. Port Art Director
Brian Sheridan Illustrator
Port Miolla Associates Design Firm
Arnold Bakeries Client
South Norwalk, CT

Chiu Dea Art Director/Designer
Peter Matsuka, Mark Schroeder Illustrators
Landor Associates Design Firm
Hiram Walker Client
San Francisco, CA

Primo Angeli Art Director
Rolando Rosler, Ian McLean, Mark Crumpacker
   Designers
Primo Angeli, Inc. Design Firm
Lavazza Premium Coffees Client
San Francisco, CA

Dennis Thompson, Jody Thompson
   Art Directors
Veronica Denny, Wendy Simons Designers
Deborah Russell Illustrator
The Thompson Design Group Design Firm
Guittard Chocolate Company Client
San Francisco, CA

Anthony P. Greco Art Director
Alfred Fuhrmann Designer
Wayne Bandur Photographer
The Design Center/American National Can
Design Firm
Moyer Packing Company Client
Oak Brook, IL

Barbara Vick Art Director
Thomas Bond Designer
Dave Stevenson Illustrator
SBG Partners Design Firm
Sun Microsystems, Inc., Tops Division Client
San Francisco, CA

Mark Oliver Art Director
Susan Edelmann, Mark Oliver Designers
Bill Boyd Photographer
Mark Oliver, Inc. Agency
Bob Evans Designs Client
Santa Barbara, CA

Bill Davis Art Director
Camille Maravegias Designer
Lister Butler, Inc. Design Firm
3M Client
New York, NY

169

Michael Livolsi Art Director
Jon Wieden, Elizabeth Cotton Designers
Landor Associates Design Firm
Safeway Stores, Inc. Client
San Francisco, CA

Debbie Smith Designer
Shay Cohen Illustrator
Monnens-Addis Design Consultants Design Firm
Kraft-Knudsen Client
Emeryville, CA

Carolyn Greathead Art Director
Jackie Schilperoort Designer
Greathead Associates Agency/Design Firm
Liptons (SA)(PTY), Ltd. Client
Johannesburg, South Africa

Mark Posnett Designer
Pentagraph (PTY) Ltd. Design Firm
Cadbury's Chocolates Client
Sandton, South Africa

170

Charles Hively Art Director/Designer
Danny Harries Illustrator
The Hively Agency Agency/Client
Hively/Fine Design Design Firm
Houston, TX

Juan Concepcion Art Director
Rafael Feliciano Designer
Richard Gerstman Overall Supervision
Michael Lucas Account Supervisor
Gerstman & Meyers, Inc. Design Firm
Nabisco Brands, Inc. Client
New York, NY

Scott A. Mednick Art Director
Loid Der Designer
Dan Arsenault Photographer
Scott Mednick & Associates Agency/Design Firm
Worlds of Wonder Client
Los Angeles, CA

Paul Miller, John Lister Art Directors
Camille Maravegias Designer
Chuck Lamonica Photographer
Lister Butler, Inc. Design Firm
The Haagen-Dazs Company, Inc. Client
New York, NY

Marc Gobe Art Director
Peter L. Levine Designer
Julian Allen Illustrator
Cato Gobe & Associates Design Firm
The Limited, Inc. Client
New York, NY

Clive Gay Art Director
Roland Meissner, Clive Gay Designers
Trademark Design Design Firm
Paul Guillame Client
Shoreditch, London, England

Nass Gherantab Art Director/Designer
Marinelli Communications, Inc. Design Firm
Chesebrough-Pond's, Inc. Client
New York, NY

Joe Selame Art Director
Selame Design Group Design Firm
Spinnaker Software Corporation Client
Newton, MA

Marc Gobe Art Director
Jerome Berard Designer
Philipe Houze Photographer
Jerome Berard Typographer
Cato Gobe & Associates Design Firm
Fotomat Corporation Client
New York, NY

Primo Angeli Art Director
Ray Honda Designer
Rick Wahlstrom Photographer
Primo Angeli, Inc. Design Firm
Supermac Technology Client
San Francisco, CA

Bob Cruanas Designer
Peterson & Blyth Associates Design Firm
The American Tobacco Company Client
New York, NY

Courtney Reeser Art Director
Mary Brucken Designer
SBG Partners Design Firm
Paccar Parts Client
San Francisco, CA

Steve BonDurant, Keith Meehan Art Directors
Susan Corey Designer
Keith Meehan, Steve BonDurant Illustrators
Gene Flanders Project Coordinator
Icon Graphics, Inc. Agency
Eastman Kodak Company Client
Rochester, NY

Roger Johnson Art Director
Bruce Hutton Designer
Silver Oaks Design Firm
Deere & Company Client
Moline, IL

174

John Neher Art Director/Designer/Illustrator
John Racila Association Design Firm
Noma International Client
Elmhurst, IL

Michael Livolsi Art Director
Quentin Murley Designer
Landor Associates Design Firm
Hiram Walker Client
San Francisco, CA

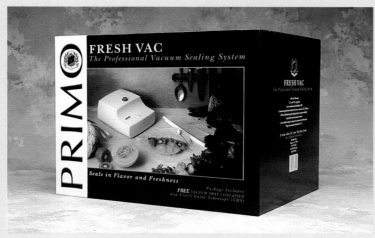

Judi Radice Art Director
Primo Angeli Creative Director
Kelly O'Kane Designer
Beatriz Coll Photographer
Primo Angeli, Inc. Design Firm
Spectrum Foods, Inc. Client
San Francisco, CA

Vasken Kalayjian, Tetsuya Matsuura
  Art Directors
Tetsuya Matsuura Designer/Illustrator
Glazer and Kalayjian, Inc. Design Firm
Letraset Client
New York, NY

175

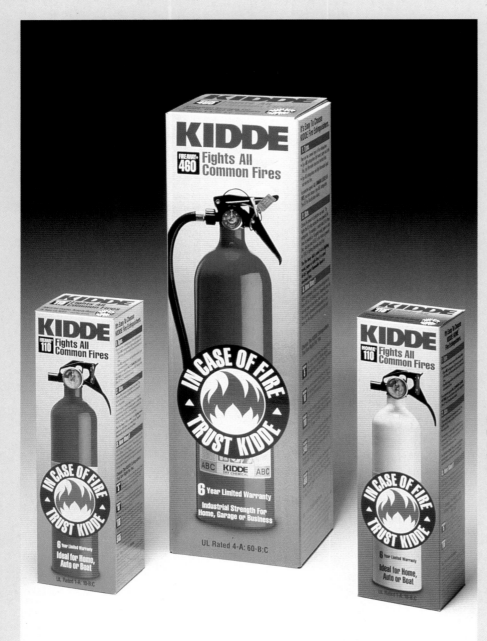

Doug Bond Art Director/Illustrator
Clay Smith Designer
FGI Agency
Walter Kidde Client
Chapel Hill, NC

Margit Kaeser Art Director
Barbara Pearson Designer/Illustrator
Kaeser & Wilson Design, Ltd. Design Firm
McMillian/McGraw Hill, School Division Client
New York, NY

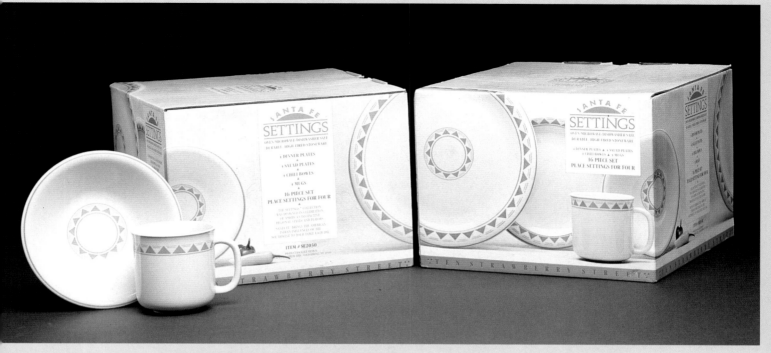

Karen Beckwith Art Director
Phyllis Rosone, Theresa Kraft, Karen Beckwith
  Designers
Beckwith Barrow, Ltd. Design Firm
Ten Strawberry Street Client
Cold Spring, NY

Carol A. Matjasich Art Director
Bette Randa, Allen Porter, Carol A. Matjasich,
  Robert Rausch Designers
Christopher Hawker Photographer
Porter/Matjasich & Associates Design Firm
Whitaker Carpenter Marquette Client
Chicago, IL

Sarah Danes, Lynette Siebert Designers
Pentagraph (PTY) Ltd. Design Firm
Adcock Ingram Client
Sandton, South Africa

Calendars

THE HÄAGEN-DAZS® 1990 CALENDAR

FORM
SUBSTANCE
PASSION

Häagen-Dazs®

Vladimir Tseytlin, Kathryn Frund Art Directors
Donna Aristo, Jerry Errico Photographers
The Guild Group Agency
The Haagen-Dazs Company, Inc. Client
Pleasantville, NY

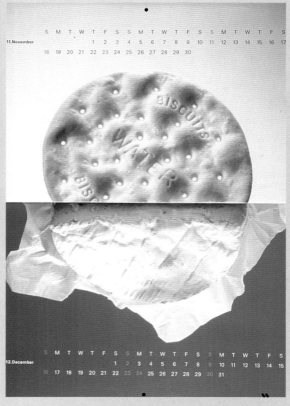

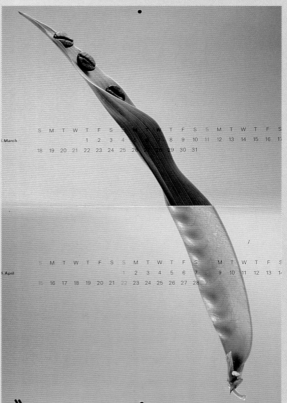

Keizo Matsui Art Director
Yuko Araki Designer
Nob Fukuda Photographer
Keizo Matsui & Associates Design Firm
Ikaruga Milk Products Client
Osaka, Japan

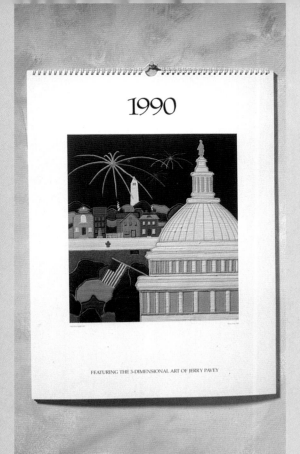

1990

FEATURING THE 3-DIMENSIONAL ART OF JERRY PAVEY

March

s	m	t	w	t	f	s
				1	2	3
4	5	6	7	8	9	10
11	12	13	14	15	16	17
18	19	20	21	22	23	24
25	26	27	28	29	30	31

Jerry Pavey Art Director/Designer/Illustrator
Tom Radcliffe, William McCaw Photographers
Jerry Pavey Design & Illustration Design Firm
S.D. Warren Paper Company/
   S&S Graphics, Inc./
   Jerry Pavey Design & Illumination Clients
Silver Spring, MD

Viktor Kaltala Art Director/Designer
Hannu Hautala Photographer
Reijo Taajaranta Copywriter
Oy Lito-Scan Ab Client
Helsinki, Finland

1990 Calendar

Harbingers of
Happiness

National

JULY

SUN	MON	TUE	WED	THU	FRI	SAT
1	2	3	4	5	6	7
8	9	10	11	12	13	14
15	16	17	18	19	20	21
22	23	24	25	26	27	28
29	30	31				

AUGUST

SUN	MON	TUE	WED	THU	FRI	SAT
			1	2	3	4
5	6	7	8	9	10	11
12	13	14	15	16	17	18
19	20	21	22	23	24	25
26	27	28	29	30	31	

National

JANUARY

SUN	MON	TUE	WED	THU	FRI	SAT
	1	2	3	4	5	6
7	8	9	10	11	12	13
14	15	16	17	18	19	20
21	22	23	24	25	26	27
28	29	30	31			

FEBRUARY

SUN	MON	TUE	WED	THU	FRI	SAT
				1	2	3
4	5	6	7	8	9	10
11	12	13	14	15	16	17
18	19	20	21	22	23	24
25	26	27	28			

National

Norio Tamaki Art Director/Designer
CDP Japan Agency
Matsushita Electic Industrial Company, Ltd.
   Client
Tokyo, Japan

1990

THE YEAR
OF THE
HORSE

Exxon Chemical Polymers Group celebrates "The Year of the Horse" in the calendar pages of its 1990 calendar. Throughout history and in the arts around the world, man has recognized the qualities of this spirited animal. The strength or the stallion, grace of a trotter, and independent disposition have made, for example, an important symbol in this special.

Imperial Oil
Polymers Group

	MAY					
Sunday	Monday	Tuesday	Wednesday	Thursday	Friday	Saturday
29	30	1	2	3	4	5
6	7	8	9	10	11	12
13	14	15	16	17	18	19
20	21	22	23	24	25	26
27	28	29	30	31	1	2

Ward Pennebaker, Jeffrey McKay
Art Directors/Designers
Pennebaker Design Design Firm
Exxon Chemical Client
Houston, TX

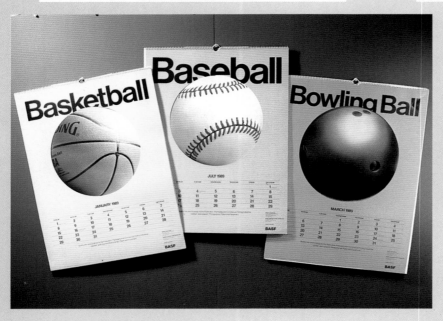

Rick St. Vincent Art Director
Edward Powell Copywriter
St. Vincent, Milone & O'Sullivan Agency
BASF Client
New York, NY

Clive Gay Art Director
Paul Hance, Clive Gay Designer
Trademark Design Design Firm/Client
Whitnall Simonson Production
Shoreditch, London, England

182

7

sun	mon	tue	wed	thu	fri	sat
1	2	3	4	5	6	7
8	9	10	11	12	13	14
15	16	17	18	19	20	21
22	23	24	25	26	27	28
29	30	31				

東洋インキ

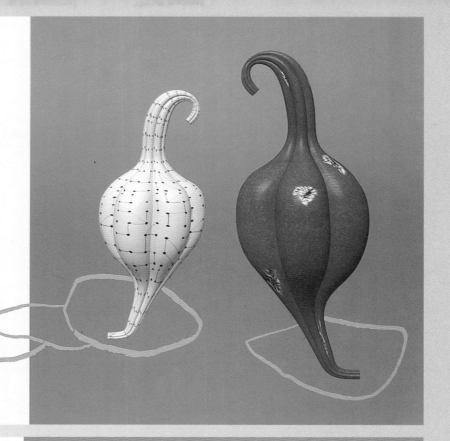

1

sun	mon	tue	wed	thu	fri	sat
	1	2	3	4	5	6
7	8	9	10	11	12	13
14	15	16	17	18	19	20
21	22	23	24	25	26	27
28	29	30	31			

東洋インキ

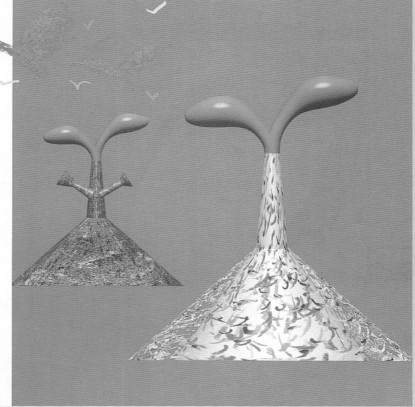

Keisuke-Nagatomo Art Director
Takashi-Nomura Designer
Seitaro-Kuroda Illustrator
Masaki-Fujihata Computer Graphics
Comart-House Company, Ltd. Agency
Kz Company, Ltd. Design Firm
Toyo Ink Company, Ltd. Client
Tokyo, Japan

Craig Butler Designer
Jay Vigon Illustrator
Butler, Inc. Design Firm
Scott & Daughters Publishing, Inc. Client
Los Angeles, CA

Richard Hamilton Smith Art Director/
   Photographer/Copywriter
Richard Hamilton Smith Photography Client
St. Paul, MN

Mogens Sorensen Art Director
Bill Riley Copywriter
Scandutch I/S Client
Klampenborg, Denmark

Jack Anderson Art Director
David Bates, Jack Anderson Designers
Jim Laser Photographer
Hornall Anderson Design Works Design Firm
Jim Laser Client
Seattle, WA

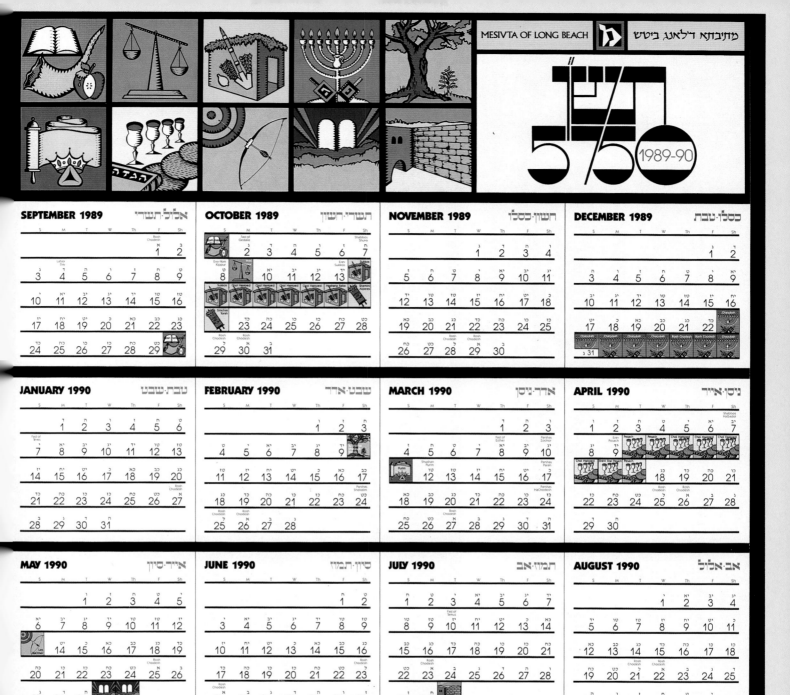

Faygie Bienenfeld
Art Director/Designer/Illustrator
Bienenfeld Design Agency
Mesivta of Long Island Client
Harrison, NY

Promotional Pieces

HERE'S THE CHANCE FOR
ANESTHESIOLOGISTS TO DO SOMETHING
ABOUT THEIR MALPRACTICE RATES.

Jerry Sullivan Art Director
Ed Koren Illustrator
Sullivan Haas Coyle Agency
Jackson Liability Solutions Client
Atlanta, GA

Lamar Ussery Art Director/Designer
Sam Harrison Copywriter
In-house Design Firm
John H. Harland Company Client
Decatur, GA

Tim Brown Art Director/Illustrator
David Gibbs Creative Director
The Design Group Design Firm
John Tesh Photography Client
Greensboro, NC

Cherly L. Oppenheim Art Director
Randy Morrow, Cheryl L. Oppenheim Designers
Meg Galea, Curtis Redhead Producers
Versatility, Inc. Production
Metropolitan Opera Guild Design Design Firm
Metropolitan Opera Guild, Inc. Client
New York, NY

Douglas Reeder Art Director/Designer/Illustrator
SHR Design Communications Design Firm
AIGA Phoenix Client
Scottsdale, AZ

Lois Slahowitz, Ralph Miolla Art Directors
Paul Port Designer
Port Miolla Assoc. Design Firm
Chesebrough Ponds, Inc. Client
South Norwalk, CT

Francois Fontaine Art Director
Lindsay Paleos Creative Director
Tabitha Seipel Illustrator
Stackig, Sanderson & White Agency
Saul Burk, Orthodontist Client
McLean, VA

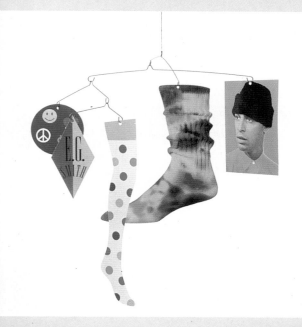

Eric Smithen Art Director
John Pirman Designer/Illustrator
E.G. Smith/World Love Productions Agency
Reddington Design Production
E.G. Smith Socks Client
New York, NY

Duane Perolio Art Director
Merri Hehr, Duane Perolio Designers
John Youssi Illustrator
Perolio Block Communications Design Firm
Rubloff Client
Chicago, IL

Steven Ferlauto Art Director
Elaine Zeitsoff Creative Director
Barbara Shapokas Designer/Illustrator
NBC Sales Client
New York, NY

Marc Gobe Art Director
Peter L. Levine Designer
Cato Gobe & Associates Design Firm
The Limited, Inc. Client
New York, NY

Cherly Doncaster Art Director/Designer
Gregg Lipman Project Coordinator
Martha Voutas Productions, Inc. Agency
S. Posner Sons, Inc. Design Firm
Izod Lacoste Client
New York, NY

Eva Stefenson, Kristin Johnson Art Directors
Greg Hom Designer
Liz Claiborne Agency/Design Firm/Client
New York, NY

Selene Danae Eymer Art Director/Designer
Eymer Design Design Firm
Quadrum Gallery Client
Waltham, MA

Martha Voutas Art Director/Designer
Gregg Lipman Project Coordinator
Martha Voutas Productions, Inc. Agency
S. Posner Sons, Inc. Production
Perry Ellis Shoes Client
New York, NY

Gun Bauchner Art Director/Designer
Max Vaduka Photographer
The Perfumer's Workshop, Ltd. Client
New York, NY

Dan Lennon Art Director
Loid Der Designer
Michael Seieroe Photographer
Lennon & Associates Design Firm
Lackawanna Leather Company Client
Los Angeles, CA

191

Bruce Crocker Art Director/Designer
Steve Marsel, David Caras Photographers
Mark Fisher, Richard Goldberg,
   Katherine Mahoney, Susan Smith,
   Karen Watson Illustrators
Innerer Klang Typographer/Letterpress
Crocker, Inc. Boston Design Firm
Deborah Lipman Artists' Representative Client
Boston, MA

Barbara McCullough Art Director
Michael Dudash Illustrator
Thomas Ferguson Associates, Inc. Agency
Sterling Regal Production
Sandoz Pharmaceuticals Client
Parsippany, NJ

Fred SanFilipo, Bruce Younger
   Art Directors/Designers
Marty Czamanske Photographer
Jerry O'Neill Copywriter
SanFilipo Younger Associates Agency
Xerox Corporation Client
Rochester, NY

Jeff Brall/Port Miolla Associates Art Direction
Port Miolla Associates Design
Jeff Weir Photographer/Design Firm
Ragu Foods, Inc. Client
South Norwalk, CT

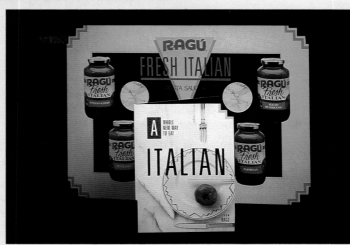

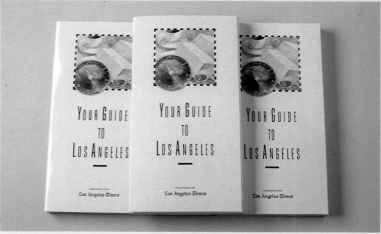

Paul Liebowitz Art Director
David Bragin Designer
Jeff Holewski Illustrator
Marinelli Communications, Inc. Agency
Sony Corporation Client
New York, NY

Julia Chong Tam Art Director/Designer
Sandra Speidel Illustrator
Julia Tam Design Design Firm
Los Angeles Times Client
Palos Verdes, CA

Greg Correll Art Director
Deborah Kaufman, Greg Correll Designers
Small Packages, Inc. Design Firm
American Savings Bank Client
New York, NY

Ken Cook Art Director
Tori Wilke, Sharon Gresh Designers
Steve Tague Photographer
Daniel Pelavin, Alan Kikuchi Illustrator
Bright & Associates Design Firm
NYNEX Client
New York, NY

Jeffrey Keyton Art Director
**Steve Byram, Stacy Drummond, Scott Wadler,
   JoAnn Agress** Designers
Herman Costa Photographer
Mark Malabrico, David Harry Stewert Illustrators
MTV Creative Services Design Firm
MTV Networks Client
New York, NY

Arthur Kaufman Art Director/Designer
**Magnum Photos, David Stoecklein,
   Life Pictures** Photography
Sandra Holtzman Copywriter
Sudler & Hennessey Agency/Design Firm
Chesebrough-Pond's, Inc. Client
New York, NY

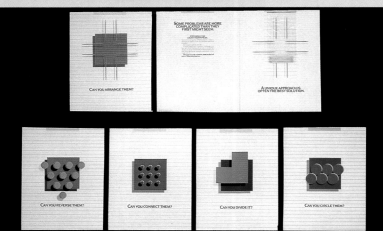

Bill Harrison Art Director/Designer
Brian Otto Illustrator
Dick Jacobs Copywriter
Frank J. Corbett, Inc. Agency
The Upjohn Company Client
Chicago, IL

Gary Hutchins Art Director
Tom Senatori Creative Director
John Ingham Copywriter
W&B Advertising Design Firm
Wisconsin Chamber Orchestra Client
Madison, WI

Carol Caroff Art Director
Megan Cash Designer
Spenser Jones Photographer
Karen Lawrence Illustrator
Widmann & Company Agency
E.I.DuPont de Nemours & Company Client
New York, NY

Ken Womack Art Director/Designer
Barry Fantich Photographer
Alan Babb Typography
Rives Smith Baldwin Carlberg Agency
Kentucky Fried Chicken Client
Houston, TX

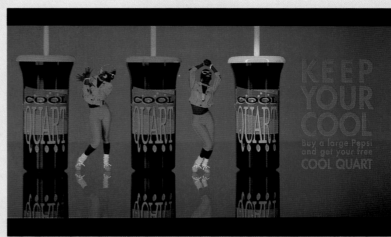

Katherine Zeppelin Art Director
Alain Paul Combe Creative Director
Steven Klein Photographer
In-house Design Firm
Revlon, Inc. Client
New York, NY

Roger Johnston Art Director
Bruce Hutton Designer
Silver Oaks Design Firm
Deere & Company Client
Moline, IL

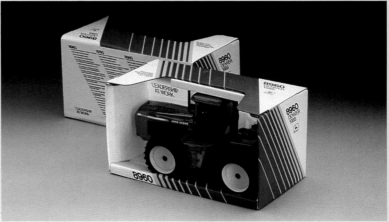

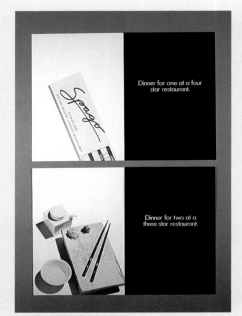

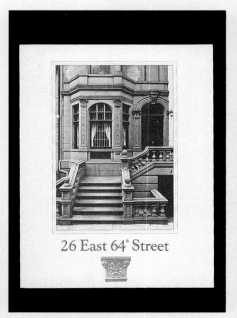

William Sidenstecker Art Director/Designer
Brendan Ross Photographer
Kathy Fawcett Copywriter
Gray & Kilgore, Inc. Agency
Franklin Fitness & Racquet Club Client
Troy, MI

Susan Loren Art Director
Howard Johnson Designer
Mario Novak Photographer
Susan Loren Associates, Inc. Agency
Kushner Seiden Properties Client
New York, NY

Patty Nalle, Arnold Wechsler Art Directors
Akiva Boker, Patty Nalle Designers
Bard Martin Photographer
Javier Romero Illustrator
Wechsler & Partners, Inc. Design Firm
Quest for Value Distributors Client
New York, NY

Aad van den Berg Art Director
Henk Schuurman Calligrapher
Marc van der Marck Concept
Arthouse, Rotterdam Design Firm
Schefferdrukkerij bv Client
Amsterdam, The Netherlands

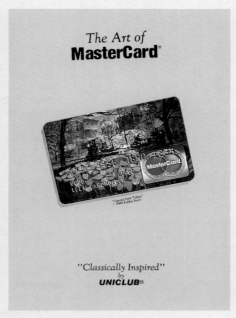

The Art of
MasterCard®

"Classically Inspired"
by
UNICLUB®

Glenn Staada Art Director
Ben Geist Designer/Illustrator
Staada & Koorey, Inc. Design Firm
Mack Trucks Client
Hackettstown, NJ

Kalika Stern Art Director/Illustrator
Creatif Licensing Agency
Kalika Design Design Firm
Uniclub Client
New York, NY

Keith Puccinelli Art Director/Designer/Illustrator
Puccinelli Design Design Firm
Santa Barbara Savings and Loan Client
Santa Barbara, CA

Jay Doniger Art Director
Debra Dymora Designer
Art Rogoff Copywriter
Abelson-Taylor, Inc. Agency
Syntex Laboratories Client
Chicago, IL

Michael Stetson Art Director
Jill Loewenthal Designer
Frank English Photographer
Patricia Raley Editor
A. Colish, Inc. Production
Metro-North Commuter Railroad Client
New York, NY

Chris Grosse Art Director
Elaine Zeitsoff x
Don Eddy Copywriter
NBC In-house Design Firm
NBC Sales Marketing Client
New York, NY

Marcia Weinberg Art Director
Wyndy Wilder Designer
Ellen von Unwerth Photographer
VOGUE Promotion Agency
VOGUE Magazine Client
New York, NY

Vickie Peslak/Quinn Art Director
Sandra Quinn Designer
Platinum Design, Inc. Design Firm
Associates of the American Craft Museum Client
New York, NY

LEGEND HAS IT THE
FIRST TAILGATE PARTY TOOK
PLACE IN OREGON.

HENRY WEINHARD'S PRIVATE RESERVE

Christie Kelley Art Director
James Woods Photographer
John Koenig Copywriter
Young & Rubicam Chicago Agency
Blitz-Weinhard Brewing Company Client
Chicago, IL

Fred Knapp Art Director/Designer/Illustrator
John Payne Photographer
Fusion Design Associates Design Firm
Opticote Client
Chicago, IL

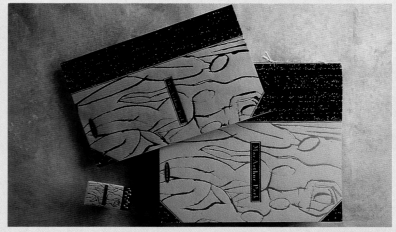

Judi Radice Art Director
Jennifer Morla Designer
Jeanette Aramburu Illustrator
Morla Design Design Firm
Spectrum Foods Client
San Francisco, CA

Amy Usdin Art Director
Janet Bates Creative Director
Arthur Meyerson Photographer
Business Incentives, Inc. Design Firm
GE Capital Client
Minneapolis, MN

Gerhard Ade Art Director
Vincent Adamo, Pam Picken Designers
Don Snyder Photographer
Ade Skunta and Company Agency
Bohme, Inc. Client
Cleveland, OH

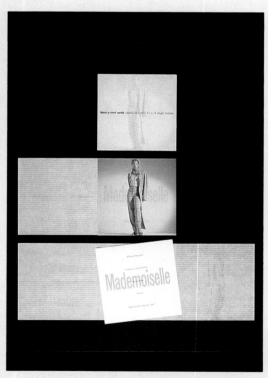

Wendy Edwards Lowitz Art Director
Joe VanDerBos Designer/Illustrator
Moira & Company Design Firm
Abbott Diagnostics Client
Chicago, IL

Ava Schlesinger Art Director
Kathleen Phelps Designer
Anthony Gordon Photographer
In-house Design Firm
MADEMOISELLE Magazine Client
New York, NY

Joel Azerrad Art Director
Elaine Zeitsoff Creative Director
Don Eddy Copywriter
NBC In-house Design Firm
NBC Sales Marketing Client
New York, NY

200

Alison Hill Art Director
Tracy Sabin Designer
Ave Pildas Photographer
Anthony Masterson Coordinator
Sabin Design Design Firm
Turner Entertainment Co. Client
San Diego, CA

Toni Schowalter Art Director/Designer
Schowalter 2 Design Agency/Design Firm
ManesSpace Client
Short Hills, NJ

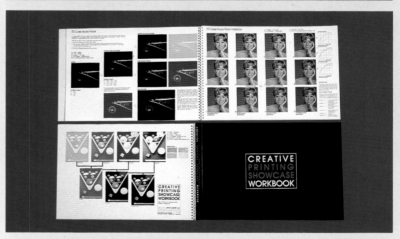

Yoh Jinno Art Director/Designer
AllStock, Inc. Photography
Jinno International Agency
**Eurasia Press (Offset) Pte. Ltd./
   Pioneer Graphic Scanning** Client
Chestnut Ridge, NY

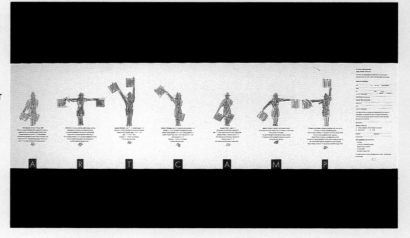

Lewis Glaser Art Director/Designer/Illustrator
Wet Paper Bag Graphic Design Design Firm
**Texas Christian University Office of
   Extended Eduction** Client
Edgecliff Village, TX

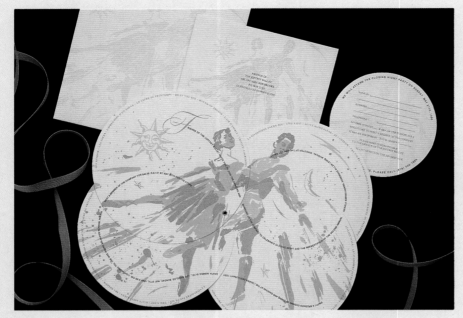

John Georgopoulos Art Director
Dan McNulty Designer
Emma Hayashida Illustrator
Georgopoulos Design, Inc. Design Firm
Friends of the Joffrey Client
Los Angeles, CA

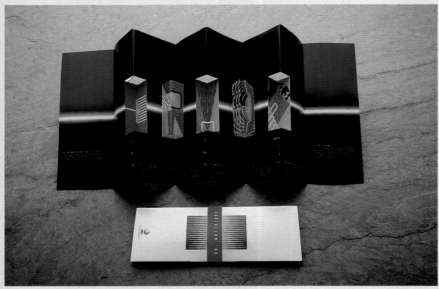

Mike Melia Art Director
Jordan Louie, Mike Melia Designers/Illustrators
Baron Leatherbury Copywriter
Melia Design Group Design Firm
AT&T Client
Atlanta, GA

Tetsuo Niwa Art Director/Designer
Daiwa Gravue Planning Room Agency
Niwa Design Office Design Firm
Daiwa Gravure Client
Nagoya, Japan

Wayne Bressler Art Director/Illustrator
Gary Van Dis Creative Director
Virginia Perry Copywriter
THE NEW YORKER Magazine Agency
American Booksellers Association Client
New York, NY

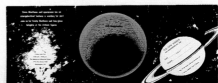

Quantum2

WE STARTED WITH THE
FINEST LENS WE'VE EVER MADE.

AND WE IMPROVED IT.

Janet Fried Art Director/Designer
George Kamper Photographer
Mark Fisher Illustrator
ICE Communications, Inc. Agency
Bausch & Lomb International Client
Rochester, NY

John Harold Art Director/Designer
Christopher Harting Photographer
Sharon Drinkwine Illustrator
Cipriani Kremer Agency/Design Firm
Honeywell Bull Client
Boston, MA

Self-Promotion

Robert Wallace, Stanley Church Art Directors
Stanley Church Designer
Marilyn Montgomery Illustrator
Wallace Church Associates, Inc.
  Design Firm/Client
New York, NY

Kan Tai-Keung Art Director
Eddy Yu Chi-Kong Designer
Kan Tai-Keung Design & Associates, Ltd.
  Design Firm
Heung Chit Kau Client
Hong Kong

Keith D. Gold Art Director/Creative Director
Stacey Harper Designer/Illustrator
Gold & Associates Agency/Design Firm/Client
Ponte Vedra Beach, FL

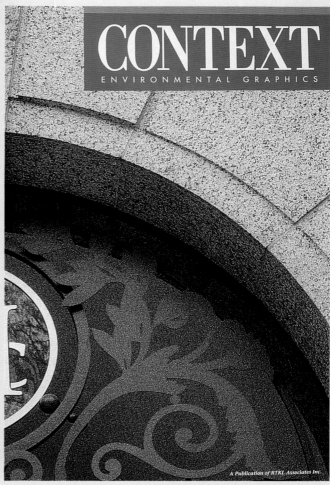

CONTEXT
ENVIRONMENTAL GRAPHICS

A Publication of RTKL Associates Inc.

Ann Dudrow, Elizabeth Brink Art Directors
Elizabeth Brink, Suzanne Redmond Designers
RTKL Associates, Inc. Design Firm/Client
Dallas, TX

Roger Cook, Don Shanosky
Art Directors/Designers
Cook and Shanosky Associates, Inc.
Photographers/Design Firm/Client
Princeton, NJ

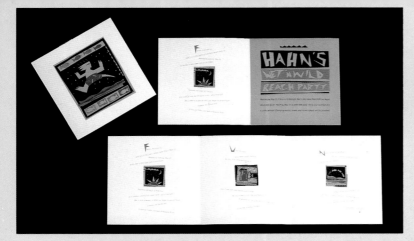

Ross Adcock Art Director/Illustrator
Kiki Tiano, Ross Adcock Designers
Barbara Lutz Copywriter
Hahn Advertising & Design Agency/Design Firm
The Hahn Company Client
San Diego, CA

Tor Pettersen Art Director
David C. Brown, Sanjay Patel, Tor Pettersen
  Designers
Fern Arfin Copywriter
Tor Pettersen & Partners Design Firm/Client
London, England

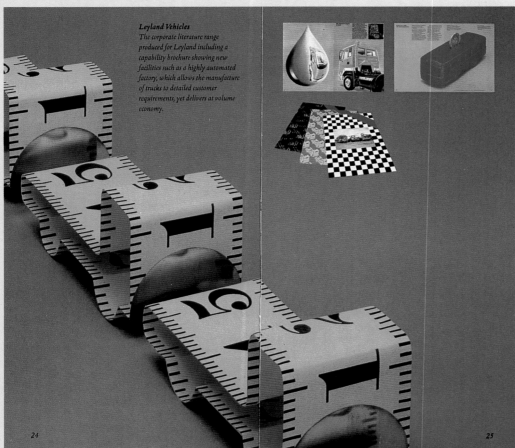

Leyland Vehicles
The corporate literature range produced for Leyland including a capability brochure showing new facilities such as a highly automated factory, which allows the manufacture of trucks to detailed customer requirements, yet delivers at volume economy.

24

25

Bruce Rubin Art Director
Jim Cordaro, Ruth Christian Designers
Rubin Cordaro Design Design Firm/Client
Minneapolis, MN

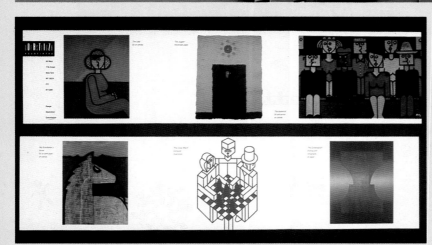

Jose Luis Ortiz Art Director/Illustrator
Denise Halpin Designer
Robert Reichert Photographer
Ortiz Design Associates Design Firm/Client
New York, NY

Carlos Segura Art Director/Designer/Copywriter
Carlos Segura Client
Armando Segura Photographer
Sol Communications Agency/Design Firm
Chicago, IL

Clifford Selbert Art Director
Melanie Lowe Designer
Clifford Selbert Design, Inc. Design Firm
The Markuse Corporation Client
Cambridge, MA

Jean C. Norland Art Director/Designer
Doug Finley Photography Photographer
Jim O'Connell Illustrator
Modular Solutions, Inc. Agency
Norland Graphic Design Design Firm
Lakeside Pharmaceuticals Client
Bloomfield, NJ

Keith Puccinelli Art Director/Designer/Illustrator
Puccinelli Design Design Firm/Client
Santa Barbara, CA

PAMELA HANSON

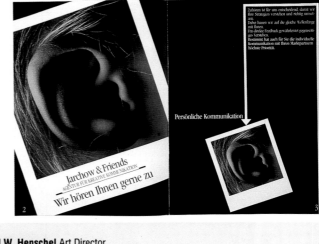

Lucy Sisman Art Director/Designer
Pamela Hanson Photographer/Client
Sisman Design Design Firm
New York, NY

Karl W. Henschel Art Director
Frank Muckenheim Designer
Dieter Waider Photographer
Studio Sign Design Firm
Jarchow & Friends Agency/Client
Frankfurt, West Germany

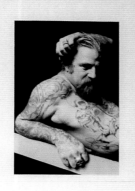

MELANIE EVE BAROCAS
photographer
ANNUAL REPORTS

MELANIE EVE BAROCAS
photographer
CONEY ISLAND

Mary Repetti, John Philion Art Directors
Susan H. Barocas, Melanie Eve Barocas
  Designers
Melanie Eve Barocas Photographer/Client
Guiford, CT

Paul Curtin Art Director
Peter Locke Designer
Paul Curtin Design Design Firm
Julie Holcomb Printers Production
Paul Curtin & Catharine Keena Client
San Francisco, CA

Peter Wong Ming Faye Art Director/Designer
Peter Wong Design & Associates
  Design Firm/Client
Hong Kong

Dick Jones Art Director
Sal Panasci, Dick Jones Designers
Dorland Sweeney Jones, Inc. Agency/Client
Philadelphia, PA

James A. Stygar Art Director/Designer
Penelope H Stygar Copywriter
Stygar Group, Inc. Design Firm/Client
Richmond, VA

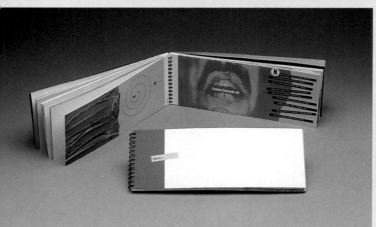

Pam Cerio, Okey Nestor, Karen Skunta
  Designers
Candace McKinley Copywriter
In-house Design Firm
TSI/Point to Point Production
Typesetting Service, Inc. Client
Cleveland, OH

Brian D. Fox Art Director
Dan Pavia Designer
B.D. Fox & Friends, Inc. Agency/Client
Santa Monica, CA

Robert L. Meyer Art Director
Betty Ball Designer
Rose DeNeve, Rita Jacobs Copywriters
Robert Meyer Design, Inc. Design Firm/Client
Stamford, CT

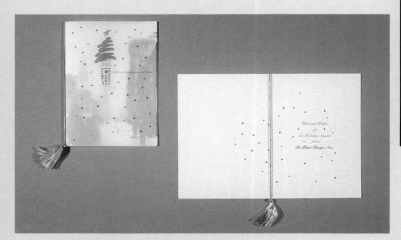

Roberta Marini de Plano Art Director
Marco de Plano Designer
Donna Slade Illustrator
De Plano Design, Inc. Agency/Client
New York, NY

Anne Kauranen Designer
Martti Korpijaakko Copywriter
USP Helsinki Oy Agency/Client
Helsinki, Finland

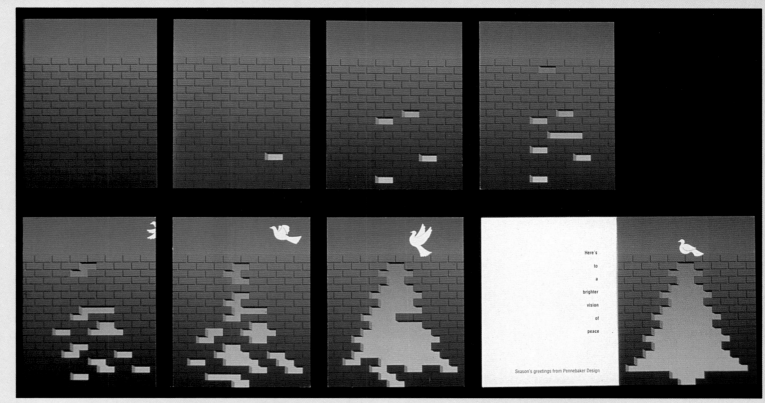

Here's
to
a
brighter
vision
of
peace

Season's greetings from Pennebaker Design

Ward Pennebaker, Jeffrey McKay Art Directors
Jeffrey McKay Designer/Illustrator
Pennebaker Design Design Firm/Client
Houston, TX

Bill Swearingen, Larry Profancik
    Art Directors/Designers
Kelly McKnight Copywriter
PriceWeber Marketing Commmunications, Inc.
    Agency/Client
Louisville, KY

Jane Kobayashi Ritch Art Director/Designer
Eric Myer Photographer
Moravaoliverberte Design Firm
Eric Myer Client
Santa Monica, CA

Sharon H. Collins Art Director/Designer
Fred Slavin Photographer
Loren 2 Design Firm/Client
New York, NY

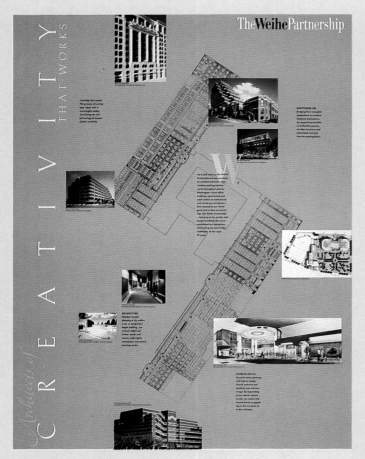

Elaine Callahan Art Director/Designer
Deborah Stocks Copywriter
MDB Communications Agency
The Weihe Partnership Client
Washington, DC

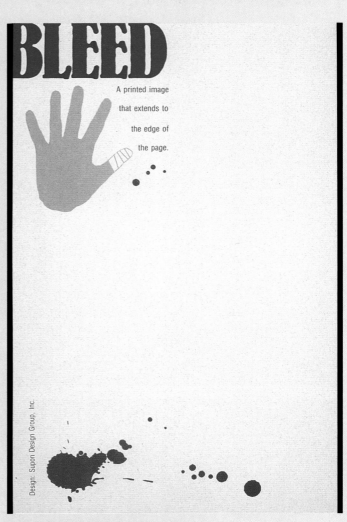

Supon Phornirunlit Art Director/Designer
Wayne Kurie Copywriter
Supon Design Group, Inc. Design Firm/Client
Washington, DC

Richard Sabean Art Director/Designer/Illustrator
Bob Brody Photographer
Joe Heighington, Michael Patti
   Copywriters/Clients
BBDO Agency
New York, NY

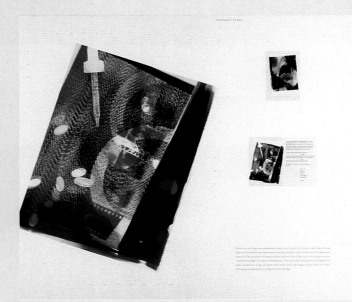

Jim Berté Art Director
John Tom Designer
Julie Suhr Copywriter
Robert Miles Runyan & Associates
   Design Firm/Client
Playa del Rey, CA

Martin Marshall Jaccoma Mitchell
ADVERTISING

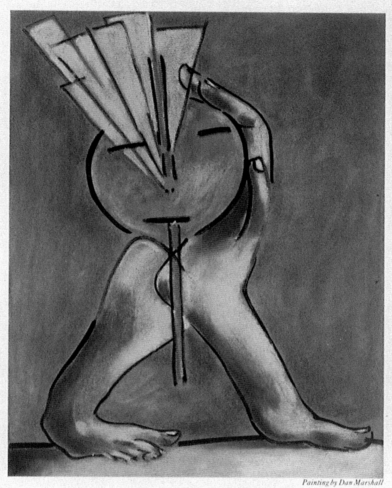

Painting by Dan Marshall

Work that Works

Dan Marshall Art Director
Dick Frank Photographer
Bill White Copywriter
Robin Keen Production Manager
Martin Marshall Jaccoma Mitchell Agency/Client
New York, NY

Trademarks & Logotypes

Greg Sabin Art Director
Tracy Sabin Designer/Illustrator
Sabin Design Design Firm
Zonk, Inc. Client
San Diego, CA

Angel L. Buñag Art Director
Alex Dennis Bolado Designer
George Cabig Photographer
Design Systemat, Inc. Design Firm
Cosmos Bottling Corporation Client
Makati, M.M., Philippines

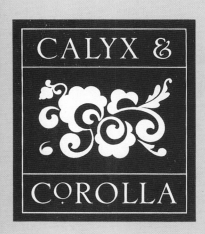

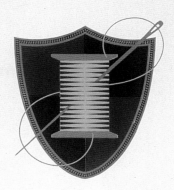

DESIGNS IN THREAD

Ken Cook Art Director/Designer/Illustrator
Ken Cook Design Design Firm
New York, NY

Barbara Vick Art Director
Mary Brucken Designer
SBG Partners Design Firm
Designs in Thread Client
San Francisco, CA

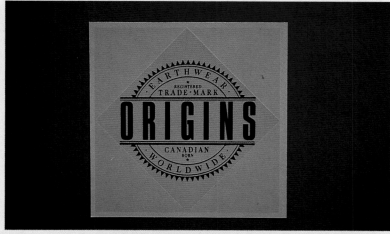

James O'Mara Art Director/Designer
O'Mara & Ryan Design Firm
Marquis of London Client
W. Vancouver, British Columbia, Canada

Nicolas Sidjakov Art Director
Amy Knapp Designer
Hank Osuna, Amy Knapp Illustrators
SBG Partners Design Firm
EurekaBank Client
San Francisco, CA

Joe Selame Art Director
Selame Design/Boston Design Firm
Townsends, Inc. Client
Newton, MA

Chan Hoyle Art Director
Kip McDaniel Designer/Illustrator
In-house Design Firm
Vermont American Tool Company Client
Lincolnton, NC

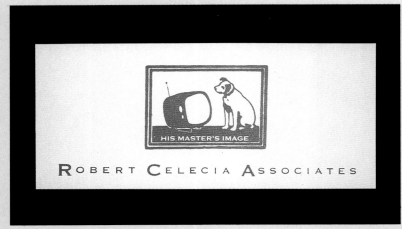

Mark Oliver Art Director
Robert Celecia, Mark Oliver, Karyn Paddon
    Designers
Mark Oliver, Inc. Agency
Robert Celecia Associates Client
Santa Barbara, CA

Charles Totaro Art Director
Shelly Meredith Designer
Jeffrey Shelly, Robert P. Zangrillo Illustrators
The Walt Disney Company Concept
Prince Client
New York, NY

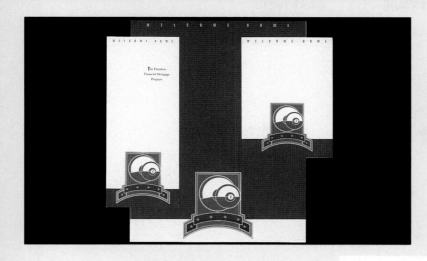

Kenneth Hoffman Art Director
Anne Endrusick, Renee Borsari Designers
Renee Borsari, June Evans Illustrators
Optima Group, Inc. Design Firm
Liberty Bank Client
Millford, CT

Jean-Francois Renaud Art Director/Designer
Nolin Laroseé et Associeś, Inc. Design Firm
**Association des medecins psychiatres du
    Quebec** Client
Montreal, Quebec, Canada

ASSOCIATION DES
MÉDECINS PSYCHIATRES
DU QUÉBEC

David E. Carter Art Director
David E. Carter, Inc. Design Firm
D&E Radar Systems Client
Ashland, KY

Dennis S. Juett Art Director
Robert N. Blatherwick Designer/Illustrator
Dennis S. Juett & Associates, Inc. Agency/Client
Pasadena, CA

DENNIS S. JUETT & ASSOCIATES INC
54 W. GREEN ST., PASADENA, CA 91105
PHONE 213-385-4373 / 818-568-8244

Tor Pettersen Art Director
Colleen Crim Designer
Claire Barnett Illustrator
Tor Pettersen & Partners Agency/Design Firm
Environmental Management, Ltd. Client
London, England

Diane Koziol Art Director/Designer
Anne Redner Illustrator
DMB&B Agency
Detroit Creative Directors Council Client
Bloomfield Hills, MI

Bob Rankin Designer
Steve Barrett Illustrator
Rankin Design For Marketing Design Firm
East Teak Client
Bellevue, WA

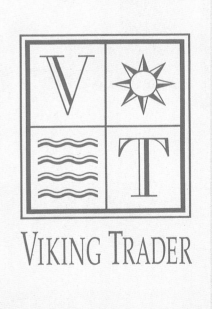

William R. Tobias Art Director/Designer
William R. Tobias Design, Inc. Design Firm
Ayuda, Inc. Client
New York, NY

Maureen Erbe Designer
Maureen Erbe Design Design Firm
Viking Trader Client
Los Angeles, CA

Jim Smarilli Art Director/Designer
Smarilli Graphics Design Firm
Pennsylvania Bar Association Client
Wormleysburg, PA

Lennart Hansson Art Director/Designer
Liberg & Company Agency
Lennart Hansson Design Design Firm
Svedala Industri AB Client
Malmo, Sweden

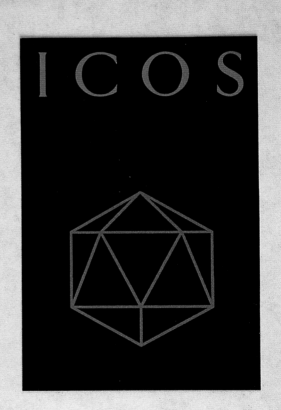

Gunnar Swanson Designer
Gunnar Swanson Design Office Design Firm
National Toxics Campaign Client
Venice, CA

Woody Pirtle Art Director
Libby Carton, Woody Pirtle Designers
Nonan/Russo Communications
Pentagram Design Firm
ICOS Corporation Client
New York, NY

FREEDOM

TAX CREDIT PLUS

Arnold Wechsler Art Director
Patty Nalle, Christie Clock Designers
Michael Schwab Illustrator
Wechsler & Partners, Inc. Design Firm
Related Capital Corporation Client
New York, NY

Mark Oliver Art Director
Donna Nakamura, Mark Oliver Designers
Mark Oliver, Inc. Agency
Easter Island Foundation Client
Santa Barbara, CA

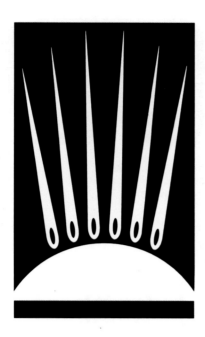

Michael M. Dula Art Director/Designer/Illustrator
Larry Pao Design, Inc. Design Firm
Planet Jupiter Client
Costa Mesa, CA

Keith D. Gold Art Director/Creative Director
Nils Lucander Designer
Gold & Associates Agency/Design Firm
Stuller Settings Client
Ponte Vedra, FL

Friends Of The Zoo

Gregg Frederickson Art Director
Lena James Designer/Illustrator
SmithGroup Design Firm
Friends of the Washington Park Zoo Client
Portland, OR

Jack Anderson Art Director
Mary Hermes, David Bates, Jack Anderson
  Designers
David Bates Illustrator
Hornall Anderson Design Works Design Firm
Consolidated Restaurants Client
Seattle, WA

Carol Mills Designer
Mills Associates, Inc. Design Firm
Eclat-The Information Automation Company
  Client
New York, NY

Supon Phornirunlit Art Director/Designer
Supon Design Group, Inc. Design Firm
Walsh Wallpaper Services Client
Washington, DC

Marcia Weinberg Art Director
Tamara Wicks Designer/Illustrator
VOGUE Magazine Client
New York, NY

Vickie Sawyer Karten Art Director
Greg Clarke Designer/Illustrator
Josh Freeman/Associates Design Firm
Sisley Italian Kitchen Client
Los Angeles, CA

Nancy Ruzow Art Director/Designer/Illustrator
Ruzow Graphics, Inc. Agency/Design Firm
Game Parts, Inc. Client
Stamford, CT

Sharon Klein Designer
Sharon Klein/Graphic Design, Inc. Design Firm
O.D.N. Productions Client
New York, NY

biosurface

Ulf Petterson Art Director/Designer
M.O.R. Agency
Biosurface Client
Malmoe, Sweden

John Georgopoulos, Ron Imada Art Directors
Jennifer Birkland, Dan McNulty Designers
Georgopoulos Design, Inc. Design Firm
Flavor Foods Client
Los Angeles, CA

Thomas McNulty Art Director/Designer
Brian Jacobson, Thomas McNulty
  Designer/Illustrator
Profile Design Design Firm
Apple Computers, Inc. Client
San Francisco, CA

Robin Brandes Art Director
Calvin Hom Designer
Sharon Shamiko Lee Illustrator
IDEAS Agency
Neville Price Developers Client
San Francisco, CA

Jani Drewfs Art Director
Denise Weir, Denise Weir Designers
Nancy Gellos Illustrator
Hornall Anderson Design Works Design Firm
Sunfresh Foods Client
Seattle, WA

Laura Kay Art Director
Donald Kay Designer
Laura Kay Design Design Firm
Specialty Design Client
Ashland, OR

Emilio V. Brunetti Art Director/Designer
Studio Brunetti Design Firm
Integrated Pre-Press, Inc. Client
Astoria, NY

Julian Naranjo, Eugenio Naranjo Art Directors
Eugenio Naranjo Designer/Illustrator
BM.A Asociados Agency
Instituto Profesional Santo Tomas, Chile Client
Santiago, Chile

Amy Leppert Designer/Illustrator
Shannon & Shannon Design Associates Design
  Firm
Chez Josephine Restaurant Client
Holland, MI

Sarah F. Huie Art Director/Designer
Barton Chambers Design Architect
Todd C. Lundgren Project Manager
RTKL Associates, Inc. Design Firm
Forest City Enterprises Client
Dallas, TX

Michael Meade Art Director/Designer
GTE Graphic Communications Design Firm
GTE Corporation Client
Stamford, CT

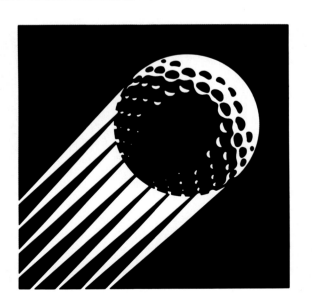

John Georgopoulos Art Director
Dan McNulty Designer
Nadene Bristow Director of Corporate
  Communications
Georgopoulos Design, Inc. Design Firm
Tishman West Companies Client
Los Angeles, CA

224

David J. Baca Art Director/Designer/Illustrator
Bob Roos Copywriter
David J. Baca Design Associates Design Firm
Orientations Client
San Jose, CA

Greg Oznowich Art Director/Designer/Illustrator
Watt, Roop & Company Agency
Atrium Cafe Client
Cleveland, OH

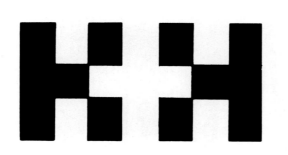

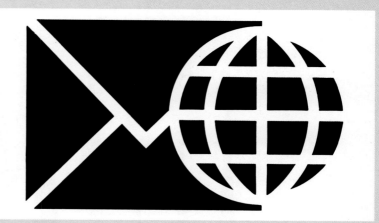

Courtland Thomas White Art Director/Designer
Courtland Thomas White, Inc. Design Firm
Haygood & Haygood Client
New York, NY

Terrence W. McCaffrey Art Director/Designer
U.S. Postal Service Design Firm/Client
Washington, DC

Joseph M. Hunt Art Director/Designer
Robin Shepherd Studios Design Firm
Live & Learn Client
Jacksonville, FL

John Dunn Art Director/Designer
Dunn and Rice Design, Inc. Design Firm
Rochester Monotype Client
Rochester, NY

THE GEGENHEIMER GROUP LTD.

Elizabeth P. Ball Art Director/Designer
Tom Fowler, Inc. Design Firm
The Gegenheimer Group, Ltd. Client
Stamford, CT

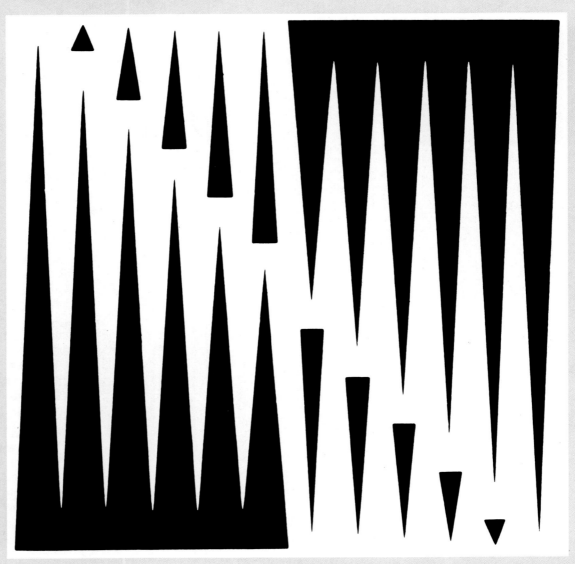

Ronnie S.C. Tan Art Director
Patricia Tan Designer
Design Objectives Pte. Ltd. Design Firm
Nippon Machine Tool Pte. Ltd. Client
Singapore

226

Chemical Bank
Pictogram - "Branch Spotlight"

Edward Walter Art Director
Beth Story Designer
Edward Walter Design Design Firm
Chemical Bank Client
New York, NY

Scott Pettit Art Director/Designer
Dick Prow Creative Director
Al Malone Illustrator
Rhea & Kaiser Advertising Agency
Vaughan's Seed Company Client
Naperville, IL

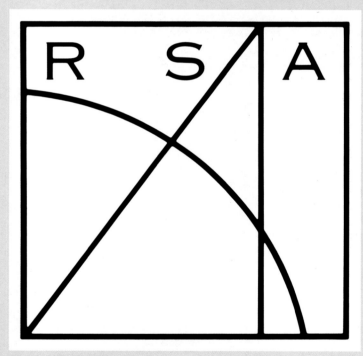

John Georgopoulos Art Director
Dan McNulty Designer
Georgopoulos Design, Inc. Design Firm
Rothenberg Sawasy Architects Client
Los Angeles, CA

Robert Froedge Art Director/Illustrator
Robert Froedge Design Design Firm
Image Design, Inc. Production
Western Civilians Band Client
Nashville, TN

etterheads

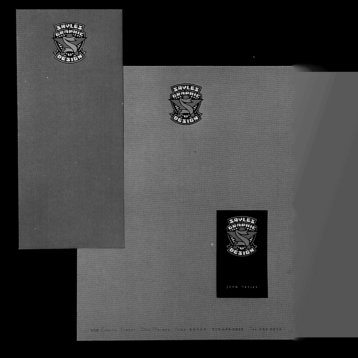

John Sayles Art Director/Desig[ner]
Sayles Graphic Design, Inc. D[esign Firm]
Des Moines, IA

Scott Ray Art Director/Designer
Keith Nichols Photographer
Peterson & Company Design Firm
Dallas Repertory Theatre Client
Dallas, TX

Clive Gay Art Director
Lynette Shebert Designer
Trademark Design Design Firm
Three's Company Client
Shoreditch, London, England

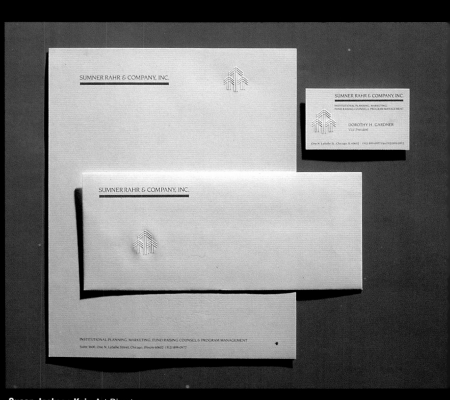

Amy Leppert Designer/Illustrator
Shannon & Shannon Design Associates
   Design Firm
Handwoven, Jean Pluta Client
Holland, MI

Susan Jackson Keig Art Director
   Designer/Illustrator
Susan Jackson Keig Design Firm
Sumner Rahr & Company, Inc. Client
Chicago, IL

George Klauber, Joseph Roberts Designers
Klauber/Roberts Design Firm
The Tuneful Company/Tommy Tune Client
New York, NY

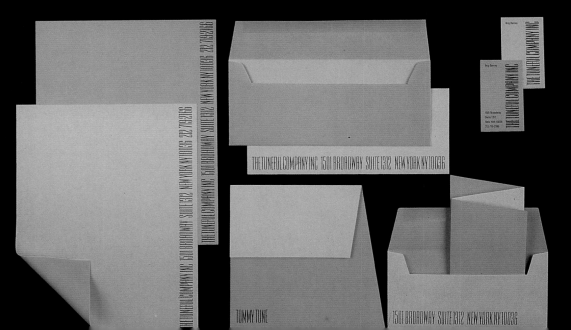

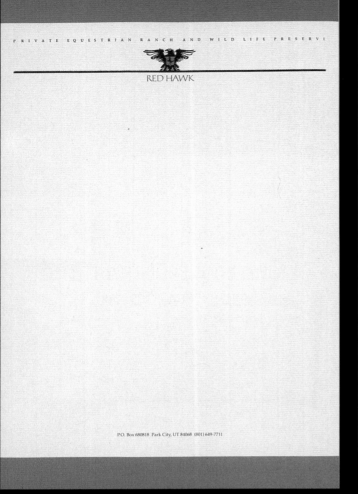

PRIVATE EQUESTRIAN RANCH AND WILD LIFE PRESERVE

RED HAWK

P.O. Box 680818 Park City, UT 84068 (801) 649-7711

McCormick/Schilling Gourmet

Quite simply, the best spices on earth.

Mary Pisarkiewicz Art Director
Bradley Olman Photographer
Pisarkiewicz Design, Inc. Design Firm
McCormick & Company, Inc. Client
New York, NY

Don Weller Art Director/Designer/Illustrator
Mike Nielsen, Don Weller Copywriters
The Weller Institute for the Cure of Design, Inc.
    Agency/Design Firm
Red Hawk Client
Park City, UT

David Gibbs Art Director/Designer/Illustrator
The Design Group Design Firm
Carol Krusch Interior Design Client
Greensboro, NC

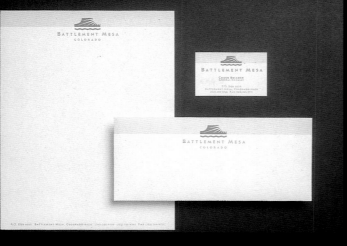

Richard Foy Art Director
David Tweed Designer
Communication Arts Design Firm
Battlement Mesa Client
Boulder, CO

Ronnie Holland, Josie Dolby Art Directors
Kiki Tingas Designer
Tingas Hills, Inc. Agency
Ingersoll-Rand Company Client
Charlotte, NC

Cheryl Doncaster Art Director/Designer
Gregg Lipman Project Coordinator
Martha Voutas Productions, Inc. Agency
Optica Client
New York, NY

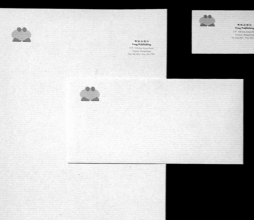

Freeman Lau Siu-hong Art Director/Designer
Kan Tai-Keung Design & Associates, Ltd. Design
   Firm
Frog & Associates, Inc. Client
Hong Kong

William R. Tobias Art Director
Jeffrey R. Olsen Designer
William R. Tobias Design, Inc. Design Firm
Nablo/Troxel Building Contractors Client
New York, NY

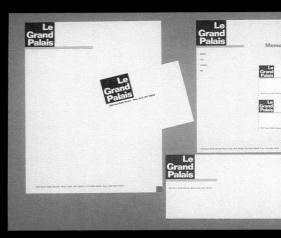

Robbi G. Muir Art Director/Designer
Lohman Organization Agency/Design Firm
Benenson Capital Company Client
New York, NY

Vickie Sawyer Karten Art Director
David Fikse Designer
Josh Freeman/Associates Design Firm
Bruce Ayres Photography Client
Los Angeles, CA

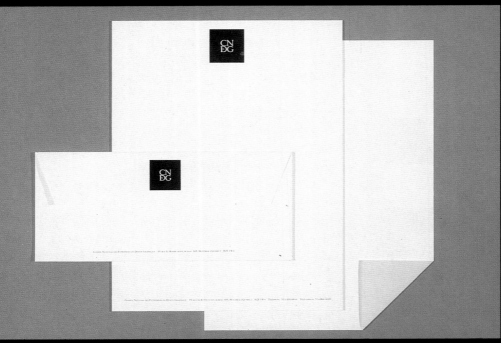

Louis Gagnon Art Director/Designer
Real Lefebvre Handlettering
Nolin Larosée et Associés, Inc. Desi
**Conseil National des Enterprises en
    Design Graphique**
Montréal, Québec, Canada

Peter Pentz Art Director/Designer
Charles Berger Illustrator
SAXX Advertising, Inc. Agency
TVC Film Laboratories Client
Melville, NY

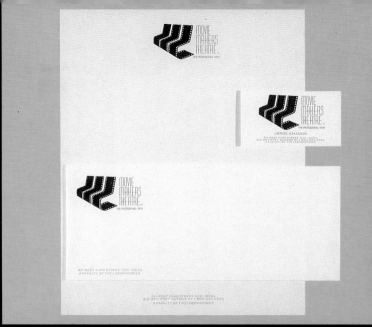

Philippe Hémono Art Director
Vittorio Illustrator
Pierre Coté Copywriter
Publicité Martin, Inc.Agency
Transports Québec Client
Montréal, Québec, Canada

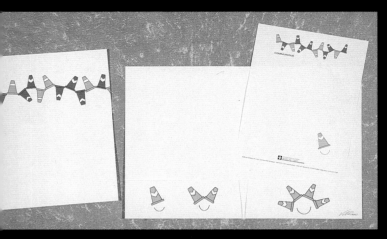

Viktor Kaltala Art Director/Designer/Illustrator
USP Helsinki Oy Design Firm
Olosneuvos Client
Helsinki, Finland

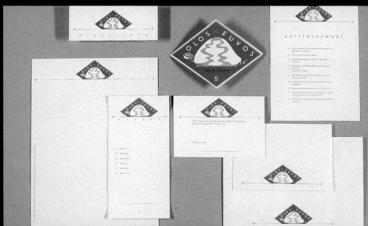

Ellen Dolinar Designer
Freelance Advantage, Inc. Client
New York, NY

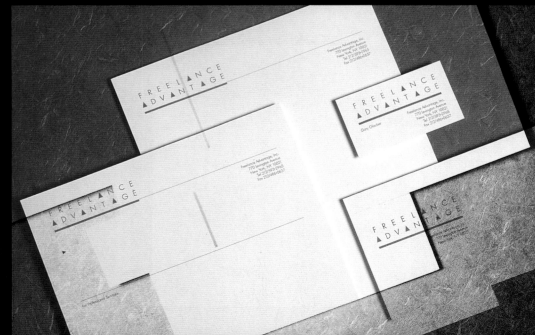

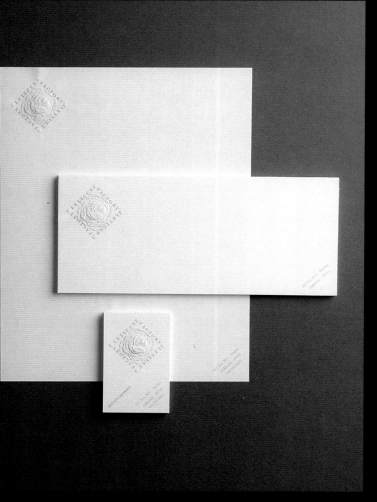

Larry Will Art Director
William Letcher, Larry Will Designers
Tom Carver Illustrator
Larry Will Design Group Design Firm
Lettuce Factory Client
Reno, NV

Marjorie Sopkin Art Director/Designer
Terence Falk Photography Client
Stony Creek, CT

Jan Uretsky Art Director
David Suit, Jan Uretsky, Margaret Marcy
    Designers
Uretsky & Company Design Firm/Client
New York, NY

Frank Collyer Designer/Client
Stony Point, NY

Paul Curtin Art Director
Peter Locke Designer
Ignatius Tanzil, Paul Curtin Illustrators
Paul Curtin Design Design Firm
Bicycle Trails Council of Marin Client
San Francisco, CA

Sachi Kuwahara Art Director/Designer/Illustrator
Sawcheese Studio Design Firm
Richard L. Segal & Associates Client
Santa Monica, CA

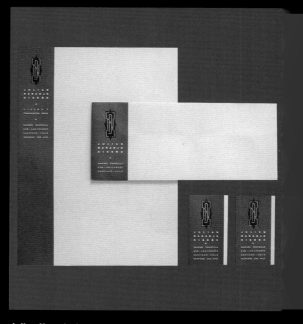

Keith Puccinelli Art Director/Designer/Illustrator
Puccinelli Design Design Firm/Client
Santa Barbara, CA

Julian Naranjo Art Director/Designer
Esteban Vasquez Photographer
Julian Naranjo Diseno, Chile Design Firm/Client

Randy Latocki Art Director/Designer
Marc A. Williams Creative Director
Larry Conely Group Creative Director
Young & Rubicam, Inc. Agency
Actcom Worldwide Client
Detroit, MI

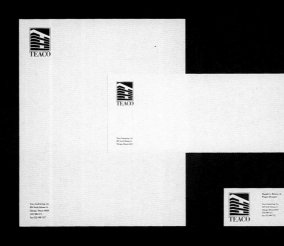

Dorothea Kutyla Art Director/Designer
James Daniels Illustrator
Kutyla Design Design Firm
Teaco Contracting, Inc. Client
Chicago, IL

Paul Ciavarra Art Director/Designer
Doug Law Illustrator/Designer
Della Femina McNamee, Inc. Agency Firm
800 Plant It Client
Boston, MA

Cheryl Lewin Art Director/Designer
Lewin Design Associates Design Firm
Twigs Client
New York, NY

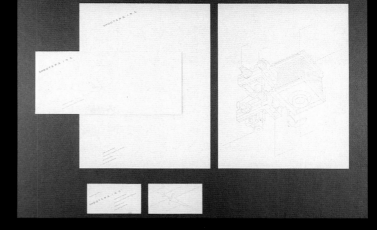

Karl S. Maruyama Art Director
Designer/Illustrator
Tom Fowler, Inc. Design Firm
Shooter, Inc. Client
Stamford, CT

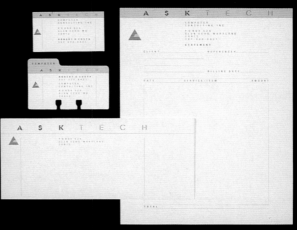

Clare Wilson Art Director
Barry Mover Designer
The Huffman Press Printer
WilsonWorks Design Firm
AskTech Computer Consulting, Inc. Client
Washington, DC

James O'Mara Art Director
Stephen Ramsden, James O'Mara Designers
O'Mara & Ryan Ltd. Agency/Design Firm
Northwestern Aircraft Leasing Corp. Client
W. Vancouver, British Columbia, Canada

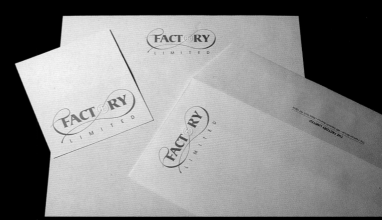

Andy H. Lun Art Director
Jeffrey Huang Designer
Toto Images, Inc. Design Firm
The Factory Limited Client
New York, NY

The

Fourth

International

Conference

on Limb

Development

& Regeneration

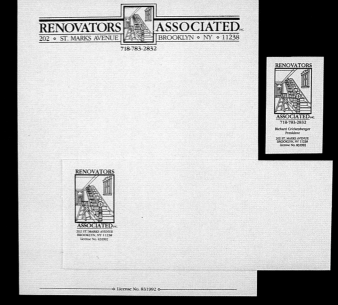

Jim Mokarry Art Director/Designer/Illustrator
Jim Mokarry Design Design Firm
Renovators Associated, Inc. Client
Brooklyn, NY

Bennett Peji Art Director/Designer
Edwin Peji Illustrator
Bennett Peji Design Design Firm
LaJolla Cancer Research Foundation Client
San Diego, CA

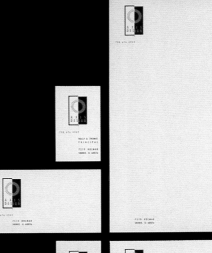

Holly (Thomas) Stein Art Director/Designer
Axis Design Design Firm/Client
Skokie, IL

Patt Mann-Berry Art Director/Designer
Geoffrey Nelson Photography Photographer
Patt Mann-Berry Design Design Firm/Client
Los Gatos, CA

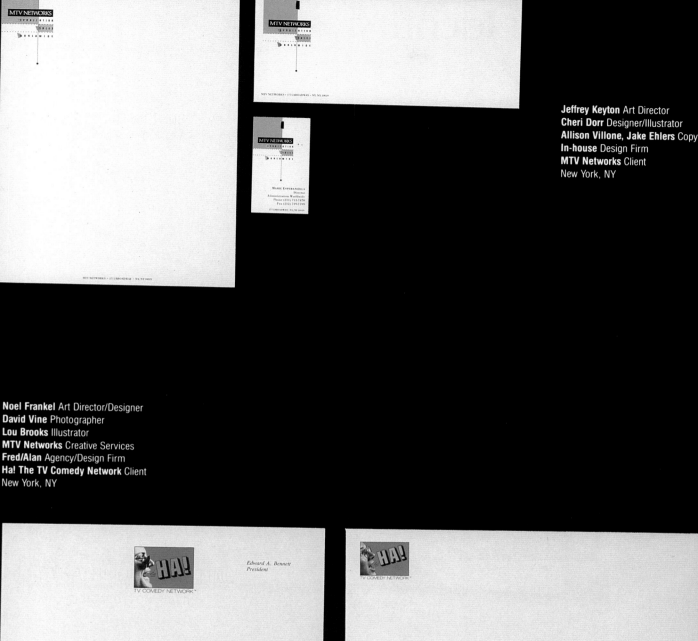

Jeffrey Keyton Art Director
Cheri Dorr Designer/Illustrator
Allison Villone, Jake Ehlers Copy
In-house Design Firm
MTV Networks Client
New York, NY

Noel Frankel Art Director/Designer
David Vine Photographer
Lou Brooks Illustrator
MTV Networks Creative Services
Fred/Alan Agency/Design Firm
Ha! The TV Comedy Network Client
New York, NY

Corporate Identity

Charles Totaro Art Director
Laurie Offenberg Cole Designer
John Loter, Robert P. Zangrillo, Murad Gumen
Illustrators
The Walt Disney Company Client
New York, NY

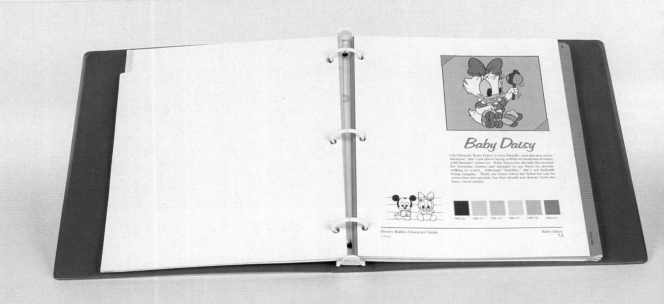

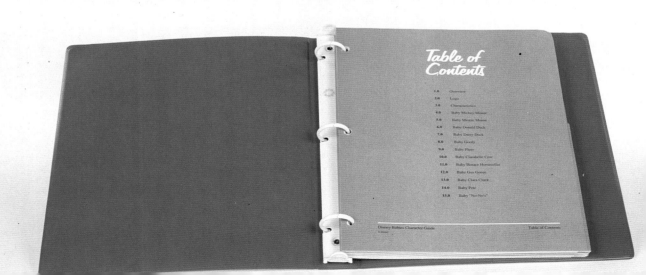

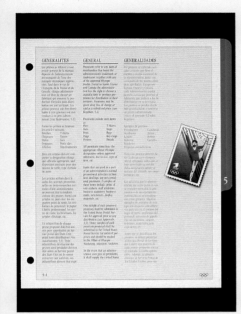
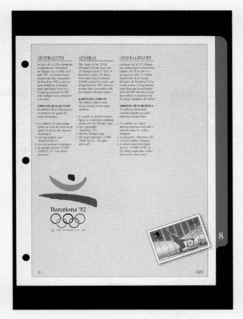
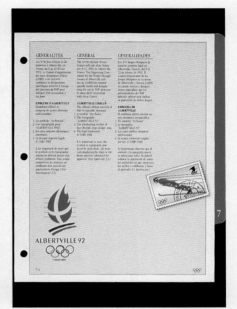

Gisele Sangiovanni Art Director/Designer
Akira Aki Otani Illustrator
CYB Yasumura Design Firm
United States Postal Service/Olympic Client
New York, NY

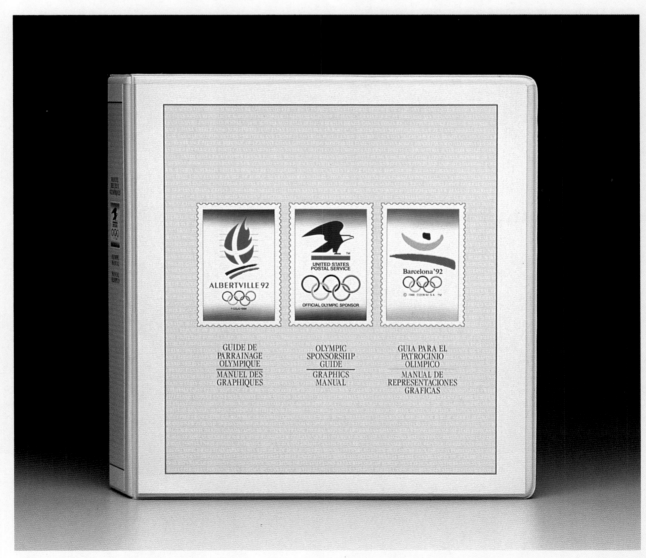

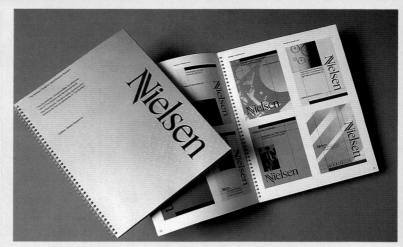

William R. Tobias Art Director/Designer
William R. Tobias, Philippa Dunne Copywriters
Lisa Breslow, Eugene J. Tava
  Mechanical Artwork
William R. Tobias Design, Inc. Design Firm
Nielsen Media Research Client
New York, NY

Deanna Farrell Art Director
Clive Jacobson Designer
Della Femina McNamee Design Group Agency
Forest-City Ratner Companies Client
New York, NY

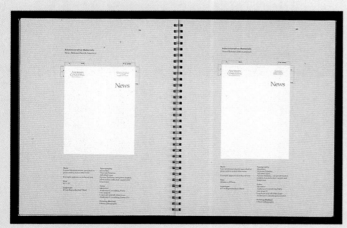

William Rosner Art.Director/Copywriter
Shari Finger Designer
Burson-Marsteller Agency/Design Firm
Andersen Consulting Client
New York, NY

Go Kariya Art Director/Designer
Audins Associates, Inc. Production
Lamd Incorporated Client
Niigata-ken, Japan

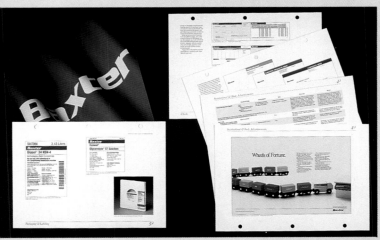

Eva Stefenson, Christopher Dangtran
  Art Directors
Christopher Dangtran Designer
Ben Rosenthal Photographer
Martin Foley, Sara Chereskin Copywriters
In-house Design Firm
Liz Claiborne, Inc. Client
New York, NY

Robin Simon Art Director
Kathleen Evans Designer
Donna Sears Copywriter
Paragraphs Design, Inc. Design Firm
Baxter International, Inc. Client
Chicago, IL

Gisele Sangiovanni Art Director/Designer
CYB Yasumura Design Firm
Lincare, Inc. Client
New York, NY

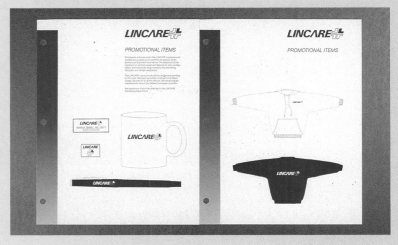

MARTIN LUTHER KING, JR.
"AS I REMEMBER HIM"
BY ROSE KING CLAIBON

At the burning bush at Mount Horeb God called Moses to become the great leader of His people. The Israelites were victims of servitude. Oppression was their daily lot. The Scriptures reveal this: "And the Lord said, I have surely seen the affliction of my people which are in Egypt, and have heard their cry, by reason of their taskmasters; for I know their sorrows" (Exodus 3:7). Moses was "the man for the job."

Centuries later another Moses arose to become a great leader. In the infancy of the civil rights movement Dr. Martin Luther King, Jr., pastored the Dexter Avenue Baptist Church in Montgomery, Alabama. The Black people, like the Israelites, were victims of servitude and a type of oppression brought about by bigotry and discrimination.

"Go therefore now, and work; for there shall no straw be given you, yet shall ye deliver the tale of bricks," cried Pharaoh. "And the officers of the children of Israel did see that they were in evil case" (Exodus 5:18, 19). For centuries, even after slavery, similar circumstances faced the Black people throughout the South. In the face of the lowest paying jobs to no jobs at all, with limited cultural advantages and separate but unequal educational and recreational institutions, Blacks were expected to pull themselves up by their own bootstraps.

Then in 1955 Rosa Parks was arrested because she refused to stand and give her seat to a White man who had boarded a bus. Few Blacks had ever dared to rebel against the "system," so designed by law to separate the Blacks and Whites. The fear of losing their jobs or their freedom, even their lives, kept the Negroes "in their place." This day, this Black woman decided on a lone rebellion. When asked, "Why?" she said, "I was just tired." Thus the sparks of the Black movement toward first-class citizenship were ignited.

The Black leaders, who were mostly ministers, were notified of Mrs. Parks' arrest. These preachers were respected by the people and were not obligated to White employers, who would fire anyone who protested in any way against segregation. But now the time was right and the fear diminished. So who would be their leader, their spokesman, their Moses? A seed organization, the Montgomery Improvement Association (MIA) became the nucleus around which the struggle was launched.

There were older ministers who had been waging a cold war for their people for many decades. They had tried to find jobs, they had gotten people out of jail, they had gone before city officials to get streets paved and to make other improvements. There were younger natives of the town, strong and energetic, who had started their families and who would grow up here. Yet nearly all of them agreed on one man, Dr. Martin Luther King, Jr. He was not an older, experienced minister as some of the others, nor a native of Montgomery, but a newcomer.

Like Moses, Dr. King was the man for the job. Why was he right? What were his credentials? What did he bring to the task? Martin Luther King received his post-high school education at Morehouse College, in his native Atlanta, Georgia. Morehouse, a maker of Black gentlemen, was where he received the B.A. degree in 1948. The next step was Crozer Theological Seminary in Chester, Pennsylvania. It was here that Dr. King was introduced to Gandhi's philosophy of nonviolence, and in 1951 received his Bachelor of Divinity. His quest for knowledge and excellence led him to Boston University and the conferral of the Ph.D. degree in 1955. Those great institutions helped him to develop into a great scholar and leader of his time, well-bred, well-read, and well-led.

He was led first by his father, whose footsteps he followed into the gospel ministry. Martin Luther King, Jr., studied and advanced the teachings of Mahatma Gandhi's nonviolent resistance. The greatest of all whom he followed was Jesus Christ, who filled his heart with love for all mankind, even those who hated him and fought against him. The most important characteristic of a great leader, second only to love, is meekness. Moses had it. The Bible acclaims him as "very meek, above all the men which were upon the face of the earth" (Numbers 12:3). Meek, according to Webster's New World Dictionary, is "patient and mild, not inclined to anger or resentment." Such a spirit was exhibited in Dr. King from the beginning to the end of his leadership in the civil rights movement. Meek but not weak, he was to become the greatest U.S. civil rights leader of the twentieth century, known not only throughout the South and the nation, but throughout the world.

But the decision to accept that leadership was not an easy one. His parishioners needed his full attention. Certainly his wife and children needed more of his time. But when the call came, Martin Luther King, Jr., decidedly and prayerfully answered, "Yes!"

The mass meetings began in the churches. Strategies were outlined by the leaders, but he was the main speaker—a born orator with a message that inspired Black people as never before. They gathered wherever civil rights meetings were held. But they came to hear him—their leader. He preached love for all men and nonviolence. When militant Blacks cried, "Burn, baby, burn," and promoted "brick-for-brick" tactics, his voice could be heard above the sometimes discouraged and angry crowd: "Put down your guns and knives; violence is not the way." He got out there and showed them the way.

Martin Luther King showed his people the way by marching—from the state capital to the nation's capital. He
Continued on page 29

A CONTEMPORARY OF DR. MARTIN LUTHER KING, JR. . . . REFLECTS UPON HIS LIFE AND IMPACT ON SOCIETY

6 MESSAGE

MESSAGE 7

Steve Hall, Lee Cherry Art Directors
Lee Cherry Designer
Ron Garnett Illustrator
Review & Herald Pub'l. Assoc. Agency
MESSAGE Magazine Client
Hagerstown, MD

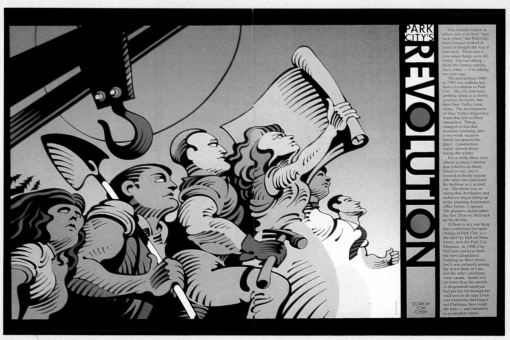

Don Weller Art Director/Designer/Illustrator
The Weller Institute For the Cure of Design, Inc.
Agency/Design Firm
PARK CITY LODESTAR Magazine Client
Park City, UT

Jeffrey Keyton Art Director
Steve Byram, Stacy Drummond Designers
David La Chapelle/Buckmaster Photographer
In-house Design Firm
MTV:Music Television Client
New York, NY

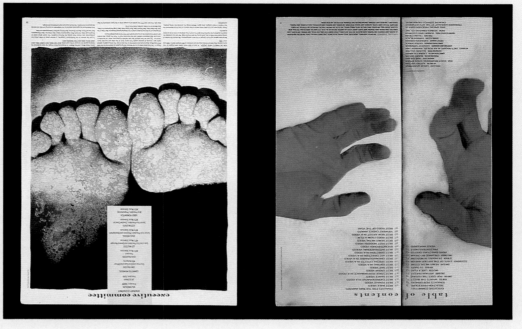

Dwayne Flinchum Art Director
Gottfried Helnwein Illustrator
OMNI Magazine Other
New York, NY

FICTION

Studebakers and flying saucer bars evoke bittersweet memories for a man who let the magic slip away

UNIDENTIFIED OBJECTS

BY JAMES P. BLAYLOCK

In 1956 the downtown square mile of the city of Orange was a collection of old houses: craftsman bungalows and tile-roofed Spanish, and here and there an old Queen Anne or a gingerbread Victorian with geminate windows and steep gables, and sometimes a carriage house alongside, too small by half to house the lumbering automobiles that the second fifty years of the century had produced. There were Studebakers at the curbs and Hudsons and Buicks with balloon tires like the illustrations of moon-aimed rockets on the covers of the pulp magazines. Science was still a professor with wild hair and a lab coat and with bubbling apparatus in a cellar; but in a few short years he would walk on the moon— one last ivory and silver hurrah—

PAINTING BY GOTTFRIED HELNWEIN

Richard Bleiweiss Art Director
Eric Schnakenberg Photographer
PENTHOUSE Magazine Client
Whitestone, NY

WORLD WAR II
When Darkness Fell
BY OTTO FRIEDRICH

Rudolph C. Hoglund Art Director
Arthur Hochstein Designer
TIME Magazine Client
New York, NY

JURGEN STOCKMAR
THE RETURN OF

Miles Abernethy Art Director/Designer
Barry Shepard Creative Director
Dougie Firth Photographer
Matthew Carter Copywriter
SHR Design Communications Design Firm
Audi of America, Inc. Client
Scottsdale, AZ

First Light

Rick Bard Art Director/Photographer
Bard Communications Design Firm
MANHATTAN Magazine Client
New York, NY

beach
my

David Carson Art Director/Designer
Art Brewer Photographer
Carson Design Design Firm
BEACH CULTURE Magazine Client
Del Mar, CA

RIDING THE BOOM
How long can this go on?

Kathy Kelley Art Director
Al Brandtner Designer
Alan Brunettin Illustrator
CHICAGO Magazine Client
Chicago, IL

THE LAST OF THE CURRITUCK BEACH COWBOYS

BY LORRAINE EATON

Out west in the desert sun, they say the light can do strange things. They say that when the heat comes broiling down and the sun's rays are hotter than a branding iron, the eyes can play tricks and make you see things that just aren't there.

Is it real, or just a mirage?

Barry Anderson, Laurie Gagnon,
Jane Krumwiede, Mark Thacker Art Directors
Advertising Design Services Design Firm
OUTER BANKS Magazine Client
Kill Devil Hills, NC

HELP FOR YOUR **HYPERACTIVE** CHILD

Charli Ornett Art Director/Designer
Lauren Sorokin Photographer
Healthy Kids Client
New York, NY

David Carson Art Director
Art Brewer Photographer
BEACH CULTURE Magazine Client
Dana Point, CA

JEWELS

Carol Mills Art Director/Designer
William Guillen Photographer
Mills Associates, Inc. Design Firm
Communications Venture Group. Ltd.x Client
New York, NY

One touch of nature makes the whole world kin.
WILLIAM SHAKESPEARE

Think Special Report

Respect for the planet

Ron Couture Art Director
Newsvision Design Firm
IBM-International Business
Machines Corporation Client
Mount Kisco, NY

249

Tom Staebler Art Director
Kerig Pope Designer
Pater Sato Illustrator
PLAYBOY Design Firm/Client
Chicago, IL

Michael Salisbury Art Director/Designer
Philip Burke Illustrator
Salisbury Communications Agency/Design Firm
General Media Client
Torrance, CA

Kent Hunter Creative Director
David Suh Designer
Mark Jenkinson, Charles Purvis, Timothy White
  Photographers
Frankfurt Gips Balkind Design Firm
MCI Communications Client
New York, NY

Jeffrey L. Dever Art Director/Designer/Illustrator
Dever Designs, Inc. Design Firm
COMMON CAUSE Magazine Client
Laurel, MD

ONE KIND of a

Peek-a-boo with Phyllis Kind, the feared and revered Mad Hatter of art

BY MARCIA FROELKE COBURN

Photography by DAVID CARTER

SOME LIKE IT

HOT

PHOTOGRAPHY BY ELIZABETH HATHON

Image Maker

After his first artistic retreat, Peter Max emerged to define an era with his art, and also to assemble some 72 licensees—with yearly sales exceeding $1 billion. He is just emerging from his second such retreat. Are you ready?

 STRESS
ストレスにハワイ 快

日本のみなさん、ストレスとうまくつき合っていますか？あぶない兆候に気づいたら、いますぐ日本を脱出してください。ハワイはストレスによく効きます。解消のツボはずばり、快、遊、味、踊、涙、描、深。ここを集中的に治療すれば五感の幸せうろおいぼけで。るりやかな自然の中で思いきりスポーツを楽しんで、爽やかになっちゃいましょう。おいしいお料理を食べ歩きするのも効果的です。踊りまくる。これは文句なしに絶快。そうそうハワイといえばやっぱりショッピング。一流ブランドのブティックめぐりもメンタルヘルスに最適です。それからレンタルもメンタルにいいみたい。高級車を借りて、ビーチフロントの一軒家でパーティーなんて素敵です。最後は探索。旅の醍醐味をたっぷり満喫して、日常生活をしばし忘れてみる。そんなこんなで、ぜんぶひっくるめてグッバイ・ストレス！保証します。

Kathy Kelley Art Director/Designer
David Carter Photographer
CHICAGO Magazine Client
Chicago, IL

Kam Wai Yu Art Director
Keith Beaty Photographer
Vit Wagner Copywriter
The Toronto Star Newspaper Ltd. Client
Toronto, Ontario, Canada

Carol Mills Art Director
Judy Kramer Designer
Elizabeth Hathon Photographer
Mills Associates, Inc. Design Firm
Communications Venture Group, Ltd. Client
New York, NY

Rick Bard Art Director/Photographer
Bard Communications Design Firm
MANHATTAN Magazine Client
New York, NY

Kunio Hayashi Art Director
Joy S. Matsuura Designer
Masahiko Wada Photographer
Media Five Limited Design Firm
Travel Plaza, Inc. Client
Honolulu, HI

OBSERVING CROWS

Is preening behavior among crows merely cosmetic, or does it accomplish something else?

MARY LEISTER

The greatest thing about birding, for me, is its absolutely boundless serendipity. Those sightings, those happenings, those thoroughly unexpected surprises we come upon in our own hedgerows, in our neighbor's woodland, in the everyday corner of an everyday field, those are the things that keep us birders tingling with a sense of quiet adventure every time we step into the out-of-doors or even glance from a window. It's not so very often that we find a new bird; but now and again, and at long, long intervals, we discover a perfectly usual bird of our long acquaintance up to some behavior we've never seen before.

MASLOWSKI PHOTOGRAPH

88

Robert Ayers, John Johanek Art Directors
John Johanek Designer
Karl Maslowski Photographer
Publication Design, Inc. Design Firm
BIRD WATCHER'S DIGEST Client
Allentown, PA

Bryan Canniff Art Director
Alan Andresen Designer
Brian Kosoff Photographer
POPULAR MECHANICS Client
New York, NY

Peter Wong Ming Faye Art Director/Designer
Michael Ma Po Shum Photographer
Peter Wong Design & Associates, Ltd.
  Design Firm
THE PACIFIC TRAVELLER Client
Hong Kong

21 TOP TIPS FOR GOOSE HUNTING

Expert advice on how to bring in, and bag, more birds, by Zack Taylor

1 A blind may be the least important element in goose hunting. You can lie out on the ground on top of a ground cloth or foam pad. The important thing is to keep still—move only your eyeballs. Keep your hand on your gun so you can sit up and swing in one easy motion.

2 Always wear a camouflage cap with a brim to hide your face.

3 Pick up any empty shotgun shells lying around the area you're shooting from. Biologists estimate that a Canada goose's vision is eight times as powerful as a man's. If the sun glints off the shells, geese can pick them out from a long way off.

4 To keep your shotgun's barrel clear of dirt before you raise up to shoot, rest it on the curve of your boot. Be sure that barrel opening clears the end of the boot.

5 Oversized silhouettes are probably the most common and least expensive decoys, followed by plastic half shells. The shell decoys look good and stack easily, but cost more. To add life to field sets, use wind socks.

6 Use natural weeds to break up your silhouette.

7 Geese can be lured with a couple dozen decoys. The more they are pursued, though, the greater the number of decoys you will need. Guides often put out several hundred silhouettes.

8 Gun the first week of the season if at all possible. Flocks are still unwary.

9 If you're gunning clear water, use monofilament for decoy leads. Geese often spot green nylon leads.

10 It can be difficult to estimate when geese are in range because they are so big. Rule: If you can make out their eyes, take them. Also, geese are faster than they appear to be.

11 As in all water-fowling, weather is key to success. Wind, snow, rain and fog are all good. Geese need to eat more in cold weather, and therefore must move around more.

A blind isn't always best. Lay out a ground cloth among some tall weeds, set up your decoys, keep as still as possible, and wait for the geese.

Illustrated by Sports Afield by Jack Unruh

Gary Gretter Art Director
Carol Rheuban Designer
Jack Unruh Illustrator
SPORTS AFIELD Magazine Client
New York, NY

Thaddeus A. Miksinski, Jr. Art Director/Designer
Barry Fitzgerald Photographer
United States Information Agency Agency
TOPIC Magazine Client
Washington, DC

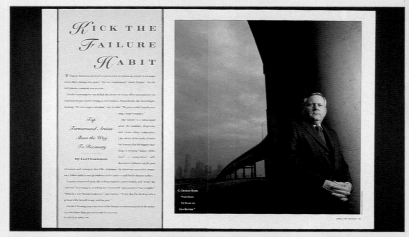

David A. Bayer Art Director
Heidi Antman Designer
Danny Turner Photographer
SUCCESS Magazine Client
New York, NY

Wendy Mansfield Art Director
Lisa Goldenberg Designer
Caroline Bowyer Design Director
Cara Rossignol Photographer
WORKING WOMAN Magazine Client
New York, NY

Editorial Design MULTIPLE UNIT

HEEL!
OPPOSITE: MANOLO
BLAHNIK SUEDE AND
PERSIAN LAMB BOOTIE,
$710. THE DOG, A PUG.
THIS PAGE: PRADA
JEWELED VELVET MULE
WITH HEEL, $290. THE
DOG, A BULLDOG. MORE
INFO, LAST PAGES.

Karen Lee Grant Art Director/Designer
Elliot Erwitt Photographer
MIRABELLA Client
New York, NY

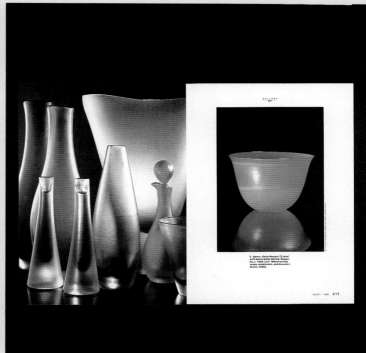

E. Gary Bloom Art Director
Carol Van Jinbo Designer
George Erml/Courtesy of Muriel Karasik Gallery
 Photographer
THE WORLD & I Magazine Client
Washington, DC

255

PARIS PRESTIGE

Jacques Robert Art Director
Pierre Berdoy Photographer
CHATELAINE-Maclean Hunter Client
Montreal, Quebec, Canada

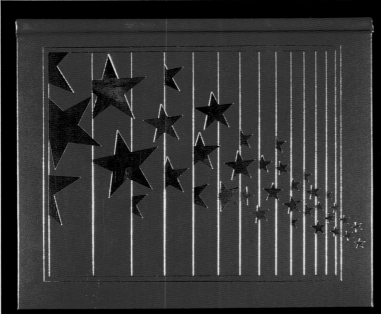

David M. Seager Art Director/Designer
National Geographic Society Agency/Client
Washington, DC

Peter Wong Ming Faye Art Director/Designer
Charles Lindsay Photographer
Peter Wong Design & Associates, Ltd.
   Design Firm
THE PACIFIC TRAVELLER Client
Hong Kong

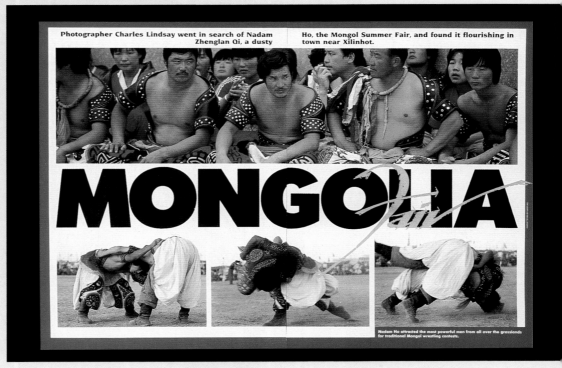

Photographer Charles Lindsay went in search of Nadam Zhenglan Qi, a dusty Ho, the Mongol Summer Fair, and found it flourishing in town near Xilinhot.

MONGOLIA Fair

Nadam Ho attracted the most powerful men from all over the grasslands for traditional Mongol wrestling contests.

Wendy Mansfield Art Director/Designer
Caroline Bowyer Design Director
Anthony Russo Illustrator
WORKING WOMAN Magazine Client
New York, NY

David M. Seager Art Director/Designer
Tom Danielson Photographer
National Geographic Society Agency/Client
Washington, DC

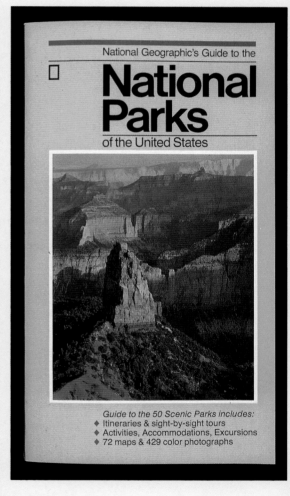

Jacques Robert Art Director
Jacques Denarnaud Photographer
CHATELAINE-Maclean Hunter Client
Montreal, Quebec, Canada

A   C

VALENTINE. *Cease to persuade, my loving Proteus:*
Home-keeping youth have ever homely wits.
Were't not affection chains thy tender days
To the sweet glances of thy honored love,
I rather would entreat thy company
To see the wonders of the world abroad,
Than, living dully sluggardized at home,
Wear out thy youth with shapeless idleness.
But since thou lov'st, love still, and thrive therein,
Even as I would, when I to love begin.
PROTEUS. *Wilt thou be gone? Sweet Valentine, adieu!*
Think on thy Proteus when thou haply seest
Some rare noteworthy object in thy travel:
Wish me partaker in thy happiness
When thou dost meet good hap; and in thy danger,
If ever danger do environ thee,
Commend thy grievance to my holy prayers,
For I will be thy beadsman, Valentine.
VALENTINE. *And on a love-book pray for my success?*

T   ONE
                                                                   SCENE I

Martin Solomon Art Director/Designer
Isadore Seltzer Illustrator
Royal Composing Room Design Firm/Client
New York, New York

Terrance W. McCaffrey Art Director/Designer
In-house Design Firm
U.S. Postal Service Client
Washington, DC

Mary Archondes Cover Coordinator
Circa '86, Inc. Design Firm
Harper & Row Publishers, Inc./College Division
  Client
New York, NY

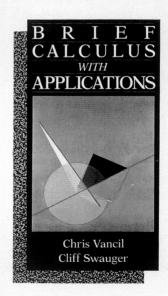

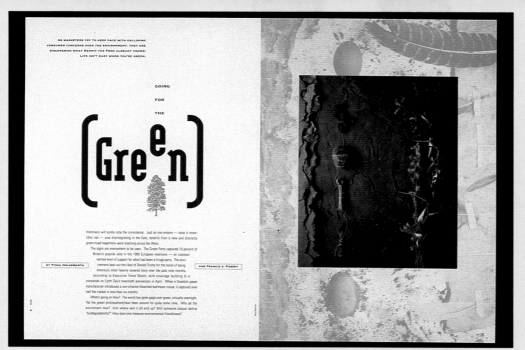

As marketers try to keep pace with galloping consumer concerns over the environment, they are discovering what Kermit the Frog already knows: Life isn't easy when you're green.

GOING FOR THE

(Gre e n)

By Fiona Holderegneth   And Francis X. Piderit

Historians will surely note the coincidence. Just as one empire — color it monolithic red — was disintegrating in the East, tendrils from a new and distinctly green-hued hegemony were reaching across the West.

The signs are everywhere to be seen. The Green Party captured 15 percent of Britain's popular vote in the 1989 European elections — an unprecedented level of support for what had been a fringe party. The environment beat out the likes of Donald Trump for the honor of being America's most heavily covered story over the past nine months, according to Executive Trend Watch, with coverage building to a crescendo on Earth Day's twentieth anniversary in April. When a Swedish paper manufacturer introduced a non-chlorine bleached bathroom tissue, it captured over half the market in less than six months.

What's going on here? The world has gone gaga over green, virtually overnight. Yet the green philosophies have been around for quite some time. Why all the excitement now? And where will it all end up? Will someone please define "biodegradability"? How does one measure environmental friendliness?

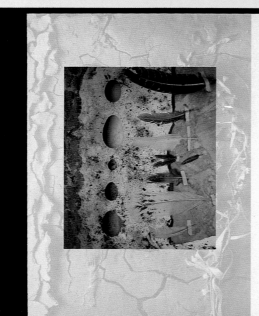

To Begin in the Beginning

One could go as far back as Rachel Carson's *The Silent Spring*, published in 1963, to find the roots of the movement. In the 1950's, green consumers were known as hippies. By the 1970's, they were known in polite company as environmental activists, and as eco-freaks behind their backs. West Germany's Greens took the movement from the streets into the corridors of power, and the Club of Rome put the fear of God into everyone with its dire warnings.

Recently, the public and media worked their way through a list of environmentally hot "hazards of the week" lead in paint and petrol, chlorofluorocarbons (CFCs) and the depletion of the ozone layer, the greenhouse effect, toxic waste dumping, nuclear winter, water pollution, acid rain, and deforestation.

Somewhere along the line, though, it finally dawned on people that the environmental movement was not an itemized list of causes, but a state of mind that touched every aspect of life. Angst is meaningless without action.

The call for practical action is evident in the pages of the much-acclaimed *Green Consumer Guide* by John Elkington and Julia Hailes, published in the U.K. in September 1988 to coincide with Green Consumer Week. The power of the pocketbook was what turned a social issue into a marketing issue. David Nichol, president of Loblaw International Merchants, put it this way in a speech last November when he said, "Consumers are beginning to comprehend the power that they have to vote for the environment at the cash register. The implications for business are potentially enormous. In the interest of the environment, and customers ... are poised to bestow rewards upon your company, or inflict devastating penalties."

Target Markets

Some of the first product categories to be hit by the green movement were those involving aerosols. CFC's, used as aerosol propellants, were implicated in the appearance of a hole in the ozone layer about the size of the U.S. As the public grasped the consequences of ozone depletion and its link with skin cancer, manufacturers were forced to introduce green aerosols, containing no harmful CFC's.

But the problem remains unsolved. These "environmentally friendly" aerosols contain butane, evident in the "WARNING: FLAMMABLE..." notices on every can. Major manufacturers are now introducing pump-action aerosols which are both truly environmentally friendly and safe, even though these tend to cost more. According to the Nielsen Retail Index, U.K. sales of pump-action sprays as a percentage of total hair spray sales went from negligible levels in early 1988 to over 13 percent in groceries and more than 20 percent in pharmacies by the end of 1989.

Nappies, or disposable baby diapers, is another market hit by green fever. Nappies are bleached white with chlorine. Reports have suggested that plant and marine life suffer from the chlorine gas effluent of the bleaching process. Even more worrying have been reports linking dioxin, the toxic chemical released in the chlorine bleaching process, with cancer. As a result, both major manufacturers in Britain — Procter & Gamble and Peaudouce — have launched nappies which they claim are environmentally friendly.

Another environmental hazard caused by disposable diapers is, in fact, their very disposability. In the U.S., an estimated 16 billion diapers were thrown away last year, with the majority entering the country's overflowing landfill sites. With little or no air or sunlight reaching them, these products degrade slowly. P&G, in addition to cutting the weight and volume of its disposable diapers, is operating a pilot program that asks for used diapers back. The company is asking 1,000 parents in Seattle to save Pampers and Luvs diapers, along with disposable diapers made by competitors, for a weekly collection.

In the detergents market, one of the major environmental controversies involves phosphates, which account for around 25 percent by weight of most washing powders. Landlocked Switzerland has had to ban phosphates altogether. The Netherlands and West Germany have both introduced restrictions. In Britain, the most serious problems are in the Norfolk Broads and Lough Neagh, where the water is being treated with phosphate removers.

West Germany's Henkel sells phosphate-free detergents under the Persil and Dixan brand names in most of Europe. "All over Europe, legislation is restricting the use of phosphates," according to Atele Linder, marketing director of Henkel Benlin. "In some countries, like Italy, Denmark and Sweden, phosphates are virtually forbidden." Spain is an exception. In October, Henkel launched Persil phosphate-free detergent in Spain, making it that country's first. Mr. Linder explains, "Henkel is launching an environmentally safe detergent here because we want to be ahead of everybody."

Shortly after the Henkel launch in Spain, P&G introduced Ariel Ultra phosphate-free concentrated detergent in the U.K., following roll-outs in West Germany and France. Two companies in the U.K. market with environmentally friendly products are Ark and Ecover. The former is an environmentally aware consumer products group which launched its range of green products in 1989. Ecover is a Belgian detergents manufacturer which has been selling its products in the U.K. since 1980.

A Tidal Wave

The environmental movement is virtually a worldwide wave, but one that is moving at different speeds in different places.

In the view of Loblaw's Mr. Nichol, "While the environment is the No.1 concern of Canadians, recent surveys indicate that in the U.S. it currently ranks in the sixth or seventh position." Dr. Deborah Anderson, director of environmental coordination for P&G, sees the wave moving in about the same way, commenting that "European consumers are five to seven years ahead of the U.S. in their environmental concerns. Even Canadian consumers are a few years ahead of the U.S."

(Angs**t** IS MEANINGLESS WITHOUT ACTION.**)**

Kent Hunter Art Director
Kin Yuen Designer
Hans Neleman Photographer
Paul Leith, J. Otto Siebold, Rob Colvin Illustrators
Frankfurt Gips Balkind Design Firm
A.C. Nielsen Client
New York, NY

ENCHANTED FOREST
KOKE'E
penetrating Kauai's misty uplands

story & photos by David Boynton

As I sit in Koke'e writing this, I feel the pull of the outdoors and step out to stand in the light mist known as "angels' breath." A cloud settles softly onto my face, the western sky blushing pink as the calls of native birds embroider the evening stillness. I can feel the rhythm of the wind as it envelops the forest, ranging here and there, sharing the airwaves with the blended trills of invisible crickets, each species with its unique song.

I can feel the *mana*, or spirit, of this ancient forest, whose twisting branches are etched onto the lacey veil of evening fog. The distant screech of an owl, the watchful *aumakua*, cuts through the chill of these uplands on the northwest side of Kauai.

This is the Koke'e that draws me back to endless amazement at forest moods that leave me standing in awe, at the endlessly varied textures of forest experience.

In the forests, on the ridges
of the mountains stands Laka
Dwelling in the source of the mists
Laka, mistress of the hula,
has climbed the wooded haunts
of the gods.

This classic translation of an ancient chant captures for me the very spirit of Koke'e.

Set like an emerald in a beautiful pendant, Koke'e's forests lie at the center of Kauai's wilderness country. Originally the name of a small stream,

"I can feel the *mana*, or spirit, of this ancient forest, whose twisting branches are etched onto a lacey veil of evening fog."

Myles Ludwig Art Director
Steve Shrader Designer
David Boynton Photographer
Inter-Pacific Media, Inc. Design Firm
THE SANDWICH ISLANDS QUARTERLY/
   Kamani Tree Press, Inc. Client
Hanalei, HI

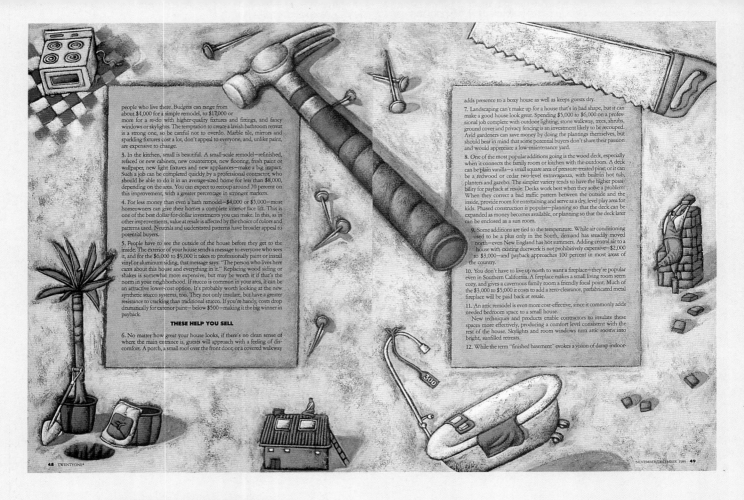

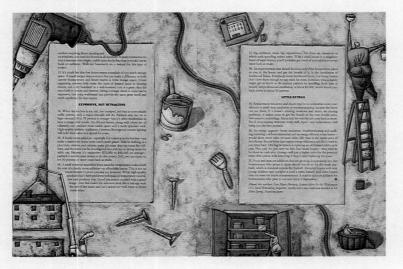

Lori Twietmeyer Art Director/Designer
Nicholas Wilton Illustrator
The Quarton Group Publishers Agency
Century 21 Real Estate Client
Troy, MI

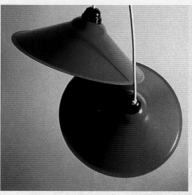

LAMPS

illuminate
a room with
individual
flair—
demure,
dynamic,
or coolly
sensual

E xtraordinary floor lamps (opposite, from left)—a stone-based model that's strong, straightforward; a metallic wave undulating with creativity. Colorful hanging lamps (above, left) recall the industrial age, now just want to have fun. A sculptural shade caps a copper sconce (above, right). Simply sensational, a trio of clean-lined sconces for a hallway or dining room (below, right). Vivid contrasts (below, left): the radiant calm of a Japanese paper shade; a futuristic floor lamp that's positively purple. Opposite page (left to right): Floor lamps, Stuber/Stone Inc., Blairhouse. This page (clockwise from top left): Hanging lamps, IKEA, Inc.; copper wall sconce, Stuber/Stone Inc.; wall sconces, IKEA, Inc.; hanging lamp, Light Inc., N.Y.; floor lamps, George Kovacs.

Phyllis Richmond Cox Art Director
Ann Marie Mennillo Designer
David Lawrence Photographer
BRIDE'S/The Conde Nast Publications, Inc.
  Client
New York, NY

beyond the
basics—a
gallery of
unique
chairs that
reflects
personality,
home style

CHAIRS

S ophisticated? Witty? Free-spirited? A single piece of furniture can speak worlds about a home. Here, a rose slipper chair for the boudoirs (above, left) captures snuggliness in bold yellow. Whimsical side chairs (above, right) spin Harlequin nifty, sleek gingko lines, Baquelina elegance, respect for tradition; a Queen Anne classic reigns (below, right). Sensualize how the smooth curves, warm tones of a bentwood (below, left). Fifties-style stacking chairs (opposite) piled with exuberance. This page: (clockwise from top left): Slipper chair, the Primary Collection, Gräce Fine USA; checkered chair, Douglas; vintage chair, Fredrick Williams; Queen Anne chair, Bakerl bentwood chair, by Michael Haslam for Thonet. Opposite page: Stacking chairs, ICF.

festive,
formal, or
fun 'n
funky,
tables set
the mood
for any
occasion

TABLES

D reamy chords or braided dubarious at (opposite) can play to party favories. Flip, Mix paired of tables (below, left) whirl to where the action is. Grounded festive tables (above, right) seeks an body-to-bodion, while a pedestal-stand, mahogany joy table (below, right) abodore proper English elegance. Moving toward the 21st century, symmetric metal and-glass (below, left). Decadent retro ornamented tables. Furniture in the Twentieth Century, N.Y. This page (clockwise from top left): Whirland ornamented tables, Douglas; seating tables, Gerrard Hartnoge; lift-top mahogany iron table, Stuber; glass top pyramid table, John Dericher, N.Y.

John Follis Art Director/Designer/Copywriter
Follis & Verdi, NY Agency
**Child Abuse Prevention Information
Resource Center** Client
New York, NY

Some abused children grow up to become famous.

Abused children grow up to become abusing adults. Not in every case, but in too many. Nine out of ten murderers, rapists and drug addicts suffered from physical or emotional abuse as a child. So did the four people pictured above.

If you need help, or want to learn about preventing child abuse, call 1-800-342-7472. Or you can write to: Child Abuse Prevention Information Resource Center, 134 South Swan Street, Albany, NY 12210.

Child Abuse. It hurts all of us.
Child Abuse Prevention Resource Center   Photos courtesy Bettmann

DROP OUT OF SCHOOL AND YOU CAN STILL GET A JOB ON WALL STREET.

NOURISH YOUR MIND. STAY IN SCHOOL. BURGER KING

DROP OUT OF SCHOOL AND YOU'LL STILL GET TO TRAVEL ON BUSINESS.

BREAK THE RULES NOURISH YOUR MIND. BURGER KING

DROP OUT OF SCHOOL AND YOU'LL STILL HAVE TO GO TO WORK IN A SUIT.

NOURISH YOUR MIND. STAY IN SCHOOL. BURGER KING

David Meador Art Director
David Hale Creative Director
Alison Grant Copywriter
DMB&B Agency
Burger King Client
New York, NY

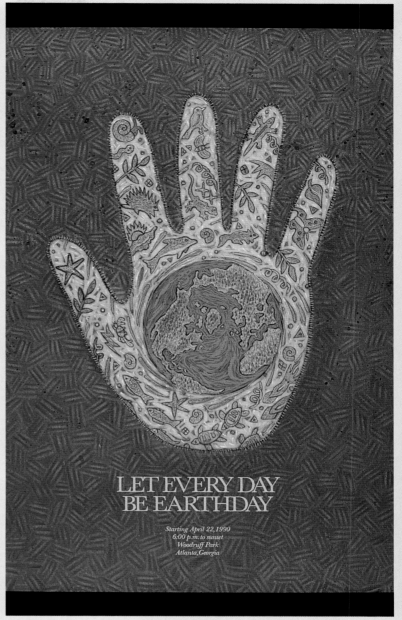

LET EVERY DAY
BE EARTHDAY

Starting April 22, 1990
6:00 p.m. to sunset
Woodruff Park
Atlanta, Georgia

Kim Youngblook, Julie Sand, John Lineweaver
 Art Directors
Julie Sand Designer
Joe E. Sanders Illustrator
Youngblood, Sweat & Tears Agency/Design Firm
Georgia Earth Day Committee Client
Atlanta, GA

Jim Mochnsky Art Director
Stephen John Phillips Photographer
Arthur Mitchell, Jim Mochnsky Copywriters
W.B. Doner and Company Agency
The World Wildlife Fund Client
Baltimore, MD

How do you fit five elephants in a box?

First find someone who'll do the killing. Arm him with a machine gun and an axe. Send him off to slaughter elephants. Pay him for the tusks. And ship them away to be carved into bracelets and necklaces.

The African elephant is being driven from the face of the earth for the sake of consumer demand for ivory trinkets. In just 10 years, the population of African elephants has been more than halved. If this rate of killing continues, the African elephant could be extinct in just 25 years. The killers and the people who pay them don't care about elephant deaths. They don't hear the world's outrage. They just want money. They're the people we must stop.

Please join World Wildlife Fund's Elephant Action Campaign. Help us put these killers and the people who finance them out of business. Your donation of $15 or more will help us support increased anti-poaching patrols. And supply equipment to those rangers who are already in the field – desperately trying to stop the senseless slaughter of one of the world's great species.

Time is running out. 143 African elephants are dying every day. So their tusks can be turned into jewelry. You can stop this. Before it's too late. Call 1-800-453-6100 to make a donation.

BOTTOMS UP!

A toast to those who know when to say "enough."

Tom Chung Art Director
Harrison Getz Creative Director
Richard Chestnut Photographer
Eric Jensen Copywriter
NBC Corporate Communications Client
New York, NY

She's gone to great pains.

Just to survive being homeless. She, and hundreds of other children like her. That's the homeless problem in Phoenix. The immense pain. The desperate look of having to grow up much too fast. ✤ Together, we can house the helpless ones. And we must do that. ✤ A special fund for the homeless children of Phoenix has been established. Call, or mail your tax deductible contributions to: *Phoenix Home and Garden Fund for Homeless Children, c/o Arizona Community Foundation, 4350 E. Camelback Road, Suite 216C, Phoenix, AZ 85018. (602) 952-9954*

PHOENIX HOME AND GARDEN
Fund for ★★★★
Homeless Children

Part of the Arizona Children's Trust Fund

Created by Nordensson Lynn Advertising

Kathryn Polk Art Director
Lois New Designer
Jon Gipe Photographer
Greg Stene Copywriter
Nordensson Lynn Advertising Agency
PHOENIX HOME & GARDEN Magazine Client
Tucson, AZ

She could be telling you she's failed for the last time.

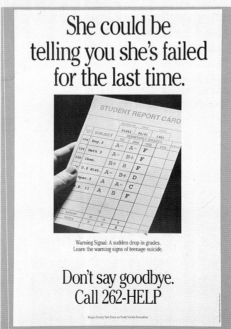

Warning Signal: A sudden drop in grades.
Learn the warning signs of teenage suicide.

Don't say goodbye.
Call 262-HELP

Bergen County Task Force on Youth Suicide Prevention

Wesley Shaw Art Director
Ed Taylor Photographer
Rhonda Smith Copywriter
Words and Pictures Agency
Bergen County Task Force on Youth Suicide Prevention Client
Park Ridge, NJ

In Asia, blue eyes, freckles and curly or blond hair are all signs of having mixed blood, most likely half American. And in most Asian societies, carrying the traits of their American fathers results in being viewed as socially unacceptable. Even being denied citizenship in the countries where they were born. It also means being excluded from receiving proper health care and, sadly, a basic education.

IMAGINE
HAVING
ILLEGITIMACY
WRITTEN ALL
OVER YOUR FACE.

Since 1964, The Pearl S. Buck Foundation has been providing AmerAsians with needed medical, educational and psychological support. But to continue, we need you. Please help us make sure these AmerAsian children are cared for and never forgotten.

The Pearl S. Buck Foundation, Inc.
HELPING AMERASIAN KIDS SINCE 1964
GREEN HILLS FARM • PERKASIE, PENNSYLVANIA • 18944 • (800) 242-BUCK

Carlos Segura Art Director/Designer
Doug Schiff Copywriter
Bayer Bess Vanderwarker Agency
The Pearl Buck Foundation Client
Chicago, IL

264

A CONDOM? I'D RATHER DIE.

Minnesota Aids Project

Gregg Byers Art Director
Allen Cohn Copywriter
DDBO/Minneapolis Agency
Minnesota AIDS Project Client
Minneapolis, MN

"Ahhh... Ohhh...Oh! Oh God. Oh. Oh my God... Oh God, Oh Oh OhGodOhGodOhGodOhGod Oh...Oh God... OH GOD!!"

Make love without a condom and you really better start praying.
AIDSLINE 870-0700

Rich Buceta Art Director
Allen Cohn Copywriter
BBDO/Minneapolis Agency
Minnesota AIDS Line Client
Minneapolis, MN

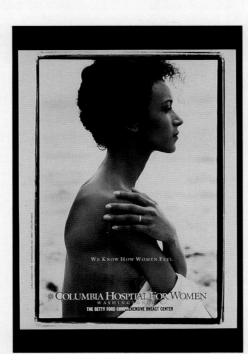

Karen Trout Art Director
Helen Norman Photographer
VanSant Dugdale Advertising Agency
Columbia Hospital For Women Client
Baltimore, MD

Roy Podorson Art Director
Ted Charron Copywriter
Charron, Schwartz & Partners, Inc. Agency
Robert Robbins Production
ABC Network News/Project Literacy U.S. Client
New York, NY

265

There's some swampland we'd like to sell you.

We plan on building something quite remarkable there. Nothing.

The Cache River Wetlands in southern Illinois is one of the most unusual wild areas left in the state. And we'd like to keep it that way-wild.

Home to 1000 year-old cypress trees, herons, and other waterfowl that migrate along the Mississippi, this fragile area is part of the 22,000 acres of irreplaceable land The Nature Conservancy has helped save in Illinois since 1957.

But soil erosion and the destruction of bottomland hardwood forests still threaten unprotected parts of the wetlands.

Right now, we have the opportunity to expand the Cache River Preserve to 60,000 acres. But we need your help.

As an international non-profit organization dedicated to protecting endangered plants and animals by purchasing the land they depend on, The Nature Conservancy itself depends on memberships and donations.

Membership in The Nature Conservancy is only $15 a year, and all contributions are tax deductible. Of course, donations of any size are welcomed and needed. As are volunteers for field work.

Please join us in saving the cypress swamps of the Cache River. After all, an investment opportunity like this only comes along once every thousand years.

For information, call 312-346-8168, or write: The Nature Conservancy, Illinois Field Office, 79 West Monroe Street, Suite 708, Chicago, Illinois 60603.

Photo: Kim Harris

THE NATURE
CONSERVANCY

We save land the American way. We buy it.

At The Nature Conservancy, we believe that the most effective way to preserve America's wildlands is the most direct way. Buy them, so nobody else will.

By purchasing land that supports endangered plants and animals we can preserve them—without legislative red tape or unnecessary controversy.

Using this approach, the Illinois chapter of The Conservancy has saved over 22,000 acres of irreplaceable wildlands since 1957.

Over 100 preserves statewide include a diversity of ecosystems—from bald eagle roosting sites along the Mississippi River to the unique Nachusa Grasslands in central Illinois, to restored prairies on the outskirts of Chicago.

With only one tenth of one percent of Illinois still in its original condition, these preserves are crucial if we are to save even part of our natural heritage for future generations.

Such preserves also cost a lot of money.

The Nachusa Grasslands were purchased by The Nature Conservancy just 15 minutes before an auction would have turned it into a housing development.

Membership in the Illinois chapter of The Nature Conservancy is only $15 and all contributions are tax-deductible.

Of course, donations of any size are welcomed and needed. As are volunteers for field work.

Help save the land of Illinois. As Will Rogers said, they ain't making any more of it.

For information, call 312-346-8168, or write: The Nature Conservancy, Illinois Field Office, 79 West Monroe Street, Suite 708, Chicago, Illinois 60603.

THE NATURE
CONSERVANCY

Tom Shortlidge Art Director
Tim Bieber, Kim Harris Photographers
Scott Burns, John Koenig Copywriters
Young & Rubicam Chicago Agency
The Nature Conservancy Client
Chicago, IL

Stephen Burdick Art Director/Designer
Mark Morelli Photographer
Carol Sutton Copywriter
Polese Clancy Design Firm
AIDS Action Committee Client
Boston, MA

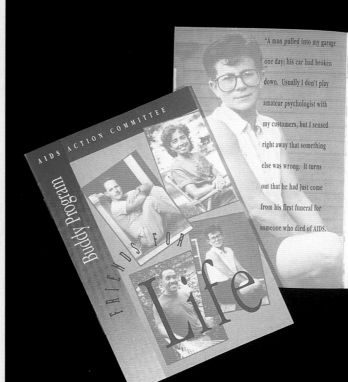

She Lives Right Near The Office.

Conventional wisdom suggests that being employed in the United States guarantees a roof over your head. But right now there are 1,000,000 Americans with jobs and no place to live. So much for conventional wisdom.

CALL PROJECT HEAT. 781-2944.

Tom Smith Art Director
Cathy Wolf Designer
William Viggiano Photographer
Wyse Advertising Agency
Project Heat Client
Cleveland, OH

It's Time We Addressed The Homeless.

Ten thousand homeless people live and die in Cleveland. If we don't address this problem now, one hundred thousand people will inhabit the streets of our city by the turn of the century. What do we do then?

CALL PROJECT HEAT. 781-2944.

TO YOU IT'S HELL.
TO US IT'S JUST ANOTHER DAY ON THE JOB.

Sunlight is rare.

Garbage piles up in the halls and stairwells. Crack vials crunch beneath your feet.

Welcome to the world of the Visiting Nurse Association of Brooklyn. A world in which we've played an important part since 1888.

Our job is often very dangerous. Sometimes so dangerous, we have to travel with security escorts. But we believe that Brooklyn residents deserve quality home health care. No matter where they live. No matter how risky the conditions.

And since being sick can happen anytime, we work 24 hours a day, seven days a week.

Providing so many varied services requires a great deal of dedication. It also requires a great deal of money.

That's why, for the first time ever, we're asking for your help. Send your check to: Development Office, Visiting Nurse Association of Brooklyn, 138 So. Oxford St. Brooklyn, NY 11217.

The Visiting Nurses are looking for more Visiting Nurses. If you want one of the most demanding, satisfying jobs in New York, contact Personnel at (718) 230-6900.

And help turn Hell into Heaven.

VISITING NURSE ASSOCIATION OF BROOKLYN
138 South Oxford Street
Brooklyn, New York 11217

Larry Aarons Art Director/Designer
Bruce Davidson Photographer
Jeff Bockman Copywriter
Taylor-Gordon, Aarons & Company, Inc. Agency
Visiting Nurse Association of Brooklyn Client
New York, NY

Turn *Turn* Turn

When there's nowhere left to turn, turn to SAFEHOUSE
449-8623

Carole Nervig Art Director
Dani Burke Designer
Andy Katz Photographer
Carole Nervig/Graphic Design Design Firm
Boulder County Safehouse Client
Boulder, CO

267

Erwin Lefkowitz Art Director
Nathaneal Neujean Sculpture
Joseph Rudavsky Copywriter
Erwin Lefkowitz & Associates Agency
Ramapo College, Center for Holocaust
and Genocide Studies Client
New York, NY

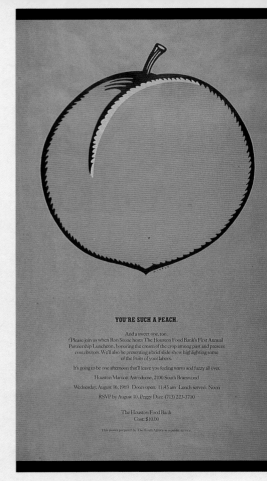

YOU'RE SUCH A PEACH.

And a sweet one, too.
Please join us when Ron Stone hosts The Houston Food Bank's First Annual
Partnership Luncheon, honoring the cream of the crop among past and present
contributors. We'll also be presenting a brief slide show highlighting some
of the fruits of your labors.

It's going to be one afternoon that'll leave you feeling warm and fuzzy all over.

Houston Marriott Astrodome, 2100 South Braeswood

Wednesday, August 16, 1989 Doors open: 11:45 am Lunch served: Noon

RSVP by August 10, Peggy Dure (713) 223-3700

The Houston Food Bank
Cost: $10.00

This poster prepared by The Hively Agency as a public service.

Charles Hively Art Director/Designer
Charles Hively Illustrator/Copywriter
The Hively Group Agency
The Houston Food Bank Client
Houston, TX

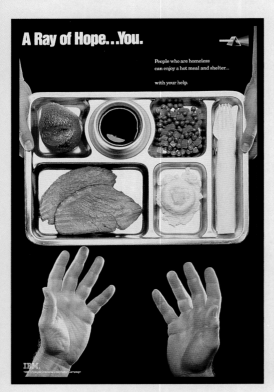

A Ray of Hope...You.

People who are homeless
can enjoy a hot meal and shelter...

with your help.

IBM.

LEAGUE
FOR THE
HEARING
IMPAIRED
Words blossom even in silence

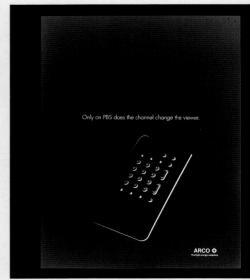

Only on PBS does the channel change the viewer.

ARCO
The high energy company.

Bob Salpeter Art Director/Designer
Larry Silver Photographer
Gloria Stashower Copywriter/Design Firm
IBM Client
New York, NY

Bill Holley Art Director
Kerry Oliver, Bill Holley, Dennas Davis
    Designers
Dennas Davis Illustrator
Buntin Advertising, Inc. Agency
League for the Hearing Impaired Client
Nashville, TN

April Mackay Thomas Art Director
Jan Craig Creative Designer
Tony Garcia Photographer
Kresser/Craig Agency
ARCO Client
Los Angeles, CA

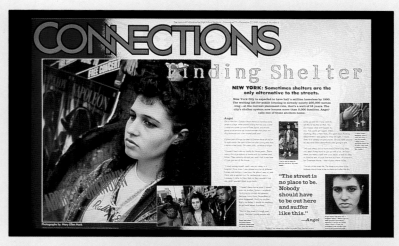

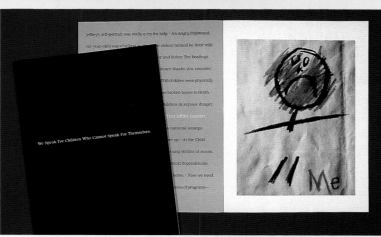

Michael Hilker Art Director
Joseph Broda, Tracy Boyd Designers
Mary Ellen Mark Photographer
Mark Wilcox Associate Art Director
Deborah Barnes Copywriter
Whittle Communications Design Firm/Client
Knoxville, TN

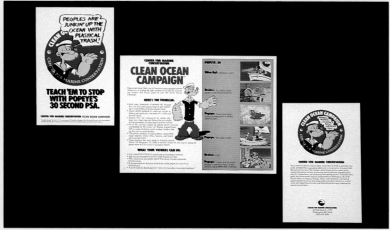

Jill Perry Townsend Art Director
James Hellmuth, Jill Perry Townsend Designers
James Hellmuth Illustrator
Phil Mendez Productions Animation
Center for Marine Conservation Agency/Client
Washington, DC

Tom Smith Art Director
Cathy Wolf Designer
Martin Reuben Photographer
Wyse Advertising Agency
Child Guidance Center Client
Cleveland, OH

TAKE ONE SMALL STEP

MAKE A DONATION NOW
Save the Children Fund

Barry Moss Art Director/Designer
IHJ Advertising Agency
Save the Children Fund Client
McMahons Point, NSW, Australia

We don't all have careers in medicine, homes in Beverly Hills, or huge bank accounts, either.

In fact, more than 45,000 elderly Jews in Los Angeles can barely afford to feed themselves. They come to us for medical care. For food and shelter. And for legal aid, as well as the transportation to receive it.

They come to us because we're dedicated to Jewish survival. And to helping people in need. They come to us because we're the United Jewish Fund, the Los Angeles arm of the worldwide United Jewish Appeal.

Not All Jews Retire To Miami.

And today, our needs are greater than ever before. But we can't do anything without your help. So please donate generously.

And if the world wants to stereotype us, let it be as givers.

My contribution is:
☐ $25 ☐ $50 ☐ $100 ☐ Other $_____
Name_____
Address_____
City/Zip_____
Phone_____
Occupation_____

Mail in with your check to:
United Jewish Fund,
6505 Wilshire Blvd.,
Los Angeles, CA 90048
Or call (800)553-9474,
Ext. 102.

UNITED JEWISH FUND

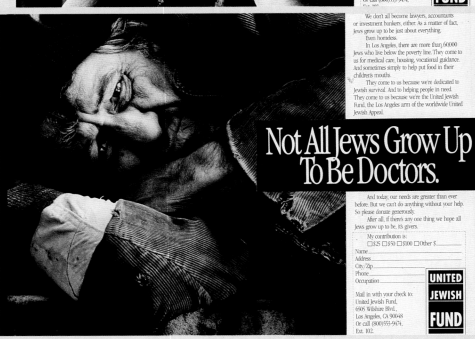

We don't all become lawyers, accountants or investment bankers, either. As a matter of fact, Jews grow up to be just about everything.

Even homeless.

In Los Angeles, there are more than 60,000 Jews who live below the poverty line. They come to us for medical care, housing, vocational guidance. And sometimes simply to help put food in their children's mouths.

They come to us because we're dedicated to Jewish survival. And to helping people in need. They come to us because we're the United Jewish Fund, the Los Angeles arm of the worldwide United Jewish Appeal.

Not All Jews Grow Up To Be Doctors.

And today, our needs are greater than ever before. But we can't do anything without your help. So please donate generously.

After all, if there's any one thing we hope all Jews grow up to be, it's givers.

My contribution is:
☐ $25 ☐ $50 ☐ $100 ☐ Other $_____
Name_____
Address_____
City/Zip_____
Phone_____
Occupation_____

Mail in with your check to:
United Jewish Fund,
6505 Wilshire Blvd.,
Los Angeles, CA 90048
Or call (800)553-9474,
Ext. 102.

UNITED JEWISH FUND

Moira Schwartz, Greg Koorhan Art Directors
Gary Wexler Creative Director
Jay Silverman Photographer
Sharon Rich, Gary Wexler Copywriters
Schwartz/Wexler Agency
United Jewish Fund Client
Hollywood, CA

270

Allan A. Haag Art Director/Designer
Frank Miller, Allan A. Haag Illustrators
Design Center Design Firm
General Mills Inc. Client
Minneapolis, MN

Shalley Doppelt Art Director
Jane Sterrett Illustrator
Brouillard Communications Agency
Salvation Army Client
New York, NY

Danny Boone Art Director
John Mahoney Copywriter
The Martin Agency Agency
The Corcoran School of Art Client
Richmond, VA

Illustration

Ronald Dunlap Illustrator/Art Director
Tony Honkawa Designer
Doglight Studios Design Firm/Client
Los Angeles, CA

I LOVE MY WORK.
I HATE MY JOB.

THE NURSING CRISIS IN AMERICA
A REPORT BY THE WYATT COMPANY

Mary Flock Illlustrator
Elizabeth Addison Art Director/Designer
Addison Design Design Firm
The Wyatt Company Client
Chicago, IL

Mel Odom Illustrator
Tom Staebler Art Director
Kerig Pope Designer
PLAYBOY Client
Chicago, IL

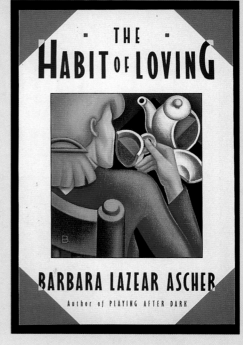

Bascove Illustrator/Designer
Robert Aulicino Art Director
Random House Client
New York, NY

Dennis Balogh Illustrator/Art Director
BEACON Magazine (of Akron Beacon Journal)
   Client
Akron, OH

Ken Dallison Illustrator
Mary Crane Art Director
Kaye Krapohl Designer
In-house Design Firm
AUTOMOBILE Magazine Client
Ann Arbor, MI

273

Bascove Illustrator/Designer
Cheryl Asherman Art Director
Wm. Morrow Client
New York, NY

Gerald Garston Illustrator
George Noszagh Art Director
Peter Swerdloff Creative Director
Brouillard Communications Agency
Municipal Bond Investors Assurance Client
New York, NY

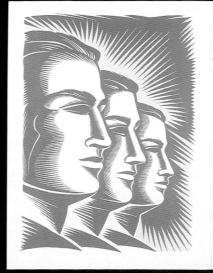

Cathie Bleck Illustrator
Arnold Wechsler, Stephen Visconti Art Directors
Stephen Visconti Designer
Bard Martin Photographer
Wechsler & Partners, Inc. Design Firm
Solomon Brothers Asset Management, Inc.
   Client
New York, NY

Cathie Bleck Illustrator
Michael Aron, Jason Calfo
   Art Directors/Designers
Calfo/Aron, Inc. Design Firm
United Way of New York City Client
New York, NY

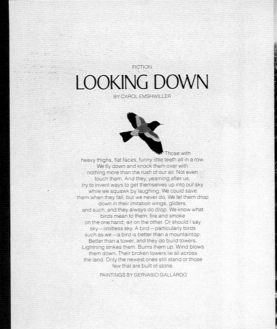

FICTION
LOOKING DOWN
BY CAROL EMSHWILLER

Those with heavy thighs, flat faces, funny little teeth all in a row. We fly down and knock them over with nothing more than the rush of our air. Not even touch them. And they, yearning after us, try to invent ways to get themselves up into our sky while we squawk by laughing. We could save them when they fall, but we never do. We let them drop down in their imitation wings, gliders and such, and they always do drop. We know what birds mean to them: fire and smoke on the one hand, air on the other. Or should I say sky—limitless sky. A bird—particularly birds such as we—a bird is better than a mountaintop. Better than a tower, and they do build towers. Lightning strikes them. Burns them up. Wind blows them down. Their broken towers lie all across the land. Only the newest ones still stand or those few that are built of stone.

PAINTINGS BY GERVASIO GALLARDO

Frances Middendorf Illustration/Art Director
Alden Burleigh Design Firm/Client
Fall River, MA

Dwayne Flinchum Art Director
Cathryn Bongiorno Designer
Gervasio Gallardo Illustrator
OMNI Magazine Client
New York, NY

---

20 AT EASE
Play's the Thing

Nathaniel Howe once defined leisure as "... time for doing something useful." Of course, that's the kind of remark one would expect from a clergyman in late 19th Century America, when the Puritan Ethic emphasized working hard in this life to be rewarded in the hereafter. Surely now, with a five-day work week and time-saving technologies, we've learned how to relax without feeling guilty, right?

Apparently not. The average woman's pocket calendar, crammed full of networking parties, fund-raising events and "educational" trips with her kids, bears mute testimony to the fact that we're still following Mr. Howe's definition of leisure.

Child psychologist David Elkind, Ph.D., of Tufts University in Medford, MA, admits that in many ways our whole American heritage is incompatible with a leisure mentality: "Americans have a 'frontier' mindset; they're constantly striving, pushing onward." Additionally, almost every American is indebted to immigrant forebears who believed that anything was possible in the "land of opportunity"—with hard work.

By contrast Europeans, with their defined borders and structured class systems, have made relaxation an art, as in the Spanish siesta and the two-hour meal in France. Even our clichés reflect our different attitudes: Where the Frenchman shrugs "C'est la vie," the American takes a deep breath and declaims, "The difficult we do at once; the impossible takes a little longer."

Naturally each stick-to-itiveness has its downside. Besides contributing to numerous health problems—migraines and heart attacks among them—new research indicates that not knowing how to relax may also defeat one's ability to get ahead. Says Elkind, "Studies have shown that truly successful people tend to have a sense of playfulness. They know how to take time out."

How does one learn to relax? First, say the experts, stop thinking of "leisure" as "doing nothing." John Neulinger, Ph.D., director of The Leisure Institute in Dolgeville, NY, uses the classic scene in The Adventures of Tom Sawyer, in which Tom's friends fight for the "privilege" of whitewashing his fence, to illustrate the true meaning of leisure. "Tim creates in his friends' minds the illusion that they're doing the task freely. Once you want to do something and it's done for its own sake (rather than for some sort of reward), it becomes a leisure experience."

Thus a Saturday museum visit scheduled because

"Everyone's seen it," or because "We ought to expose the children to such culture early," can actually be more stressful than trekking to the North Pole. While Neulinger admits the latter hardly fits most people's definition of relaxing, he also points out, "I've never heard of anyone being forced to go."

Following one's instincts and inclinations is critical to a true sense of relaxation, according to Reston, VA, psychoanalyst, Herbert Weinstadd, M.D., "Most people try to legislate their feelings and it really doesn't work. You don't tell yourself what to see, it just happens. The same thing should happen with your feelings—just experience them."

Meredith Titus, Ph.D., a clinical psychologist with the Menninger Clinic in Topeka, KS, suggests this test: "Lie down on a bed, hammock, whatever. If after a few minutes you find yourself thinking, 'Gee, that fence really needs painting,' instead of daydreaming or reading, chances are it's difficult for you to relax."

That doesn't mean it's impossible, though. Michael Marsden, Ph.D., professor of popular culture at Bowling Green State University in Ohio, suggests some "workaholics" can benefit from a gift certificate for an unstructured day, one in which they have no responsibilities. "Or a totally different environment—camping, for instance—might help, by making it difficult to follow one's daily routine."

The experts seem to agree that becoming just a bit selfish is a major step in carving out some leisure time. "Women have a particularly hard time with the concept of just doing what they want," says Titus. "So much of our identity, a positive sense of ourselves as women, comes from how much we do for others." The key, she tells her patients, is to recognize, as she finally did, "that when I feel good, I'm not only good for me, I'm better for everyone else. If that means twenty green beans instead of fresh for dinner, so be it."

Titus also recommends that people take a "health" instead of "sick" day from work. "Some companies offer you 'personal days,' but most people use them to take care of specific chores, like painting the kitchen. They'd be better off using such time to do something they've wanted to, but just haven't had time for." And if your company doesn't offer a personal day? "You may just have to play hooky."

Take that, Mr. Howe. **WENDY MEYEROFF**

ILLUSTRATION BY BETSY EVERITT

Couch potatoes and laid-back Californians aside, relaxation is a concept that doesn't sit well with the American psyche.

Betsy Everitt Illustrator
Carol Mills Art Director/Designer
Mills Associates, Inc. Design Firm
Communications Venture Group, Ltd. Client
New York, NY

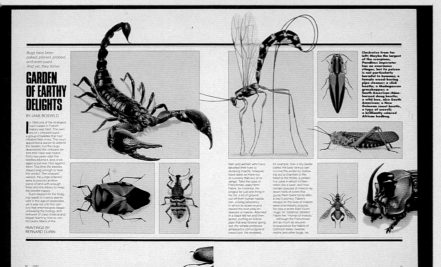

Bugs have been poked, pinned, probed and even sued. And yet, they thrive

GARDEN OF EARTHY DELIGHTS
BY JANE BOSVELD

In 1545 one of the strangest court cases in French history was filed. The owners of a vineyard sued a group of beetles that had infested their vines. The court appointed a lawyer to defend the beetles, but the bugs abandoned the vineyard before their case was heard. Forty-two years later the beetles returned, and once again a suit was filed against them. This time the beetles stayed long enough to hear the verdict. The vineyard owners, the judge ordered, were to provide another piece of land with enough trees and shrubbery to keep the beetles happy.

Such respect for the foraging needs of insects seems odd in this age of pesticides, yet it was not until this century that entomologists began unraveling the biology that beleaguers insects and began learning how to control pests. Many of the earliest pioneers...

Clockwise from far left: Maybe the largest of the scorpions, Pandinus imperator has an enormous stinger, but its poison is not particularly harmful to humans; a female wood-boring pine cleaner; a click beetle; a Madagascan grasshopper; a South American rhino-horned dung beetle; a wild bee, also South American; a New Guinean jewel beetle, a type of weevil; a brilliantly colored African beetle.

PAINTINGS BY BERNARD DURIN

Bernard Durin Illustrator
Dwayne Flinchum Art Director
Rani Levy Designer
OMNI Magazine Client
New York, NY

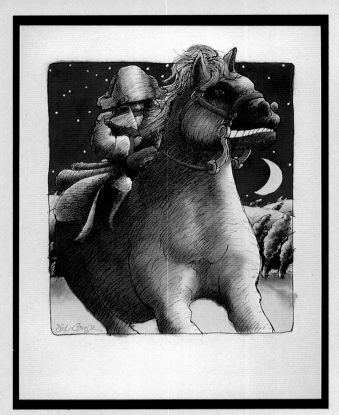

Bob Conge Illustrator
Andrew Danish Art Director
STANFORD Magazine Client
Rochester, NY

Gottfried Helnwein Illustrator
Dwayne Flinchum Art Director
OMNI Magazine Client
New York, NY

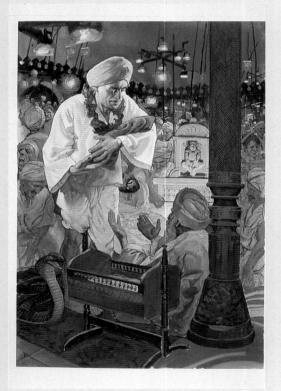

Christopher Magadini Illustrator
Larissa Lawrynenko Art Director
Reader's Digest General Books Client
New York, NY

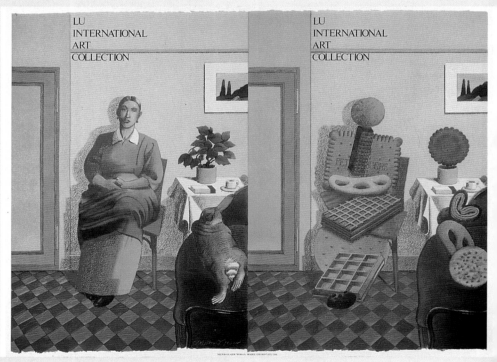

Milton Glaser Art Director/Designer/Illustrator
Milton Glaser, Inc. Design Firm
LU International Client
New York, NY

276

TO TALK, OR NOT

There's an old Armenian proverb: The tongue has no bone.
"I never gossip," my source tells me, "but if you want to know
about gossip, call X. Call her in the morning."
    "Oh?"
    "When she's still sober."   The
THE ASSIGNMENT WAS TO WRITE ABOUT GOSSIP, WHICH IS NOT THE SAME
             Art
as writing gossip, poking into people's private lives for public consump-
          of
tion. Kup and INC. and Sneed do that. The gossip column has a venerable
        Gossip
tradition in this country dating back to 1730, when Benjamin Franklin
wrote for the *Pennsylvania Gazette.* ❖ The idea was to gossip about
by BRENDA SHAPIRO
gossip, to define or, at least, to describe it. What I discovered, as I
thought it over, was that I also wanted to defend it. As honorable,
therapeutic, and utilitarian. As good fun. ❖ What kept running through
Illustration by MARY ANN SMITH
my mind was a sweet memory of my family—aunts, uncles, grand-
                             continued on page 53

18 CITY LIVING March 1992   March 1992 CITY LIVING 19

Mary Ann Smith Illustrator
Al Brandtner Art Director/Designer
Kathy Kelley Design Director
CHICAGO CITY LIVING Client
Chicago, IL

Paul Jermann Art Director/Designer/Illustrator
Triggerfish Studio Design Firm
Paul Jermann Client
Los Angeles, CA

able to manage a larger volume of assets with fewer employees than larger institutions.
Furthermore, with only two domestic offices, an extensive branch network is eliminated
through the utilization of a courier system to service deposits.

    Among our peers, the amount spent by Lincoln on overhead is con-
sistently less. While similar institutions spend 33.5% of their operating income on
personnel-related costs, Lincoln spends only 22.7%. As far as banks with the same
number of offices, Lincoln's occupancy costs amount to approximately 5% of operating income, while other institutions of similar size spend over 10%.

Our operating strategy has

resulted in an organization

with the strength   and ability

to provide the services of larger institutions

with better efficiency.

    Marketing and Business Strategy Lincoln's marketing and business strat-
egy has been and continues to be clearly defined. Emphasizing service to the unique
needs of lower middle-market businesses, our bankers maintain a constant state of
readiness to be responsive to the customer's needs.

    The Bank's typical customer is a business which grosses $10 million
or less in sales and whose credit needs are less than $2 million at any given time. The
focus on these customers is providing consistency in terms of personnel and high quality service. These customers are not primarily interested in how much the services may
cost, but on whether they have to familiarize a new cadre of account officers with their
business every few months. Consistency in terms of lack of officer turnover is what Lincoln provides. At Lincoln, there is no new cadre of trainees every six months. Quite the
opposite, the typical lending and account officer is a seasoned professional with ten to
fifteen years experience and knowledgeable of the local business community.

    Active involvement is a tradition at Lincoln. We do not adhere to the

Steve Johnson Illustrator
Rik Besser, Douglas Joseph Art Director
Douglas Joseph Designer
Besser Joseph Partners Design Firm
Lincoln Bancorp Client
Santa Monica, CA

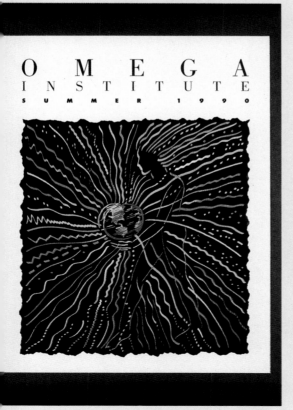

OMEGA
INSTITUTE
SUMMER 1990

Tim Girvin Illustrator/Art Director/Designer
Tim Girvin Design, Inc. Design Firm
Omega Institute For Holistic Studies Client
Seattle, WA

277

GEOFFREY BEENE'S
SMASHING TAFFETA SCARF—
IRIDESCENT, TASSLED

Ruben Alterio Illustrator
Karen Lee Grant Art Director
Michael Rand, Karen Lee Grant Designers
MIRABELLA Client
New York, NY

Barbara Buck Art Director
Keith Birdsong Illustrator
Pocket Books Client
New York, NY

Terri Davis Art Director
Nick Gaetano Designer/Illustrator
Ballantine Books Client
S. Orange, NJ

Douglas Fraser, Bob Hambly,
  Jennifer Hewitson, Brian Cronin Illustrators
Kent Hunter Creative Director
Danielle Joffe Designer
Norman Mauskopf, Mark Weiss, Dan Borris,
  Britain Hill Photographers
Frankfurt Gips Balkind Design Firm
MCI Communications Client
New York, NY

Mike Kressley Illustrator/Photographer
Ellen Clancy Art Director/Designer
Mike Kressley Photo Designer
Polese/Clancy Design Firm
American Society of Magazine Photographers
  Client
Boston, MA

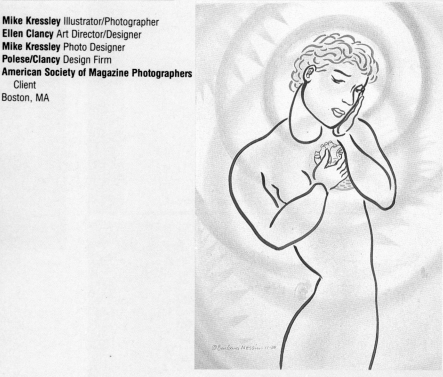

Barbara Nessim Illustrator
Joy Makon, Maxine Davidowitz Art Directors
HEALTH Magazine Client
New York, NY

Dru Blair Art Director/Designer/Illustrator
Coca-Cola Client
New York, NY

Betsy Everitt Illustrator
Naomi Burstein Art Director/Designer
Division of AIDS Program Services Copywriter
Burstein/Max Associates, Inc. Design Firm
The New York City Department of Health Client
New York, NY

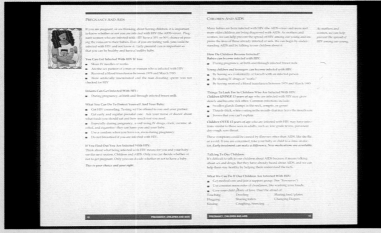

Jeffrey Keyton Art Director
Scott Wadler Designer
Warren Linn Illustrator
In-house Design Firm
MTV Networks Client
New York, NY

Attila Hejja Illustrator
Bryan Canniff Art Director
POPULAR MECHANICS Client
New York, NY

Lawrence W. Duke Illustrator
Jerry Greenstein Art Director
TFB/BBDO Agency
Everex Sytems, Inc. Client
Palo Alto, CA

Jim Stanton Illustrator/Art Director
Marina Kiriakou Project Manager
Hill & Knowlton, Inc. Agency
Jacob K. Javits Convention Center of New York
  Client
New York, NY

Crystal Palace lobby during New York International Boat Show.

John Berkey Illustrator
Bryan Canniff Art Director
POPULAR MECHANICS Client
New York, NY

Steven Guarnaccia Illustrator
Robert L. Lascaro Art Director
Will Kefauver Creative Director
Liza Wai Designer
Scholastic, Inc. Client
New York, NY

Bidjan Assadipour
Illustrator/Art Director/Designer
Zohreh Agheli Photographer
Rush Graphics Design Firm
The Rouhollah Khaleghi Orchestra Client
Eatontown, NJ

Raffi Anderian Illustrator
Catherine Pike Art Director
Marion Kane Editor
The Toronto Star Newspaper Ltd. Client
Toronto, Ontario, Canada

Blair Drawson Illustrator
Tom Staebler Art Director
Eric Shropshire Designer
PLAYBOY Client
Chicago, IL

Jeffrey Perch Illustrator
Christine Mathews Art Director/Designer
United Federation of Teachers Client
New York, NY

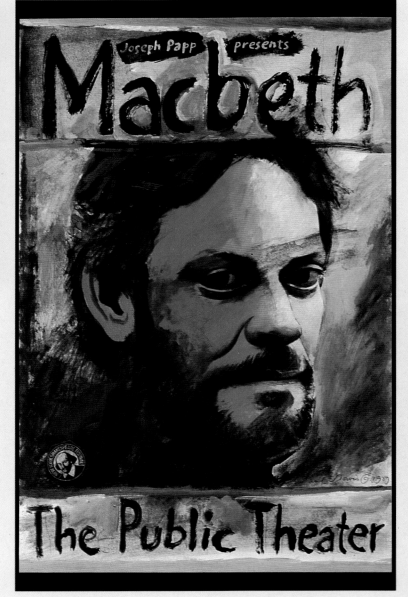

Paul Davis Illustrator/Art Director/Designer
Paul Davis Studio Design Firm
New York Shakespeare Festival Client
New York, NY

Conrad Jorgensen Art Director
Mary Brucken Designer
SBG Partners Design Firm
Kobacker Fashion Affiliates Client
San Francisco, CA

Barbara Vick Art Director
Amy Knapp Designer
SBG Partners Design Firm
The Promus Companies Client
San Francisco, CA

Faye Kleros Art Director
Young & Rubicam Chicago Agency
WXRT-FM Radio Client
Chicago, IL

Lon Levin Art Director/Designer
Georgene Boyd Illustrator
Levin Creative Group Agency
Inspired Fun, Inc. Client
Beverly Hills, CA

Laurie Szujewska Art Director/Designer
In-house Design Firm
Adobe Systems Inc. Client
Mountainview, CA

Guy Daniels Art Director
John Holt Photographer
Cipriani Kremer Agency
Raytheon Client
Boston, MA

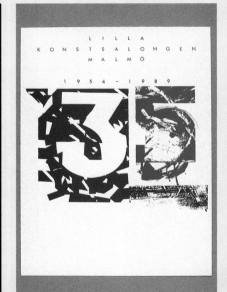

Peter Day Art Director
Alexandra Cresswell Production
Deacon Day Advertising Agency
BMW Canada, Inc. Client
Toronto, Ontario, Canada

Lennart Hansson Art Director/Designer
Lennart Hansson Design Design Firm
Lilla Konstsalongen Client
Malmo, Sweden

Lennart Hansson Art Director/Designer
Studio 54, Falun Agency
Lennart Hansson Design Design Firm
Nordic World Ski Championships 1993 Client
Malmo, Sweden

Jack Anderson, John Hornall Art Directors
**John Hornall, Jack
    Anderson, Roselynne Duavit-Passion**
    Designers
Glenn Yoshiyama, Scott McDougall Illustrators
Hornall Anderson Design Works
    Design Firm/Client
Seattle, WA

Jennifer Morla Art Director
Jeanette Aramburu, Jennifer Morla Designers
Katheryn Kleinman Photographer
Morla Design Design Firm/Client
San Francisco, CA

John Dunn Art Director
Cynthia Hummel, John Dunn Designers
Lori Farr Photographer
Dunn and Rice Design, Inc. Design Firm
Rochester Monotype Client
Rochester, NY

Hennie La Grange Typographer
Bruce Paynter Art Director
Greg Burke Creative Director
Jan Verboom Photographer
Ogilvy & Mather, Rightford Searle-Tripp
  & Makin (Cape) Agency
Volkswagen of South Africa Client
Cape Town, South Africa

Laurie Szujewska Art Director/Designer
In-house Design Firm
Adobe Systems Inc. Client
Mountainview, CA

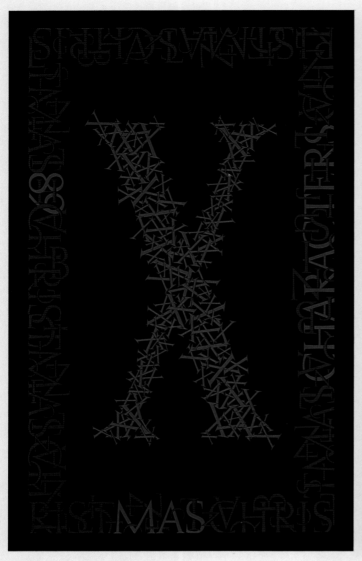

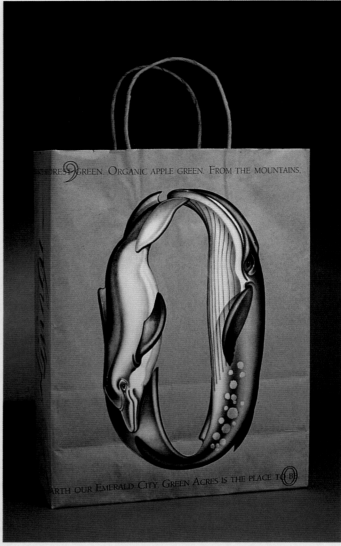

Scott Paramski Art Director/Designer
Peterson & Company Design Firm
Characters Typography Inc. Client
Dallas, Texas

Robert Valentine Art Director
Jozef Sumichrast Designer/Illustrator
Bloomingdale's Client
Lake Forest, IL

306

Philip Gips Creative Director/Designer
Frankfurt Gips Balkind Design Firm
AIGA/New York Client
New York, NY

j. Charles Walker Art Director/Copywriter
Paul Sahre Designer
Tarragon Graphics Design Firm
**The University & College Designers
    Association and Kent State University** Client
Kent, OH

HOG*vet*

Murry Handler Art Director/Designer
Feeks Communications Agency
Mehand Consultants, Inc. Design Firm
A.L. Laboratories, Inc. Client
Peekskill, NY

Jack Anderson Art Director
Heidi Hatlestad, Jack Anderson Designers
Yutaka Sasaki Illustrator
Hornall Anderson Design Works Design Firm
UNICO Properties Client
Seattle, WA

Jack Anderson Art Director
Juliet Shen, Jack Anderson, Mary Hermes
  Designers
Hornall Anderson Design Works Design Firm
Lane, Powell, Moss & Miller Client
Seattle, WA

ONE
UNION
SQUARE

LANE
POWELL
MOSS
&
MILLER

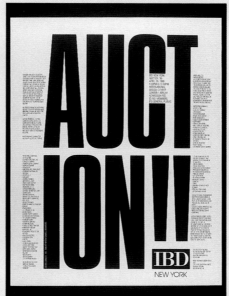

Donald L. Kiel Art Director
Joan Bittner, Donald L. Kiel Designers
Marie Van Buren Project Coordinator
Type Consortium Limited Typesetting
Swanke Hayden Connell Architects Design Firm
**The Institute of Business Designers, New
   York Chapter** Client
New York, NY

Michael Richards Art Director/Designer
Richards & Swensen, Inc. Design Firm
Salt Lake Airport Hilton Client
Salt Lake City, UT

Carol Denison, Jun Toyoda
   Art Directors/Designers
Denison/Toyoda International Design Firm
ARSOA Corporation Client
Sausalito, CA

Supon Phornirunlit Art Director/Designer
Beverly Johnson, Elizabeth Jeppsen
   Project Directors
Supon Design Group Inc. Design Firm
Association for the Care of Children's Health
   Client
Washington, DC

VERY SURE FOOTED

SCENE: WHIPPETS AND STAFFORDSHIRE TERRIER ARE LINED UP FOR A RACE ON A TEST TRACK. DOGS SHOWN IN SLOW MOTION RACING. EVENTUALLY THE TERRIER OUT RACES THE WHIPPETS AS THEY RACE THROUGH WATER HAZZARD, ETC. THE WHIPPETS RUN INTO A BLIND ALLEY WHILE THE TERRIER MAKES A SHARP TURN AND WINS.

VO: Introduction SP 33. . . . . . . .Very tenacious. . . . . very sure footed. . . . .gripping in the dry and in the wet.
SUPER: *New Dunlop SP 33. It grips*

Richard Bates Art Director
Brian Searle-Tripp Creative Director
Janet Sender Agency Producer
Ogilvy & Mather, Rightford Searle-Tripp & Makin (Cape) Agency
David Feldman Productions Production
Dunlop Client
Cape Town, South Africa

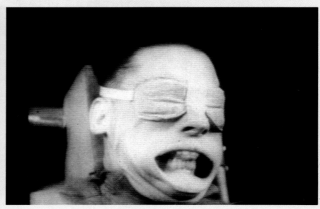

Fritz Westenberger Art Director
Michael Albright Creative Director
The Shalek Agency Agency
Verticle Pictures Production
Ocean Pacific Sunwear Client
Santa Monica, CA

Isn't that what you'd expect from Volkswagen?

Bruce Paynter Art Director
Brian Searle-Tripp Creative Director
Peter Gird Agency Producer
Ogilvy & Mather, Rightford Searle-Tripp &
Makin (Cape) Agency
David Feldman Productions Production
Volkswagen of South Africa Client
Cape Town, South Africa

VILLIANS
IN A TAKE-OFF ON A JAMES BOND MOVIE BAD GUYS
PLOT TO TRAP OUR HERO: SHOWN IN LUXURIOUS
APARTMENT. WHEN HE LEAVES BAD GUYS SIGNAL
FOR AN OLD WREAKERS BALL TO BE PLACED OVER
VOLKSWAGON JETTA TO BE DROPPED AS OUR HERO
ENTERS HIS CAR.
ON A COMPUTER GRAPHIC, BALL IS SHOWN BOUNC-
ING OFF THE JETTA BACK UP INTO THE AIR.
BALL LANDS ON BAD GUYS' VAN AS THEY LEAP TO
SAFETY; VAN IS FLATTENED.
SUPER:*New Jetta. It's obviously in a different class.*
OUR HERO: (into his car phone) "I've got something I'd like to
bounce off you"

BMW 750iL 4-Door

Paul Burrows Art Director
Joe Suskin Copywriter
McCann Agency
Patrick Latham Productions Design Firm
Johnson and Johnson Client
Sandton, South Africa

SPLASH
QUICK CUTS OF VARIOUS PEOPLE BEING SPLASHED
Music: Queen "Flash Gordon"
CHORUS: Splash, Ah-haa
Splash Ah-Haa
Splash Ah Haa
VO: Stay splashed with Shower to Shower
A new range of refreshing toiletries
SUPER: *JOHNSON & JOHNSON*
VO: And if that hasn't hit you go take a bath.

Jaguar XJ6 Sedan

Mark Oliver Art Director/Copywriter
Robert Celecia Director
Mark Oliver, Inc. Agency
Robert Celecia Associates Production
Gregg Motors Client
Santa Barbara, CA

POLYNESIAN DREAMS
(HAWAIIAN STEEL GUITAR MUSIC:UP AND UNDER
THROUGHOUT)
VO: We can't promise to have the automobile of your dreams,
but what other dealership has this many dreams?

Saab 900 Turbo Convertible

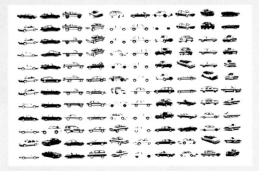

GREGG
MOTORS
The Santa Barbara Auto Center.
Highway 101 and La Cumbre/Hope Avenue offramp.

311

Bruce Soloway Art Director
Fred Olmstead Designer
Ted Charron Copywriter
Charron, Schwartz & Partners, Inc. Agency
ABC Network News Client
New York, NY

RUNNING PROFILE OF SEVEN ABC NEWS JOURNALISTS
VO: ABC we're changing the face of television news.

Kathy Aramondo Art Director
Kathy Cortenay Producer
Paul Giraud Director
Berenter Greenhouse & Webster Agency
The Big M Corporation Client
New York, NY

SUPER STARS
QUICK CUTS OF WOMEN LOOKING FASHION-Y.
SUPERS:
HAS BEEN DOING IT SINCE SHE'S 14.
DOES IT WITH HER BOYFRIEND.
DOES IT WITH HER GIRLFRIEND.
EVEN GOT HER MOTHER INTO IT.
WILL ONLY DO IT ALONE.
WITH VOICE: (ON CAMERA) I HAVEN'T DONE IT YET,
BUT I'M DYING TO.
VO: Once you pay Annie Sez prices for designer clothes, you'll
want to do it all the time too.
SUPER: *ANNIE SEZ, IT'S NOT JUST A STORE, IT'S AN*
OBSESSION.

Beverly Okada, Harvey Hoffenberg Art Directors
Harvey Hoffenberg Creative Director
Terry Gallo Copywriter
Saatchi & Saatchi Advertising Agency
Hanes Hosiery, Inc. Client
New York, NY

Jamie Way Art Director
Terry O'Reilly Copywriter
Deacon Day Advertising Agency
Fiberglas Canada, Inc. Client
Toronto, Ontario, Canada

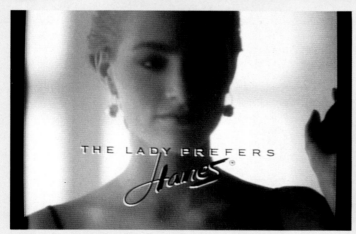

DESIGNER FORECAST

(WOMAN WATCHES DESIGNER ON TELEVISION WHILE GETTING DRESSED)
DESIGNER: See, a woman's body is merely a framework.
My designs are created to release
Pants are mandatory, metallics...
You won't see a leg in Paris this year.
Purple and fuchsia...
The short skirt is dead.
My designs—
WOMAN (VO): No matter what the gentlemen prefer, the lady prefers Hanes.

DREAM RENOVATION

MAN & WOMAN SHOW PICTURE OF DREAM SEWING ROOM. IN RENOVATION IT IS ON TOP OF HOUSE. WIFE WAVES FROM INSIDE. ROOF POPS OPEN AND WHOLE FAMILY APPEARS IN NEW ROOM.
MAN: I promised Winnifred that one day she would have her own sewing room. That promise has been fulfilled very comfortably. Warm in winter, cool in summer.
VO: To complete your dream renovation use Fiberglas Pink and Glasclad home insulation.
SUPER: *Fiberglas Canada*
When you renovate, insulate

313

Richard Long Art Director/Director
Celia Williams Copywriter/Producer
Creative Field's Agency
Marshall Field's Client
Chicago, IL

SCHOOL THANG
SONG: Mmmmmmarshal Field's
School Thang
Marshall Field's has the facts in line
lookin so cool, lookin so fine.
You'll be the one they talk about, Mmmmarshall Field's has all
the clout.
Mmmmarshall Field's
School Thang

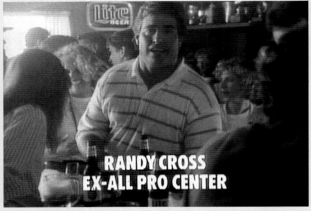

David Piatkowski Art Director
Jim Callan Agency Producer
Bob Giraldi Director
Backer Spielvogel Bates Agency
Giraldi/Suarez Productions Production
Miller Brewing Company Client
New York, NY

RANDY CROSS
RANDY: I'm tired of us centers getting no recognition. I've
played 13 seasons, in front of millions of fans. Yet, no one
knows who I am. Hey even if I'm not well known, at least my
beer is. Miller Lite.
WOMAN: Oh excuse me.
RANDY: Let me get that for you
WOMAN: Hey, aren't you Randy Cross
VO: It's well known.
When it's Miller Lite, less filling tastes great.

Jerome Faillant-Dumas Art Director
Yves Saint Laurent Designer/Illustrator
David Lynch Director
Premiere Heure Production
Yves Saint Laurent Perfumes Client
Neuilly Sur Seine, France

OPIUM
A FAN UNFOLDING-THEN A HAND, A CLOSE-UP OF AN
EYE THEN A WOMAN WALKING UPSTAIRS, CARESSES
PERFUME BOTTLE, WOMAN IN A BRONZE LAME
GOWN, MORE CLOSE-UPS OF WOMAN.
VO: For those who adore Yves St. Laurant

314

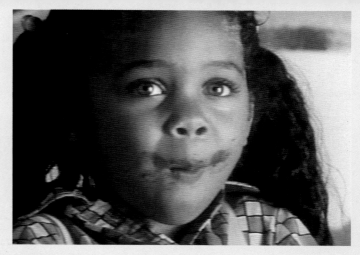

Jon Williams Art Director
Ashley Bacon Copywriter
Klerck & White Agency
David Feldman Productions Design Firm
ISCOR-Privatisation Client
 Benmore, South Africa

IT'S FOR YOU
QUICK CUTS OF PEOPLE OF ALL RACES AND INCOMES.
(Percussive Music throughout. No Voice Overs)
SUPER: *OWN SHARES.*
SUPER: *IN ISCOR*
SUPER: *DON'T BE THE ONE TO SAY "IF I ONLY HAD. . ."*

Darrel Fiesel Art Director
Ken Dudwick Creative Director
Anne Walker Agnecy Producer
Ketchum Advertising Agency
Barry Dukoff & Associates Design Firm
Beatrice/Hunt-Wesson Client
San Francisco, CA

Gabi Wagner Art Director
Edmund Petri Creative Director
Igor Luther Photographer
Sabine Muhlberger Copywriter
Young & Rubicam Agency
Gazelle Client
Vienna, Austria

SWIMSUITS
VO: Gazelle-What a feeling!

Oliver Hoffman Art Director
Marc A. Williams Creative Director
Larry Conely Group Creative Director
Young & Rubicam, Inc. Agency
Birbrower/Thomas Productions Design Firm
Michcon Client
Detroit, MI

WARM HOME
CHILD USES SIGN LANGUAGE
My hearing is not so good. I'm happy Warm Home (MichCon) has programs to help people like me. If you need help too just contact Warm Home (MichCon)
VOICE: I don't hear very well. So it's a good thing MichCon has programs for people like me. If you can use help too just get in touch with MichCon.
SUPER: MICHCON
Putting more Warmth in your life

John Pace Art Director
Jono Shubitz Creative Director
Janet Sender Agency Producer
Ogily & Mather, Rightford Searle-Tripp & Makin
   (Cape) Agency
David Feldman Productions Design Firm
South Africa Breweries Client
Cape Town, South Africa

WORK SONG
LEADER: "From the time the sun rises
CHORUS: From the sun's birth
LEADER: Till the sun sets
CHORUS: Till the dust settles on the earth
ALL: We are one with life, we are one with work...
LEADER: Time for friends to be one
ALL: With a beer that gives you more..."
VO: More refreshment, more reward at the end of the day.
Carling black Label.

Richard Bates Art Director
Brian Searle-Tripp Creative Director
Janet Sender Copywriter
Ogilvy & Mather, Rightford Searle-Tripp & Marin (Cape) Agency
Patrick Latham Productions Design Firm
Lion Match Company, Ltd. Client
Cape Town, South Africa

Gary Ennis Art Director
Michele Salmon Copywriter
Lowe & Partners Agency
Coca-Cola Foods Client
New York, NY

TRAIN
WOMAN IN TRAIN DISCARDS CAN OF DIET PEPSI.
STEPS OFF TO GET DIET SPRITE FROM MACHINE.
TRAIN START UP WOMAN RACES-CLIMBS INTO SIDE
AND THEN ROOF OF TRAIN TRYING TO GET BACK TO
HER COMPANION. SHE ARRIVES BACK IN COMPART-
MENT VERY DISHEVELED.
WOMAN: I've changed my mind
VO: When you want a change. . .there is only one diet soft
drink with the great taste of lymon.
MAN: Oh, you've changed your mind about your hair. It's
different but I like it.

MATCH SOCCER
MAN PLAYS WITH LION MATCH BOX. CATCHES IT ON
THE BACKS OF HIS HANDS, HIS ELBOW, HIS INSTEPS.
WITH HIS FOOT LIFTS INTO AIR, HEADS IT, CATCHES
IT ON HIS INSTEP AGAIN.
VO: As long as you've got a lion, you've got a friend, friend.

Owen Mundel Art Director
Dave Cockburn Editor
Mundels Agency
Toron Television Design Firm
Helios Minolta Client
Northcliff, South Africa

SIMPLE LIFE
SONG: I don't belive in Fretting and Grievin'
Don't like commotion
I want a promotion
Give Minoltafax!
SUPER: *Minoltafax (logo)*

Jerry Torchia Art Director
Mike Hughes Copywriter
Randy Shreve Other
The Martin Agency Agency
Smillie Productions Design Firm
Wrangler Jeans Client
Richmond, VA

DRIVING LESSON

A WOMAN'S VOICE: It's great. They fixed up that old truck and went out for the big driving lesson. You know they'll never forget this day as long as they live.

ANNOUNCER: Here's to fathers and sons, first time driving lessons and comfortable blue jeans.

SUPER: WRANGLER *AMERICAN HERO*
THE MOST COMFORTABLE JEANS KNOWN TO MAN

Kate Anthony Art Director
Jane Bongers Copywriter
Kelly Cavanaugh Agency Producer/Design Firm
The Directors Film Company Production
Beef Information Centre Client
Toronto, Ontario, Canada

TODAY'S BEEF

VO: So what's your beef?

VO: Today a serving of sirloin steak has as little cholesterol as an equal serving of roast chicken without the skin...
...So what's your beef?

SUPER: RETAIL SIRLOIN—120g SERVING RAW, FAT 10.6g, POLYUNSATURATES 0.4g, MONOUNSATURATES 4.8g, SATURATES 4.6g, CHOLESTEROL 59mg.

SIGNET℠
One day we'll be your bank

Signet Bank/Virginia, Signet Bank/Maryland, Signet Bank, N.A. Members FDIC. ©1989 Signet Banking Corporation.

Jerry Torchia Art Director
Mike Hughes Copywriter
Randy Shreve Other
The Martin Agency Agency
Leslie Decktor Production
Signet Bank Client
Richmond, VA

DR. J.
DR. J. WITH KIDS
VO: If you're on the basketball court and you're aggressively pursuing the basketball and you're always looking for it and you're yelling "pass me the ball, pass me the ball." And the guys look at you and say "hey, calm down."—And they pass the ball to someone else if you keep yelling at them. Where as if you just run and you just free yourself and you let it find you, it's so much easier.
SUPER: IN EVERY FIELD, SOME PEOPLE STAND OUT.
SUPER: SIGNET. ONE DAY WE'LL BE YOUR BANK.

Tim Shortt Art Director
Penny Hawkey Copywriter
Barbara Gans Russo Producer
The Bloom Agency Agency
Film Syndicate-Jerry Apoain Production
Witco Corp.:Kendall/Amalie Division Client
New York, NY

POUR IT IN, POUR IT ON
SINGERS: Kendall's the cool for your caddy. The juice for your jag. It's the jolt in your colt. . . . . And what wins you the drag.
VO: You wanna add life to the life of your car? Give it the good stuff! Kendall Moter Oil. And pour it on.
SINGERS: It's the push in your pick up. The zap in your z. The revs in your turbo. . . And the heart of your little gt.
SUPER: A WITCO PRODUCT
SUPER: KENDALL MOTER OIL

319

John Lasseter, Joe Catena Art Directors
Don Conway Photographer
Yail Milo Technical Director
FCB/Leber Katz Partners, New York Agency
Colossal Pictures/Pixar Design Firm
RJR Nabisco/Planters Lifesavers Company
Client
San Francisco, CA

BABIES
VO: What d'ya know, the Life Savers family just got a little
smaller! New Life Savers Holes. Tiny, little bites of candy in all
your favorite Life Savers flavors. Holes. . . more fun than you
could ever imagine. Delicious new Holes candy from Life
Savers. Watch out for Holes.. they're gonna be big!

Take time for lunch.

There's a name for food this good.

Hormel

Brad Cohn Art Director
Allen Cohn, Tim Pegors Copywriters
BBDO/Minneapolis Agency
Young & Company Production
Hormel Client
Minneapolis, MN

Philip Halyard Art Director
Bernie Owett Creative Director
Larry Volpi Copywriter
Judi Nierman Producer
J. Walker Thompson Agency
Nestle Nestea Client
New York, NY

BUS

ON HOT DAY PEOPLE WAIT FOR BUS. BOY DRAWS LINE IN SAND WITH HEEL MAKES SHAPE OF SWIMMING POOL. DIVES IN

RADIO ANNOUNCER: The heatwave continues. . . another hot day. . . . Make sure you got plenty of. . .
WOMAN: Hey, What are you doing?
VO: When it comes to 100% instant iced tea refreshment. . . more people choose Nestea over any other. Take the Nestea Plunge.

John Slater Art Director
Brian Johnston Copywriter
Andy Crosbie Producer
Baker Lovick, Limited Agency
The Partners'/USA Design Firm
John Deere, Inc. Client
New York, NY

Nothing Runs Like a Deere

BAD DAY

ALARM CLOCK FALLS, SHOELACE BREAKS, TOAST BURNS, NEWSPAPER IS SOGGY, CAR KEY SNAPS IN LOCK. MAN OPENS GARAGE AND CLIMBS ON MOWER AND SMILES.

VO: When you find something in life that works as well or lasts as long as a John Deere lawn mower or garden tractor. . . buy it
SUPER: *John Deere (logo)*
Nothing Runs Like a Deere

Barbara Scardino Art Director
Steven Vaughan, Samn Holcombe Directors
Earle Palmer Brown, Maryland Agency
The Partners'/USA Design Firm
U.S. Air Client
New York, NY

USAir
America's Most Frequent Flyer.

TOO SHORT

MUSIC IN BETWEEN ACTIVITIES: VACATION SCENES
VO: By Law, German Citizens Get 4 Weeks Vacation Every Year.
In France, Workers Get 5 Weeks Off.
Australians Get 1 Month, Plus Extra Vacation Pay.
Most Americans Get Just 2 Precious Weeks.
VO: US Air Low Fares The Most Departures Go for it
SUPER: *America's Most Frequent Flyer*

Stephen Blair Art Director
Jeff Lewis Copywriter
Rosnick Convery Productions Music
McCann-Erickson Advertising of Canada, Ltd.
 Agency
Toronto, Ontario, Canada Design Firm
Coca-Cola, Ltd. Client
Toronto, Ontario, Canada

TRIBES OF SUMMER
QUICK CUT OF TRIBAL CHILDREN RUNNING,
EUROFASHION PEOPLE LEAVING A CLUB, SURFERS ON
A TRUCK, SARONG-CLAD GIRLS, PEOPLE IN THE POOL
HALL, ETC. ALL DRINKING COCA-COLA CLASSICS.
SINGERS: yay-a-oooh
yay-yay-yay
yay-a-oooh
yay-a-oooh
COCA-COLA
Can't beat the feeling.

Alan Pafenbach Art Director
Steve Connelly Copywriter
John Goodman Director
Arnold Advertising Agency
September Production Production
McDonald's Co-ops of Boston, Hartford, Maine,
 Albany, Syracuse & Rochester Client
Boston, MA

WINTER
OPEN ON MAN SITTING IN CHAIR. WALLS INSTANTLY
CLOSE IN ON MAN. LEFT CONFINED BETWEEN THE
CLOSED-IN WALLS.
VO: Strange things can happen when you spend too much
time inside during the winter.

Larry Bennett Art Director
John Russo Copywriter
John Pace Producer
McKinney & Silver Agency
R. Greenburg Design Firm
North Carolina National Bank Client
Raleigh, NC

WIN WHAT YOU WANT
VO: Want a vacation? Play the Win What You Want game at
NCNB Need a car? Want an interest-free loan for college? Win
the kind of prizes that let you buy what you want. Like a boat.
Win cash—like our $100,000 grand prize. Pick up a game card
and play Win What You Want at NCNB.

Steve Feldman Art Director
Susan Jurick Producer
David Deahl Director
TBWA Advertising, Inc. Agency
Big Deahl Productions Production
E & J Gallo Winery Client
New York, NY

TOTT'S CHAMPAGNE
VO: Tott's. The premium choice.

Dean Bastian Art Director
Tim Kane Copywriter
Young & Rubicam Chicago Agency
Smillie Films, L.A. Design Firm
Peter Smillie Director
G. Heileman Brewing Company Client
Chicago, IL

WEDDING
QUICK SHOTS OF WEDDING PARTY AT RECEPTION
MUSIC: My Days are Sad and Lonely
VO: A subtle Strength
MUSIC: For You I Cry, For You dear Only
VO: A Complex Character
MUSIC: Why Haven't You Seen it
VO: A Light Beer with Body & Soul
VO: Special Export Light
SUPER: *Body and Soul*

Jim Mochnsky Art Director
Gill Cope Designer
Janet Mockard Agency Producer
W.B. Doner & Company Agency
Lovinger, Grasso and Cohen Design Firm
Bell Atlantic Mobile Systems Client
Baltimore, MD

30 MILES FROM HOME
VO: 30 miles from home. Next exit 15 miles. They're about to close. It's your only hope.
ANNOUNCER: Don't take a chance on anything less than Bell Atlantic Quality, Technology, and Service. Make sure your cellular phone is on the Bell Atlantic System. Bell Atlantic Mobile. We're more than just talk.
SFX: *PHONE RINGING*

323

BREWERY
FIRST SHOTS SHOW BREWERY ACTIVITY AND DELIVERY THEN SPLIT SCREEN OF RESTAURANT AND LOWENBRAU LIGHT BOTTLE
VO: Strong Character.
The product of Lowenbrau for over 600 years. So when it came time to brew a great light beer-one with a strong character-no effort was spared. Introducing the one light beer with a strong character. 90 calorie Lowenbrau Light.

FACTORY
VO: Strong character, the product of hard work. So when it came time to brew a great light beer—one with a strong character—no effort was spared.
Introducing 98 calorie Lowenbrau Light.
The one light beer with a strong character..

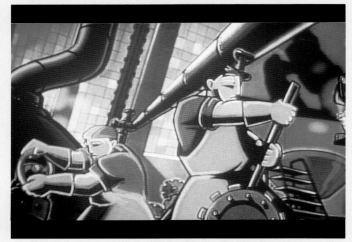

Michael Brunsfeld, Joe Sciarrotta,
Matt Canzano Art Directors
Doug Fraser, Michael Brunsfeld Designers
Lisa Dearing, Weston Giunta Photographers
Doug Fraser, Tia Kratter Illustrators
J. Walter Thompson/Chicago Agency
Colossal Pictures Design Firm
Miller Brewing Company Client
San Francisco, CA

Jeanette Elliott Creative Director
Steven Vaughan Director/Cameraman
Lael Erickson Producer
Ackerman Hood & McQueen Agency
The Partners'/USA, Inc. Design Firm
Besnier USA Client
New York, NY

John Speakman Art Director
Peter Moss Director/Cameraman
Stress Inc./Mark Stafford
 Music Production House
Terry Bell Copywriter
Scali, McCabe, Sloves (Canada), Ltd. Agency
Labatt Brewing Company, Ltd. Client
Toronto, Ontario, Canada

FRENCH CULTURE
ALTERNATING CUTS OF SLENDER GIRLS AND
BON LAIT PACKAGES.

VO: This is not yogurt. It's a whole new form of French
Culture.
Bon Lait Fromage Frais. Creamier. . . more milk. . . more
protein. . . more calcium but no more caleries than regular
yogurt.
SUPER: *Bon Lait Package*

PLAYING WITH FIRE
MEN AND WOMEN IN BATHING SUITS
ARE SPRAWLED ON A DECK
THERE ARE CANS OF "BLUE" BESIDE THEM.
A HAND FUMBLES WITH A WRISTWATCH
ALARM AND ALL TURN OVER IN UNISON.
Cut to Can
SUPER: *IT'S THE WAY WE PLAY*

Bill Jarcho Art Director
Julie Zammarchi Illustrator/Animator
Fred Macdonald, Lisa Werner Producers
Noble & Wecal Agency
Olive Jar Studios Design Firm/Production
Store 24, Inc. Client
Brookline, MA

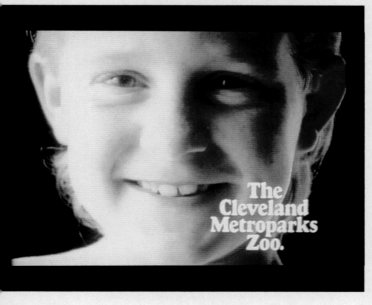

The Cleveland Metroparks Zoo.

Don Fibich Art Director/Designer
Michael Dreyfuss Music Director
Ann Russo, Roseanne Lowe, Celeste Sciortino
   Producers
Wyse Advertising Agency
Kenny Mirman Productions Production
Cleveland Metroparks Zoo Client
Cleveland, OH

FACES AD
SHOTS OF FACES OF ZOO ANIMALS DISSOLVING ONE
TO THE OTHER.
VO: One of the most beautiful things about faces like
these. . . is the look they'll bring to a face like this.
The Cleveland Metroparks Zoo. It's wild.
SUPER: *Metroparks Zoo logo*

Carl W. Jones Art Director/Designer
Joe Biafore Illustrator
Mark Dwyer Copywriter
Vickers & Benson Advertising, Ltd. Agency
Studio 412 Production
Ontario Jockey Club Client
Toronto, Ontario, Canada

NEIGHBOURS

OPEN ON BLACK SCREEN.

SUPER: Neighbours

HORSE'S FOOTPRINTS APPEAR ON BLACK, RUNNING FROM BOTTOM UP, FOLLOWED BY WHEEL TRACKS. AS THE BLACK TURNS TO WHITE, GRADUALLY THE NORTH AMERICA CUP IS REVEALED.

ANNOUNCER: The neighbours are dropping in this Saturday. They're bringing horses. They're very fast pacers. Because there's one million dollars at stake. Our neighbours are from the statesThey think their pacers are faster than ours. But the Canadians have won four years out of five. It's a good thing we get along with the neighbours. The North America Cup. This Saturday at Greenwood Raceway.

June Manton Art Director
Sue Read Copywriter
Stan Noble Producer
Lintas:New York Agency
Coco-Cola USA - Diet Coke Client
New York, NY

ELTON JOHN

VO: Not for the way it puts a smile on your face Not for the way it quenches a big thirst Just one reason Just one reason Just for the taste of it The real thing taste of it Just for the taste of it. Diet Coke

Joan Honner Art Director
Greg Miller Copywriter
BBDO Chicago Agency
HSI (NY) Production
Kemper Client
Chicago, IL

SAND CASTLE

HANDS BUILD SAND CASTLE. SHOTS ALTERNATE WITH SHOTS OF WAVE. CASTLE IS SHOWN GROWING IT INTRICATE SCULPTURE. WAVE CRASHES OVER IT LEAVING CASTLE IN TACT

VO: Building security for today-and tomorrow-is a fragile task. You need to protect what you've worked for while investing in your dreams. It can all be washed away without the right foundation. For insurance-for investments Kemper is the name to build on.

SUPER: Kemper Insurance-Investment

SUPER: Kemper The name to build on

Richard Smith Art Director
Jeff Millman Copywriter
VanSant Dugdale Advertising Agency
Capital Blue Cross Client
Baltimore, MD

MIRACLE

VO: The first miracle here is an astounding new technology. The second miracle allows the family to afford it.
SUPER:*Capital Blue Cross* (Logo)

328

Warren Lewis Art Director
Kevin Willis, Gregg Steward Copywriters
Taylor Brown Smith & Perrault Agency
Gibson, Lefebvre & Gartner Design Firm
The Houston Post Client
Houston, Tx

DINER

WOMAN SITTING AT A TABLE IN A SMALL DINER. DEEPLY INVOLVED IN THE HOUSTON POST. THE SHOT REMAINS ON THIS WOMAN THE ENTIRE SPOT. SHE IS BEGINNING TO TAKE HOLD OF HER INTEREST IN THE PAPER. AS SHE DOES, ALL SOUNDS BEGIN TO FADE AWAY, UNTIL WE REACH TOTAL SILENCE.
SUPER: *THE HOUSTON POST*
TODAY'S PAPER
TO SUBSCRIBE CALL 840-5000.

Larney Walker Art Director
Norm Kantor Copywriter
Paulette Cary Producer
Bender, Browning, Dolby & Sanderson Advertising Agency
Film & Tape Works Production
SBEZ Radio Client
Chicago, IL

GARRISON'S COMING

THE SCREEN IS EMPTY FOR THE FIRST 20 SECONDS
2 Men Talking: He's back... No kidding... Where'd you hear that?... Ralph's.. Wasn't sure he'd be back... After what he did to this town... Put Lake Wobegon on the map... Sure did... lots of tourists showin' up... Had to wait for a table at the Chatterbox t'other night... Hard to believe... Heard he's different this time... Nice to see Garrison again, though... Nice boy
SUPER: *On Saturday at 500 p.m. Garrison Keillor returns to your imagination on 91.5 F.M. WBEZ. Hear the whole picture.*

Darren Warner Art Director
Leslie Collie Designer
David Martin Copywriter
Scali, McCabe, Slover (Canada), Ltd. Agency
Champagne Pictures Production
William Neilson, Ltd. Client
Toronto, Ontario, Canada

CRUNCHIE

MULTI-LINGUAL WORDS AND GRAPHIC SYMBOLS REPRESENT slow AND fast.
SINGER: Live my life the two speed way. It may come easy it may go the long way. Just don't tell me the way to go. I could make it last I could make it go
SUPER: *TWO SPEED BAR (Cadbury's crunchie logo)*

Marty McDonald Art Director
John Parlato, Jim Lansbury Copywriters
W.B. Doner & Company Agency
The Production Company Design Firm
Baltimore Symphony Orchestra Client
Baltimore, MD

TEAM

MUSICIANS WARMING UP ORCHESTRA STAGE BASE-BALL STADIUM
MAN 1: I think they're one of the best teams playing today.
WOMAN: I just love their uniforms.
MAN 2: Great stadium, no rain delays.
MUSICIAN: We're feeling good, we're looking good, we're playing good.
FRANK ROBINSON: We could never play like that.
SUPER: *The BSO. Baltimore's other major league team. 873-8000.*
MAN: They don't chew tobacco, they don't spit, and they're very polite.

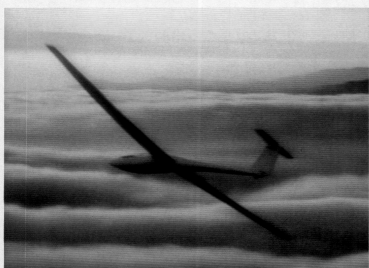

Tom Conrad Art Director
Alan Saperstein Copywriter
Mary Ann Kurasz Producer
Campbell Mithun Esty Agency
The Travelers Client
New York, NY

GLIDER
GLIDER TAKING OFF AND SOARING THROUGH SKY

VO: Financial serenity. The Confidence to spread your wings.
The Travelers gives forty million Americans financial piece of
mind.
SUPER: *(Umbrella and Logo)*
VO: The Travelers you're better off under the umbrella.

330

David Harner Art Director
Cavid Johnson Copywriter
Barbara Mullins, Dale Bramwell Producers
BBDO Agency
Pytka Productions Production
Pepsi Cola Company Client
New York, NY

RAY CHARLES

RAY CHARLES: You know when you got it right, you got it right. Whether your talking about this or whether your talking about the one and only diet cola that does it for Ray. Diet Pepsi. You know nothing tastes as good to me as Diet Pepsi.

RAY: Ah alright, now who's the wise guy?

RAY: Now that's the right one baby.

Bob Tore Art Director
Fred Stesney Copywriter
John Scarola Producer
Lintas:New York Agency
Klasky-Csupo, Inc. Production
RJR Nabisco-Planters Butterfinger Client
New York, NY

Lou Coletti Art Director
Neal Dearling, Irv Weinberg Copywriters
Maureen McKeon Producer
Lintas:New York Agency
RSA/USA Production
Eastern Airlines-Texas Air Corp. Client
New York, NY

SHARING

BART: Behold! The last Butterfinger in the whole house and I have it!
LISA: No teasing. That's what Dad says.
BART: Check out the smooth, chocolatey outside! While lurking inside is a crunchy peanut butter delight!
LISA: Dad says if you make us scream, you're dead meat.
LISA: Bart's learning to share
VO: Peanut buttery Butterfinger

Robert Billings Art Director
Tom Ackerman/GMS Photographer/Director
Ron Burkhardt, Bob Haigh Copywriters
Ron Burkhardt Creative Director
Burkhardt & Christy/N.Y. Agency
BMW of North America/Motorcycles Client
New York, NY

Phil Triolo Art Director
Robert Greenbaum, Jimmy Siegel Copywriters
Bob Emerson Producer
BBDO Agency
HSI Productions Production
Federal Express Client
New York, NY

INVICTUS

VO: Out of the night that covers me,
I thank whatever fates may be
For my unconquerable soul.
I am the master of my fate;
I am the captain of my soul.
SUPER: BMW Motorcycles.
Worth the Obsession

BEFORE 10:30

VO: On Wall Street,
Fortunes are won and lost,
And won again,
Before 10:30.
And on the backlots of Burbank,
Love often blooms and fades
Before 10:30.
Which is why it's important
That Federal Express's 10:30 deliveries
Get there before 10:30.
After all,
We found you get to be first
By getting there first.
SUPER: FEDERAL EXPRESS.
THE BEST WAY TO SHIP IT OVER HERE.

333

You depend on your car

But parts aren't important

NAPA

Because there are
no unimportant parts.

Dick Gage, John Boone Art Directors
Bob Richardson Photographer
Carroll Ballard Director
Fahlgren Martin Agency
Chelsea Pictures Design Firm
NAPA Auto Parts Client
Atlanta, GA

TRAIN
CAR STALLS ON TRAIN TRACKS
SUPER: *Conventional Wisdom Says*
SEVERAL SHOTS OF ATTEMPTS TO START CAR
BETWEEN SUPERS
SUPER: *You Depend on Your Car*
SUPER: *Your Car Depends on it's Parts*
SUPER: *But Parts Aren't Important Are They?*
SUPER: *There Are No Unimportant Parts*
VO: NAPA, Because There are No Unimportant Parts

C.B. Harding Art Director/Director
Eric Edwards Cameraman
C.B. Harding Studios Agency
Zapis Communications Client
Portland, OR

Joe McDonagh, Bob Crantz Art Directors
Eric Aronin Copywriter
Marguerite Birnbaum Producer
DCA Advertising, Inc. Agency
Highlight Commercials Production
Canon U.S.A., Inc. Client
New York, NY

FIRE SWALLOWER
WE ARE IN AN INDOOR CIRCUS. SUDDENLY A FIRE
SWALLOWER LEAPS INTO FRAME AND BLOWS A BALL
OF FLAME AT CAMERA. FADE TO PRODUCT & LOGO.
KID: Dad, Your Hair!!
VO: This breathtaking moment was brought to you by the
Canon E 51 Camcorder and it's brilliant low light capability.

Karl Shaffer Art Director
Marc A. Williams Creative Director
Joseph A. Puhy Group Creative Director
Young & Rubicam, Inc. Agency
Howard Guard Productions Production
Lincoln-Mercury Division Client
Detroit, MI

MOTERCADE
A GROUP OF MOTORCYCLES SURROUNDS A NEW
LINCOLN TOWN CAR. THE WORDS, "IT'S COMING
OCTOBER 5 TO YOUR LINCOLN-MERCURY DEALER"
AND THE "THE NEW TOWN CAR" "LINCOLN. WHAT A
LUXURY CAR SHOULD BE." ALSO APPEAR ON THE
SCREEN.
MUSIC TRACK ONLY—No Words

  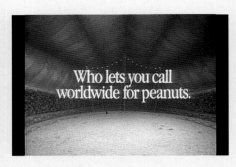

JoAnn Meyer Art Director
Martha Voss Copywriter
Roseanne Horn Agency Producer
Young & Rubicam New York Agency
Craig Hazen Agency Music Producer
AT&T Communications Client
New York, NY

TINY

VO: "Ladies and gentlemen, Tiny will now call Quebec."
VO: "Bonjour"
VO: "And now Guadalajara!"
VO: "Hola"
VO: "Milan"
VO: "Pronto"
VO: "Who lets you call worldwide for peanuts?"
VO: AT & T International Long Distance

Clark Frankel Art Director
Michael Ward Copywriter
Texas East Agency Producer
Young & Rubicam New York Agency
Dr. Pepper Company Client
New York, NY

LIKE NOTHIN' ELSE

MAN: There's something about it.
MAN: It's great!
WOMAN: It's just different.
MAN: Diet Dr Pepper is.
WOMAN: It's like nothin' else.

Woddy Swain Art Director
Andrew Landorf Copywriter
Diane Flynn Agency Producer
Young & Rubicam New York Agency
Mitchell Wirth Agency Music Producer
United States Postal Service Client
New York, NY

DINOSAURS

MAN RUNS INTO TRAFFIC THEN INTO POLICE
STATION. WOMAN APPEARS TO CORROBERATE MAN'S
STORY

MAN: Wait Stop! Wait Stop Stop! Don't You Know They're
Coming
DRIVER: Look Out
MAN: Doesn't Anyone believe me?
POLICE OFFICER: You Hear that fellows? Dinosaurs are
coming to this town. Ha! Ha!
WOMAN: They're already here.
VO: Dinosaur Stamps they're exiting. They're History. They're
at your Post Office Now
MAN: Now do you Believe me?
SUPER: *Dinosaur Stamps*
SUPER: *Get Them before it's too late!*

Woody Swain Art Director
Mike McKenna Copywriter
Ted Storb Agency Producer
Young & Rubicam New York Agency
Hunter Murtaugh Agency Music Producer
Adidas Client
New York, NY

337

Roy Grace Art Director
Cosimo Photographer/Director
Rosemary Barr Producer
Grace & Rothschild Agency
Range Rover Client
New York, NY

338

DRESSED FOR DINNER.

Steve Noxon Art Director
Kevin Fahey Copywriter
Leslie Rose, Doug Chase Agency Producers
Young & Rubicam, Inc. Agency
Sundog Productions, Inc. Design Firm
Lincoln-Mercury Division Client
Detroit, MI

DRESSED FOR DINNER
VO: I'm gonna eat 'em alive.
SONG: Nothing Moves You Like a Mercury.
SUPER: *Lincoln-Mercury Brand Sign*

Consumer Campaign TV

Goeff Hayes Art Director
Jeff Linder Copywriter
Ed Pollack Producer
Bruce Dowad Director
TBWA Advertising, Inc. Agency
Bruce Dowad Associates Production
Evian Waters of France Client
New York, NY

MORNING
VO: Morning. Three hundred sixty five chances every year for you to start doing something healthy. To keep yourself in balance. One way is with Evian Natural Spring Water from the French Alps. Like a new day, it's always there for you to do something healthy.
SUPER: *(Evian Logo)*

NATURE

VO: Nature's gift is the earth. And you can use all that it provides to do something healthy. To keep yourself in balance. There's also Evian Natural Spring Water from the French Alps. Another of nature's gifts you can use to do something healthy.

SUPER: *(Evian Logo)*

Christopher Dean Art Director
Seth Werner Creative Director
Jamie Hoeman Copywriter
The Bloom Agency Agency
Griner Cuesta & Schrom Design Firm
Team Bank Client
Dallas, TX

THE SPIKE

ANNOUNCER: When Texas American Bridge Bank became Team Bank you may noy have noticed the difference in the tellers. And the loan officers may look the same. But now we're the largest Texan run bank in Texas, with assets of over 5 billion dollars. And that, we think you'll notice.

THE WAVE

ANNOUNCER: Texas American Bridge Bank has become team Bank, giving us 5 billion dollars in assets. Making us the largest Texas run bank in Texas. Needless to say, it was good for morale.

Michael Hart Art Director
Hal Friedman, Jim Patterson, Naomi Schwartz
   Copywriters
Bob Shriber Producer
Goodyear Client
New York, NY

SMALL HOUSE
MOTHER AND CHILD ARE DRIVING ON WET ROAD.
JUST MISS ACCIDENT.
GIRL: Mommy Why do we have to travel so much?
MOTHER: that's my job, honey. That's how we get to live in a big house and have the things we need.
VO: One day, it could down to a few inches. For those few inches, it's good to know you have Goodyear tires
GIRL: We could get a smaller house.
SUPER: *GOODYEAR*
The Best Tires in the World

BROTHERS
TWO BROTHERS DRIVING ALONG WET ROAD, SINGING
BARELY MISS ACCIDENT.
BILL: So what do you think mom's going to do when we both show up out of the blue?
JOHN: Hopefully, she'll feed us. I was just thinking of how much time we could spend not together.
BILL: I Guess we're home. I miss you.
VO: That's why we say, the best tires in the world have Goodyear written all over them.
SUPER: *GOODYEAR*
The Best Tires in the World

343

BILLY'S BACK!

YOUNG MAN IN HOT CAR PULLS INTO CONOCO
STATION IN OLD-TIME WESTERN TOWN. FILLS HIS CAR
AND RIDES OFF IN THE SUNSET.

MAN: Who was that man?
LADY: I don't know, but I sure like how he rides.
VO: CONOCO-Hottest Brand Going

Don De Pasquale Art Director
Dick Smith, Jane Child Copywriters
Taylor Brown Smith & Perrault Agency
Greenbriar Productions Production
Conoco, Inc. Client
Houston, TX

GOOD GUY, BAD GUY

"HIGH NOON" SET. GOOD GUY IN WHITE CAR, BAD
GUY IN BLACK CAR.

GOOD GUY: You boys having a little trouble?
YOUNG BAD GUY: I told you we shoulda used Conoco.
GOOD GUY: If you'd been usin' Conoco you might not be
spendin' all your money on that engine.
YOUNG BAD GUY: I told you we shoulda used Conoco.
VO: CONOCO, Hottest Brand Going

GUARANTEED CARROTS
WOMAN: At Apple Tree, we hand pick all our produce. So it's Apple Tree fresh. We guarantee it. But if you get something your not happy with, we want it back.
(SFX: rapid fire thudding of carrots into wall)
WOMAN: (Gulp) Thank you.
VO: Guaranteed Apple Tree fresh.

Sherri Oldham Art Director
Laura McCarley Copywriter
Chuck Carlberg Copy Director
Rives Smith Baldwin Carlberg Agency
Leroy Koetz Productions Production
AppleTree Client
Houston, TX

GUARANTEED BREAD
MAN: At Apple tree, we bake all our own bread fresh, every single day. We're so sure it's fresh, we guarantee it. So if you don't like it, just send it on back.
(SFX: Whoosh! Thock!)
MAN: Thank you
VO: Guaranteed Apple Tree Fresh

Randee Paur Art Director
Seth Werner Creative Director
Jim Weber Copywriter
The Bloom Agency Agency
M. Leaman & Associates Production
Skaggs Alpha Beta Client
Dallas, TX

SHOPPERS DON'T STOP

ANNOUNCER: WE're just stopping people in the neighborhood. Not for very long, but just long enough to tell them about the specials at Skaggs. Here comes somebody now. Hi. Oh, here comes somebody. We'll see if they have got their circular and know about the specials this week at Skaggs.
ANNOUNCER: Hi, how are ya. Goodbye. I guess they already know. She gave me that kind of, I know already signal. Hi. Excuse me, can you roll your window down? Well at least they didn't hit me.

SAY IT AGAIN

JIM: Skaggs Alpha Beta. I'm just out crusing around. A lot of people are inside picking up Christmas ornaments, Christmas decorations, Christmas baking goods, stuff like that. I can smell it from out here.
JIM: Skaggs Alpha Beta is a great place to pick up those last minute items, huh Santa?
SANTA: You can say that again.
JIM: Skaggs Alpha Beta is a great place to pick up those last minute items.

Charlie Gennarelli Art Director
Linda Kaplan, Brian Sitts Copywriters
Judi Nierman Producer
J. Walter Thompson Agency
Bell Atlantic Client
New York, NY

BROTHERS
SUPER: The Best Call
DAVID: When I was a kid all anybody ever told me was that I was adopted. I figured that's all I was ever gonna know. One night, I get a call. this voice says, "Is this James Foster?" So I said, "Yes, who's this? Then the voice...
JOHN: And then I said, "My name is John. And I'm your brother. And I've been looking for you for forty-two years."
VO: Call your brother tonight.
SUPER: Call your brother tonight
BELL ATLANTIC
We're more than just talk.

BEST FRIEND
SUPER: *The Best Call*
WOMAN: Every Saturday, I get a call from my friend, Ellen. We've been gabbing on the phone since high school.
Back then we talked about boyfriends and teachers and now we talk about husbands, and children and grandchildren and what are you having for lunch and don't get too fat.....
When I pick up that phone on Saturday... I'm seventeen again. And believe me that's been a long time!
VO: Call your best friend
SUPER: *Call your best friend.*
BELL ATLANTIC
We're more than just talk.

347

INTRODUCING
THE NEW CELICA
BY TOYOTA

INTRODUCING
THE NEW CELICA
BY TOYOTA

INTRODUCING
THE NEW CELICA
BY TOYOTA

348

Egon Springer Art Director
Rick Pregent Copywriter
Charles Braive Agency Producer
Saatchi & Saatchi Compton Hayhurst, Ltd.
  Agency
L.T.B. Productions Production
Toyota Canada, Inc. Client
Toronto, Ontario, Canada

COUNTRY ROAD

MAN LEANING AGAINST THE 1990 TOYOTA CELICA ON
A DESSERTED COUNTRY ROAD.

MAN: There are two kinds of people. Those who lead and
those who follow. They'll be along.

SUPER: *CELICA*

BACK ALLEY

OPEN ON YOUNG MAN IN A BACK ALLEY WITH
BASKETBALL IN HIS HAND. HE'S STANDING BESIDE A
1990 TOYOTA CELICA.

MAN: Some people say a car is something you wear.
How do you like my new outfit?

SUPER: *CELICA*

DOWNTOWN

WOMAN LEANING AGAINST THE 1990 TOYOTA CELICA
IN A DOWNTOWN AREA. SHE HAS A NEWSPAPER IN
HER HANDS.

WOMAN: They say you can't have everything in life.
Who are they?

SUPER: *CELICA*

Hans Fahrnholz Art Director
Charles Stedwell Agency Producer
Carla Stedwell, Millie Olson Copywriters
Ketchum Advertising Agency
Group One Design Firm
Beef Industry Council Client
San Francisco, CA

UTOPIA
QUICK SHOTS OF SMALL TOWN AND TOWNSPEOPLE
INTERCUT WITH PREPARATION OF HAMBURGERS.

VO: Take my word for it: This is Utopia
VO: Am I talking 'bout scenery, harp music, the betterment of man? No. I'm talking burgers. I had the most perfect hamburger of my life in Utopia. It was so juicy and delicious thoght I was in heaven–so to speak. And if you ever reach Utopia, take my advice, order the hamburger.
SUPER: *Beef. Real food in Utopia, Texas.*

MANHATTAN
QUICK SHOTS OF SMALL TOWN AND TOWNSPEOPLE
INTERCUT WITH PREPARATION OF STEAKS

VO: There's only one place in the world looks like that: Manhattan.
VO: Where the air's clean, the living's easy and the food's great. Every time I'm in Manhattan I order my personal favorite–the New York Strip. Delicious. Manhattan is known for it's famous restaurants. So be sure to try all three.
SUPER: *Beef. Real food in Manhattan, Montana.*
SUPER: *Beef Industry & Beef Board.*

Mark Zapico, Dave Tschirhart Art Directors
Noel Nauber, Rob Hendrickson, Bob Daykin
  Copywriters
Bob Rashid Producer
DMB&B Agency
Pontiac Division Client
Bloomfield Hills, MI

WESTERNERS

There's somethin' coming! (Trans Sport). Like you've never seen! (Trans Sport) It's a new kind of driving machine! Get on your Pontiac and Ride!

VO: The space vehicle of the nineties. Introducing the Pontiac of minivans: The new Pontiac trans Sport.

SUPER: *(Pontiac Logo)*
We build exitment

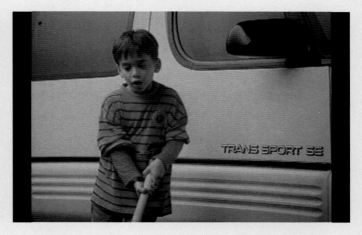

STRENGTH

"CRASH" DUMMIES AND "CRASH" DOG IN WITH TWO MORE VANS ON TOP. SMALL BOY STAND NEXT TO VAN HITS IT WITH BASEBALL BAT. NOTHING HAPPONS TO VAN.

VO: How strong and secure is the advanced space frame chassis of the new Pontiac Trans Sport? Let's just say it carries it's own weight... and then some. Trans Sport is rust-proof lower body panels resist dents... and even Eddie Jankowski. Trans Sport... the Pontiac of minivans.

SUPER: *"Pontiac Trans Sport... we build exitment."*

CREAMED BERRIES

DORIS: Hi! Today's show Creamed Berries.
Start with Reynolds new Sure-Seal freezer bags.
Pour in one pint overripe blackberries.
Take one Louisville Slugger and very carefully batter the berries.
Voila! Creamed Berries. No other freezer bag can do that.
VO: They're the toughest plastic bags ever built.
New Sure-Seal bags from Reynolds. It's Reynolds Sure-Seal or bust.
DORIS: Next week...Bashed Borscht.

BRICK

DORIS: Hi! Some of you have written to ask, "Does it matter which plastic bag you use?" A question not to be taken lightly. So we placed a brick in a Ziploc storage bag. And then in the new Sure-Seal storage bag from Reynolds.
Proving once again—it's Sure Seal or bust.
VO: They're the toughest plastic bags ever built. New Sure Seal bags from Reynolds.
It's Reynolds Sure Seal or bust.

Brent Mellett Art Director
Drake Sparkman Creative Director
Stephanie Apt Producer
Michaele Lowe Copywriter
J. Walter Thompson Agency
Reynolds Metals Client
New York, NY

HE WHO HESITATES

PLANE PASSENGERS ARE SERVED TOAST. MAN WISH-
ES HE HAD ORDERED CREAM CHEESE. TRIES TO GET
STEWARDESS'S ATTENTION. FAILS.
STEWERDESS: Toast with butter, sir.
2nd PASSENGER: Do you have any Philly?
1st PASSENGER: Could I get...
STEWERDESS: I'll take that now please.
ANNOUNCER: Next time butter your bread with Philly
instead.

DOG

MAN HAS BAGEL WITH BUTTER. WOMAN READING
NEWSPAPER AND WITH DOG HAS HERS WITH CREAM
CHEESE. MAN TRIES TO USE PHILLY. DOG GROWLS
THEN BARKS. MAN PRETENDS NOTHING HAPPONED.
SUPER: *BUTTER YOUR BREAD WITH PHILLY INSTEAD.*

Steve Foster, Ken Kimura Art Director
Tom Reilly, Mark Fisher Copywriter
Ed Maroney Producer
J. Walter Thompson Agency
Gibson, Lefebvre, Gartner Production
Kraft, Inc. Client

BLUE MONDAY/MURPHY BROWN

A DAD HOLDS HIS DAUGHTER. ROY SITS IN FROM
WITH HIS GUITAR

DAD: I didn't show up this morning
I got to take little Erin to work
She learned a new word today
She called the boss a jerk.
It's Blue Monday
I sure could use a good launch
Maybe watch a little Murphy Brown
VO: Murphy Brown and the CBS Monday night Comedies
the Cure for Blue Monday

BLUE MONDAY/BLUESMAN

ROY GAINS SINGS: Every Monday I hear sad stories From
the Good People in this town They talk about stuff that makes
life rough And bring a body down
Just one way to beat Blue Monday
Is Monday Night Comedies on CBS
SUPER: *GET THE CURE FOR BLUE MONDAY*

Scott A. Mednick Art Director
Jack Halpern Designer
Myles Reed, Robert Roll,
    Dana Precious-Stevens Copywriters
Scott Mednick & Associates Agency/Design Firm
Imagine One Production
CBS TV Client
Los Angeles, Ca

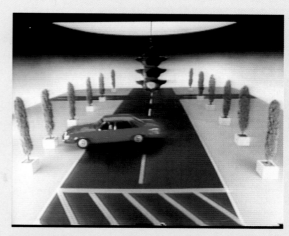

CIRCULATION
ENGINEER SHOWS PARTS OF CUT-DOWN CAR.
ANNOUNCER: The circulatory system of your car. That's where Texaco's New System 3 Gasoline starts to bring new life to fuel injectors and valves. It can keep new cars running like new and actually restore performance to older cars. You'll get more power from every octane.
SUPER: *(Texaco Logo)*
Star of the American Road

PURR
ANNOUNCER: Listen, (SFX: CAT PURRING) You're engine can sound like that with Texaco's new System 3 Gasoline. It can keep new cars running like new... (SFX: CAT MEOWS) and actually help restore performance to older cars. (SFX GROWL) It'll give you more power from every octane. Five tanks is all we ask.
SUPER: *(Texaco Logo)*
Star of the American Road

Rich Karnbach Art Director
Dick Johnson Creative Director
Craig Mungons Photographer
Bob Joseph Copywriter
Campbell Mithun Esty Agency
Texaco, Inc. Client
New York, NY

NO-BRAINER CHECKING
One Less Thing To Think About.

BancFlorida
FDIC INSURED • FSB

Tim Ward Art Director
Doug Hardee Creative Director
Sarah Fader Agency Producer
West & Company Agency
Image Point Productions, LA Production
BancFlorida Client
Tampa, FL

Tim Ward Art Director
Doug Hardee Creative Director
West & Company, Tampa Agency
David Krystal Music Music
Associates Nadel & Butler, NY Production
Publix Super Markets, Inc. Client
Tampa, FL

356

Ared Spendjian Art Director
Peter Swerdloff Creative Director
Leonard Sorcher Copywriter
Brouillard Communications Agency
Sandbank & Partners Production
Empire Blue Cross and Blue Shield of NY Client
New York, NY

WE WILL

LITTLE BOY: I think I got a yellow fever, mom.
MAN IN SUIT: It's the post nasal.
OLD LADY: No it's arterial sclorosis
OLD MAN: I got heart trouble, I got rheumatism.
RUNNER: I gotta get out of here.
OLD MAN: My back's killing me. The doctor's, the hospital
MAN: The hospital and the labs
OLD LADY: Somebody's got to help me.
VO: EMPIRE BLUE CROSS AND BLUE SHIELD. YOUR
HEALTH IS OUR ONLY BUSINESS.
RUNNER: I got to go buy oat bran.

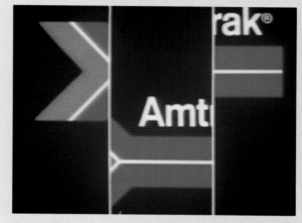

David Garcia Art Director
Alan Fraser, Jay Morales Creative Directors
Stephen Crane Copywriter
DDB Needham Agency
Charlex Production
Amtrak Client
New York, NY

357

CIRCLE RESEARCH

"UFO" LANDS IN FIELD. RESEARCHER TAKES REESES PEANUT BUTTER CUP OUT OF PACK IN HIS POCKET. COMPUTER ISOLATES "UFO." BLOWS IT UP ON MONITOR FOR EXIMINATION. PEANUT BUTTER CUP FLIES IN AND LANDS BESIDE PACK

IN THE PRAIRIES

FOOTAGE OF CIRCLES FROM EXISTING NEWSCASTS ANNOUNCER SEES REESES PEANUT BUTTER CUP LAND. ANNOUNCER INTERVIEWS RESEARCHER. LOCALS CARRY AWAY PEANUT BUTTER CUP THAT LANDED.

Vickie Wild Art Director
Sally Smallwood Copywriter
Pat White Producer
Young & Rubicam Ltd. Agency
Directors Film Company Production
Hershey Canada, Inc. Client
Toronto, Ontario, Canada

LEMMINGS

LEMMINGS RUNNING THRU FIELD TURN AROUND
AND RETURN THRU FIELD.

VO: If your best friend jumped off a cliff would you? Did your
mother ask you this? Ask yourself this. Are you... a lemming?
Lemmings jump off cliffs every four years. There are no five
year old lemmings. Unless they've learned to think for themselves.

SUPER: *THINK FOR YOURSELF.*

LIZARD

FRONT VIEW OF LIZARD. REAR VIEW OF LIZARD. SIDE
VIEW OF LIZARD. LIZARD RUNS OFF SCREEN

VO:The Dune Lizzard lifts his feet so they don't burn. this is his
life. Running in place and eating insects. What's the point?
Why bother? Why not move someplace cooler?

SUPER: *MOVE SOMEPLACE COOLER.*
WXRT. 93. RADIO CHICAGO.

Faye Kleros Art Director
Scott Burns Copywriter
Ellen Israel White Agency Producer
Young & Rubicam Chicago Agency
Highlight Commercials/Edit Express
  Design Firm
WXRT/FM Radio Client
Chicago, IL

Joe Sciarrotta Art Director
Tenny Fairchild Copywriter
Lisa Von Drehle Producer
J. Walter Thompson Agency
HKM Productions Production
Southland Corporation Client
Chicago, IL

HUNGRY-DELI

VO: Americans are busy. Yet somewhere between here and there, they find time to do a thing called "eat." That's when those who know, find a 7-Eleven the only place they can grab a Fresh deli Sandwich and a Super Big Gulp, or a Quarter Pound Big Bite and a cup of fresh ground 7-Eleven coffee. And still have time to enjoy them.
SUPER: *OSCAR MAYER*
AT PARTICIPANT STORES

EASY BREAKFAST

VO: Every morning, everybody must wake up and go to work. What takes place in between is an art form we call "the commute." And any "commuter" who knows a shortcut, knows where there's a 7-Eleven. The only place you can fuel yourself, and fuel your car. You could stop somewhere else, but those who know the easy way, stop at 7-Eleven. The sign of the times.

DAD

KID BITES SANDWICH AT THE TOP. SAME SHOT TURNED UPSIDE DOWN, BITE MISSING FROM TOP AND BOTTOM OF SANDWICH.

BEN: You know, I really owe a lot to my Dad. He's taught me a lot over the years. Like sports, fishing, camping. All that neat stuff. He even taught me the most important thing about Sunbeam Bread sandwiches. He said, "Son, always eat them from the top down.

VO: Soft, fresh Sunbeam Bread. Kids love it. Just because.

SUPER: *Kids love it. Just because.*

BEN: Unless, of course, you're in Australia.

CHOLESTEROL

KID SNAPS HIS FINGERS AND GRAPHIC OUTLINE IN SHAPE OF BREAD SLICE APPEARS. KID STEPS OUT OF FRAME, LEAVING SET EMPTY MOMENTARILY. CUT TO PRODUCT SHOT. PEANUT BUTTER AND JELLY SANDWICH. KID LEANS HIS HEAD BACK INTO FRAME AND OUTLINE OF BREAD.

KID: The people who bake Sunbeam bread asked me to remind you that Sunbeam has no cholesterol. Me to make a big deal about. Zero! Zip! Nada! I mean, if your TV screen (SNAP) was a slice of Sunbeam Bread and I was some cholesterol... lie... I'd be outa here!

VO: Soft, fresh sunbeam bread. Kids love it. Just because.

KID: Get the picture?

Bill Holley Art Director
Kerry Oliver Copywriter
Anne V. Birke Agency Producer
Buntin Advertising, Inc. Agency
Bob Ebel Productions Design Firm
Quality Bakers of America Client
Nashville, TN

Mike Bade Art Director
Lori Korchek Copywriter
Margoetes, Fertitta & Weiss Agency
Filmfair Production
New York Newsday Client
New York, NY

QUEEN
INTERIOR OF NEWSPAPER OFFICE.

VO: He was born in Queens. He lives in Queens. He writes about Queens for New York Newsday. We call him Mister Queen, but you can call him Joe. Nobody knows New York neighborhoods like we do. New York Newsday. True, Justice and the Comics.

SUPER: *(Logo)*
"True, Justice and the Comics."

SOPHOCLES
SUPER:
¢ "The truth is always the strongest argument"
¢ Sophocles
¢ "Injustice anywhere is a threat to justice everywhere"
¢ Martin Luther King
¢ "Aaugh! I've been kissed by a dog!"
¢ Lucy Van Pelt
SUPER: *New York Newsday Logo*
"Truth, Justice and the Comics"

362

Rick Hanson, Scott Schindler Art Directors
Dennis Berger, Stacy Wall Copywriters
Bob Emerson Producer
BBDO Agency
Gibson-Lefebvre-Gartner Production
Pizza Hut Client
New York, NY

RIGHT FIELD

VO: Then suddenly everyone's looking at me, my mind has been wandering, what could it be? They point to the sky, and I look up above, and a baseball falls into my glove. I play right field, it's important to know. You gotta know how to catch, you gotta know how to throw. That's why I play in right field, way out where the dandelions grow.

ANNOUNCER: As a proud sponsor of Little League Baseball, Pizza Hut welcomes all the kids who make it great.

DRIVEWAY

FATHER: Atta boy Charlie, atta boy.
CHARLIE: Mitchell with the ball. Up to the right he comes in...
FATHER: When in traffic, use the board...
CHARLIE: To the basket, he shoots...
FATHER: Use the board Charlie. Atta boy, yeah that's it. The board Charlie, use the board.
VO: As a proud sponsor of the NCAA, Pizza Hut salutes all the Charlie Mitchells out there because we know how hard it is not just to make it but to make it great.
SPORTS CASTER: Four seconds remaining. Eastern Regional finals. Mitchell right side of the lane, jumps, shoots, he scores. Charlie Mitchell at the buzzer.

Bill Argus Art Director
Ron Thomson Copywriter
Vickers & Benson Advertising, Ltd. Agency
The Partners' Film Company, Ltd. Production
McDonald's Restaurants of Canada Limited
   Client
Toronto, Ontario, Canada

KIDS TALK

SUPER: *"Kids Talk on Moms & Dads"*
RENESSA: A mother has to wash clothes almost everyday.
ANDREW: He used to be an engineer, but now he cuts the lawn.
ANTHONY: He drives an airplane.
JONATHAN: My mom's just a normal person like me.
ARI: He's a lawyer.
JONATHAN: He doesn't do much except goes to his office and photocopy things.
ARI: And he can also help someone sue someone.
.... don't you have a lawyer.
SUPER: *(McDonald's Logo.)*

 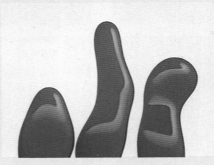 

Angelika Lang Art Director
Lester Bookbinder Director
Kaethe Pietz, Michael Conrad, Leo Burnett
   In-house TV Producers
RSA, London Production
Margaret Astor AG Client
Frankfurt, West Germany

FIRE RED

RED LIPSTICK COMES UP. LIPS ARE DOWN WITH LIPSTICK. WOMAN OPENS HER MOUTH AND BLOWS FIRE. SCREEN TOTALLY IN FLAMES.
VO: Fire Red by Margaret Astor
SUPER: *Margaret Astor*

BANG RED

WOMAN WITH LONG RED NAILS TAKES PISTOL OUT OF HER BAG. SHE DRAWS TRIGGER: EXPLOSION. NAIL VARNISH RUNS DOWN THE SCREEN.
VO: Bang Red by Margaret Astor
SUPER: *Margaret Astor*

Jeff Weiss Art Director
Moshe Brakha Photographer
Paul Opperman Copywriter
Margeotes, Fertitta & Weiss Agency
Moshe Brakha, Inc. Design Firm
Maccabee Beer Client
New York, NY

WORLD PEACE
TWO MACCABEE BOTTLES HELD UP BY PAIR OF
HANDS DANCE TO ISRALI MUSIC. OTHER DANCERS
APPEAR. ZOOM OUT TO REVEAL FILM CREW
DANCING.

VO: Life is like a beer...
VO: Sometimes it's a celebration just drinking it
VO: Do life!
SUPER: *DO LIFE*
MACCABEE BEER
(Overlay spray-paint of 60's peace sign)

DESERT
WOMAN IN DESERT SEES BUCKET OF ICE WITH
MACCABEE BEER BOTTLE.

VO: Life is like a beer. It's the wait... That heightens... The
ecstacy... Do life.
SUPER: *DO LIFE*
MACCABEE BEER

Corporate Campaign TV

COME HOME
SINGERS: Our place is your place
Our house is your house
Come celebrate with us at home this fall
Share in the good times
Home is something you can believe in
Home is somewhere you can get it all
CHORUS: Only on NBC, NBC
Join the family
Come home to the best
Only on NBC
ALL: Home, Sweet Home
You've got the best for company
The nest is never empty when you're
Home to NBC

Chuck Stepner, Chris Carlisle, Steve Lowe,
Martin Brierly Designers
Marc Reshovsky Cameraman
Steve Lowe, Martin Brierly Directors
NBC Advertising & Promotion Agency
Propaganda Films Production
NBC Entertainment Client
Burbank, CA

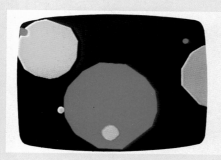
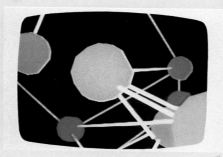

Bill Fogarty, Sherry Scharschmidt Art Directors
Andrea Trotenberg Creative Director
Christa Velbel Copywriter
Bayer Bess Vanderwarker Agency
Rhythm & Hues Production
Ameritech Client
Chicago, IL

INLAND STUDY

VO: When Inland Steel wanted to build business they looked
for a total communications solution from Ameritech.
Beginning with a digital system in a centralized office with
thousands of lines at multiple sites Ameritech moved informa-
tion to more locations.
Because Inland Steel has the highest standards only
Ameritech could fill this tall order.
(Ameritech Logo)
Ameritech solutions that work.
SUPER: *SOLUTIONS THAT WORK*

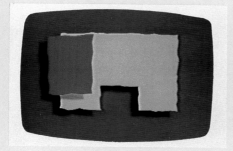
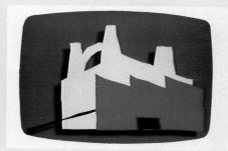

DOW STUDY

ANNCR: The people at Dow needed to find the right formula
of voice and data communications. The solution came from
Ameritech.
A system designed, installed, and managed by an Ameritech
team, in partnership with Dow. Now that's good chemistry.
(Ameritech Logo)
SUPER: SOLUTIONS THAT WORK

Dave Golden Art Director
BBDO Chicago Agency
GKO (Chicago) Production
Centel Corporation Client
Chicago, IL

AUCTION
MAN STARTS OUT IN TRUCK. HIE FRIEND IS AT HORSE
AUCTIO. TRUCK BREAKS DOWN AND MAN USES
MOBILE PHONE TO HAVE FRIEND BID ON HORSE. MAN
ARRIVES AT AUCTION. RIDES OFF ON HORSE.
SUPER: W H E R E
SUPER: P E O P L E
SUPER: C O N N E C T
SUPER: CENTEL (Logo)

CHURCHILL

MAN 1: He was an author, an orator and a great statesman and an amateur painter.

MAN 2: the way he painted was the way he lived life. He slashed the paint on.

WOMAN 1: This man ran the country for as long as he did and still had time to do all the other things.

MAN: We had just crossed the Rhine into Germany. Churchill was sitting there with this great big ciger and his victory sign and he said "Well Done Chaps!"

SUPER: Sucess is Doing More Than One Thing Well
SUPER: *BellSouth Logo*
SUPER: *Telecommunications*
SUPER: *Information Systems*
SUPER: *Mobile communications*
SUPER: *Advertising Systems*
SUPER: *Everything You'd Expect from a Leader*

SCHWEITZER

WOMAN: Albert Schweitzer was a genius! I remember as a child when we heard about him that at twenty-eight he already had three Doctorates.

DAUGHTER: He was my boss and he was my father. Philosophy and Technology and Music were his great interests and medicine would lead him to what he wanted to do.

MAN: In the morning he would operate on people. In the afternoon he would build houses. In the evening he would make his rounds as a Doctor and at night he would play the organ and write. Now who can do that?

SUPER: Success is doing more than One Thing Well
(Logo BellSouth)
SUPER: *Telecommunications*
SUPER: *Information systems*

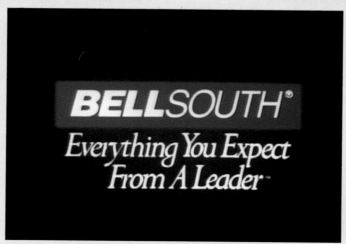

Andy Lewis Senior Art Director
Albert Maysles Cinematographer
Nell Archer, Sherry Lubbers Producers
Earle Palmer Brown Agency
Maysles Films, Inc. Production
BellSouth Communications, Inc. Client
New York, NY

Rich Martel Art Director
Al Merrin, Ted Sann Copywriters
BBDO Agency
Pytka Productions Design Firm
General Electric Corp. Client
New York, NY

HUNGARIAN RHAPSODY

SUPER: Budapest, Hungary

VO: There's a new light shining over Eastern Europe.
MAN: The Hungarians have been waiting for a very long time.
VO: A light of hope, joy and most of all, a new light of freedom.
WOMAN: Everything is changing, it's wonderful.
VO: And in this spirir GE has entered into an historic partner-
ship with a company called Tungstrum, Hungary's leading
lighting company.
WOMAN: It's like a dream, a beautiful dream.
VO: At GE we're proud to play even a small part helping the
Hungarian people build what promises to be a truly brillant
future.
SUPER: GE. We bring good things to life.

JIM

VO: Peoples bank is giving this time to their customers to do whatever they want.

JIM: I'd like to take this opportunity to tell you what Kiwanis does for charity. We raise thousands of dollars for hospitals, scholarship funds, and children's homes. I even embarrass myself for a good cause. these legs are the legs that won the local "Mr. Incredible Legs Contest" for charity. Went onto the state finals and lost. My wife says it's because of my socks.

RAY WISNEWSKI

VO: People's Bank is giving this time to their customers to do whatever they want.

RAY: I'd like to tell you about my hobby, bees. They're a lot like people. they all have specific jobs, from the day they're born until the day they die. They are very interesting, they are like society, they have a queen, they have males that are only there to service the queen. Other than that, the male comes back to the hive, sits around, does nothing, and eats. The females do all the work.

VO: If you think it's important, we do, too. People's Bank of Connecticut, menber FDIC. An equal housing lender.

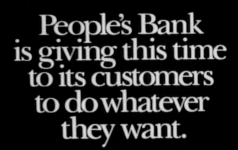

Arnie Arlow Art Director
Peter Lubalin Copywriter
Susan Jurick Producer
TBWA Advertising, Inc. Agency
Charenton Productions Production
People's Bank of Connecticut Client
New York, NY

372

CITIES

VO: In paris they lined up in the streets. In Rome it was standing room only. In LA & NY his concert sold out in an hour.
In cities all across America Paul McCartney and his new band is the hottest ticket in town.
So if you want to go, get in line early and get out your Visa card.
Because a concert like this doesn't take place everyday and it doesn's take American Express.
Visa. It's everywhere you want to be.

CHANGE OF HEART

WOMAN: they want me to use a computer. I mean, what do I need a computer for? I'm not an accountant. I've been in this business elevan years. Why do I need wone now? Can you imagine me working on a computer?
FRIEND: They figure if you can use one, then anybody can.
VO: Macintosh has the power to change your mind about computers. The power to be your best.
SUPER: *The power to be your best.*
WOMAN: So, I was wrong.

Art Mellor Art Director
Robert Greenbaum, Andrew Killey Copywriters
BBDO Agency
H. Kira Films Production
VISA Client
New York, NY

Susan Westre Art Director
Chris Wall Copywriter
Pat Walsh, Bob Belton Producers
BBDO Agency
Pytka Productions Production
Apple Computers Client
New York, NY

Public Service TV

Warren Eakins Art Director
C.B. Harding Director/Cameraman
Steve Sandoz Copywriter
Steve & Warren's Excellent Adventure Agency
American Lung Association of Oregon Client
Portland, OR

SMOKING GUN
"This year nearly 20,000 americans will lose their lives to hand guns."
"But over 390,000 of us will lose our lives to cigarettes."

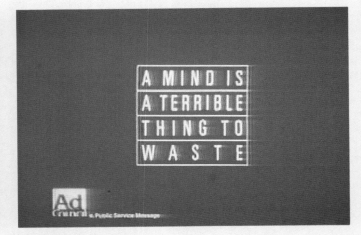

Mark Shap Art Director
Marvin Waldman Copywriter
Wendy Sasse Agency Producer
Young & Rubicam New York Agency
United Negro College Fund Client
New York, NY

GRANDFATHER
KID: Look what I drew in school today, grandpa.
GRANDFATHER: Oh my, the heart. Very good. The aorta, the left and right ventricles and the auricles.
KID: Grandpa, how do you know so much about the heart? Did you want to be a doctor when you were little?
GRANDFATHER: Well...
VO: Being black once meant forgetting about your dreams. Today the United Negro College Fund keeps these dreams alive but without your support these dreams will die.
KID: Can I be a doctor?
SUPER: *A MIND IS A TERRIBLE THING TO WASTE*

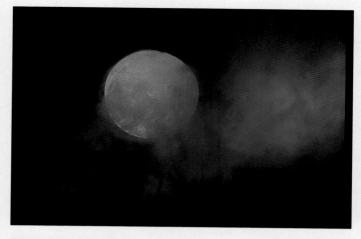

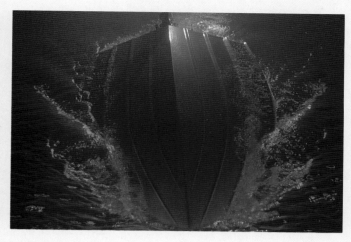

Doug Hardee Creative Director
Mirch Walker Director
Barrett Batson Copywriter
West & Company Agency
Big City Films/Walk On Water Production
Lowry Park Zoo Client
Tampa, FL

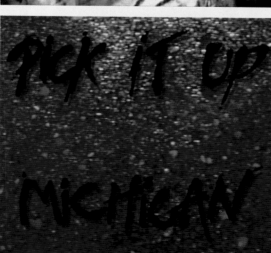

Marge Sroka Art Director
Mark Domin Copywriter
Marge Sroka, Beth Harrison Agency Producers
Young & Rubicam, Inc. Agency
The Big Picture Production
Macomb, Oakland, Wayne County Task Force on
    Freeway Clean Up Client
Detroit, MI

LITTER PIGS
VARIOUS PEOPLE DISCARD TRASH ONTO HIGHWAY
VO: This litterpiggy played the market
This Litter piggy liked to roam.
This Litter piggy had a roast beef sandwich
This Litter piggy had gum
And these Litter piggies went OINK! OINK! OINK!
All over our home.
Pick it up Michigan!
SUPER: *Pick it up Michigan*

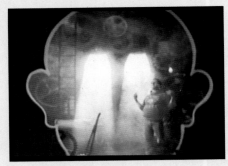

Norman Schwartz Art Director
Ted Charron Copywriter
Charron, Schwartz & Partners, Inc. Agency
ABC Network News/Project Literacy U.S. Client
New York, NY

LIGHTBULB

BRAIN VO: Hello? Anybody home?... Listen knucklehead, this is your brain speaking...your B-R-A-I-N... and uh, frankly things are a little slow up here.
I mean... Can we use a computer? No. Have we gotten any job training? Gone back to school? Read a book lately? No.
What's going to happen to us? I don't even want to think about it.
VO: Over 25 million American workers need to upgrade their skills.
BRAIN: C'mon. Smarten up. Use your brain.
You can do anything if you put your mind to it.

No one wins
with child abuse.

John Follis Art Director
Jacques Hennequet Director
Priscilla Watts Producer
Follis & Verdi, NY Agency
Picture Deuxville Production
National Committee for the Prevention of Child Abuse/Announcement furnished by the NBA and its players Client
New York, NY

ROBERT

VO: The reason Robert isn't leaving isn't because he doesn't want to be beaten at the basketball court.
It's because he doesn't want to be beaten at home.
SUPER: *No one Wins with Child Abuse.*
SUPER: *National Committee for Prevention of Child Abuse.*

Vince Cook Art Director
Dan Roettger Copywriter
Dan Geiger Producer/Director
TBWA Kerlick Switzer Agency
Big Brothers/Big Sisters of St. Louis Client
St. Louis, MO

SHANE

SHANE TALKING TO LITTLE JOE. JOE LOOKING INTO DISTANCE AT DEPARTING SHANE.
SHANE: You'll go home to your mother and father and grow up to be strong and straight.
LITTLE JOE: Yes, Shane.
LITTLE JOE: Shane...come back.
VO: Give a year to a boy and you'll both be better men.

Chris Wedge Creative Director
Michael Ferraro Animation and
    Technical Direction
Carl Ludwig Lighting Design
Ogilvy & Mather-NY Agency
Blue Sky Productions, Inc. Production
The Glass Packaging Institute Client
Ossining, NY

TRANSFORMATION
SUPER: *The Jelly Jar That Wouldn't Die*
VO: Every jar
Every bottle
Can lead more than one useful life
It can lead as many as we allow it to
Please don't bury glass while it is still alive
SUPER: GLASS
100^6 Recyclable

Jane Child Art Director/Copywriter
Taylor Brown Smith & Perrault Agency
The James Gang Production
Houston Ballet Client
Hoston, TX

PEER GYNT TV
MUSIC: Edvard Grieg
VO: Out of control. Deceiving only himself.. consumed by
money, lust and power... Spining from darkness... Into the light
of true love.
Houston's Ballet's season, premieres with Ben Stevenson's
masterful "Peer Gynt."
SUPER: HOUSTON BALLET
Peer Gynt

Tom McManus Art Director
David Warren Copywriter
T.B.W.A. Advertising, Inc. Agency
The Hudson River Sloop Clearwater Client
New York, NY

U.S.S. IOWA
VO: The United States Navy is now building a naval base on
Staten Island...In the heart of the most heavily populater area
on the continent...
The Navy says it's safe, Senator D'amato says it's safe, And
Governor Cuomo says it's safe...
So why should you worry?
after all, this base will be the new home of the U.S.S. Iowa.
You remember the U.S.S. Iowa, don't you?
SUPER: *The Hudson River Sloop Clearwater.*
Please help us prevent another tragedy...
call 1-800-67-SLOOP...

SCARRED FOR LIFE

ANNOUNCER: Two years ago, I was a victim in drinking and driving accident that left me permanently disabled.
It affects my work. And I have a lot of trouble sleeping.
At times the pain is unbearable.
the ironic thing is, I walked away without a scratch. You see, I killed someone.
And that left the kind of scars that will never heal.
VO: Drink and drive, and it could sober you up for the rest of your life.
SUPER: *Drink And Drive And It Could Sober You Up For The Rest Of Your Life.*
Governor's Highway Safety program.

PLAY YOUR PART

MUSIC UNDER: Gimmie Shelter''
The Rolling Stones
VO: Randt Travis on strings.
VO: Branford Marsalis on the horn.
VO: Paul Shaffer on keys.
VO: Carly Simon on lead.
VO: There are a lot of different parts to play in the American Red Cross. Play your part.

Steve Davis Art Director
Odette Arnold Copywriter
Laura Pless Producer
McKinney & Silver Agency
Pfeiffer Lopes Production Production
Governor's Highway Safety Program Client
Raleigh, NC

Domingo Perez Art Director
Robin Schwarz Copywriter
Bob Shriber, Michael La Gattuta Producers
J. Walter Thompson Agency
American Red Cross Client
New York, NY

YOUNG MAN

VO: Hanging out in the city might look cool in a 30 second jeans commercial.
But when you do it all summer long you really do get the blues.
VO: Support the Summer Fund and help a kid go to camp, instead of going to waste.
SUPER: *The Summer Fund*
Associated Grantmakers of Massachusetts, Inc.

WATER BABIES

A CHILD FALLS INTO WATER, SINKS TOWARDS THE BOTTOM.
AND THEN FLOATS UPWARD.
AN ADULTS ARMS COME IN AND CRADLE IT.
VO: There's a lot people can't do on their own. That's why there's a Red Cross.
But the Red Cross is human too.
And sometimes we need help.
SUPER: *WHAT WILL YOU DO FOR YOUR RED CROSS?*
SUPER: *THE CANADIAN RED CROSS SOCIETY*

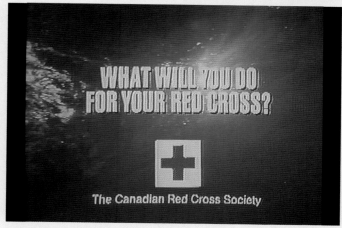

Todd Riddle Art Director
Mike Lescarbeau Copywriter
Dan Driscoll Director
Hill, Holliday, Connors, Cosmopulos Agency
September Productions Productions
Associated Grantmakers of Massachusetts
Client
Boston, MA

Sandy Kedey Art Director
Maura MacNeill Copywriter
Kelly Cavanaugh Agency Producer
Saatchi & Saatchi Compton Hayhurst, Ltd.
Agency
Derek Vanlint & Associates Production
Canadian Red Cross Society Client
Toronto, Ontario, Canada

Darrel Fiesel Art Director
Ken Dudwick, Millie Olson Creative Directors
Cathy Carolan Agency Producer
Ketchum Advertising Agency
Smillie Productions Production
United Way of the Bay Area Client
San Francisco, CA

John Lionti Art Director
Rick Dechant, Maura Mooney Producers
Tom Woodward Copywriter
Liggett-Stashower Agency
Hi-Tech Productions Production
United States Coast Guard Client
Cleveland, OH

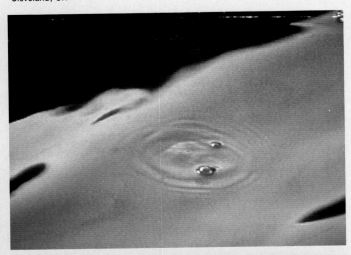

FLOATER
LIFE PRESERVER POPS UP FROM UNDER WATER
BUBBLES EMERGE FROM BELOW SURFACE.
ANNCR: If you're wearing your life preserver in a boating accident, you'll be floating on top immediately.
If you're not wearing one, it might take a week or so.
SUPER: *Wear Your Life Preserver.*
SUPER: *Guardians of the Great Lakes*

Kay Hairgrove Art Director
Kevin Willis Copywriter/Director
Houston Ad Federation Agency
East Egg Productions Production
AIDS Foundation Houston Client
Houston, TX

POOL

WOMAN: We grew up to be one of those "long distance" phone commercials–calling each other up just to say "hi". Well I just found out jack has AIDS and he's not doing so hot. I have to call him, I mean I want to. But what do you say to somebody who's probably...What do I say to him? What do I do?
SUPER: *Assistance.*
SUPER: *Education.*
SUPER: *Support.*
SUPER: *Lighting the way in the age of AIDS*
AIDS FOUNDATION HOUSTON

COWBOY

MAN: I guess having a place to live is a part of life I always took for granted. But a lot of things change when you have AIDS. I can't work as much as I used to, I'm behind on the rent–I'm being evicted. I don't know how much more time I have, but I need a place I can call home.
SUPER: *Assistance.*
SUPER: *Education.*
SUPER: *Support.*
SUPER: *Lighting the way in the age of AIDS*
AIDS FOUNDATION HOUSTON

Miranda Patterson, Scott Chalk Producers
Alex Weil Designer/Designer
John Semerad Paintbox Artist
Steve Chiarello Production Coordinator
Charlex Production
National Broadcasting Company Client
New York, NY

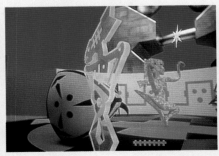

Kim Johnson, Glen Claybrook, Steve Oakes
 Art Directors/Designers
Jamie Jacobson Photographer
David Starr, Richard Winkler, Russ Dube
 Producers
Densu Advertising Agency
Broadcast Arts Production
J-Wave Radio/Japan Client
New York, NY

C.R. Russell Art Director/Designer
R/Greenberg Associates Agency/Production
Thirteen/WNET Design/Arts & Features
 Design Firm/Client
New York, NY

Alex Weil Director/Designer
Steve Chiarello Producer
John Semerad Harry Artist
Charlex Production
Ha! TV Comedy Network Client
New York, NY

Tom Corey Art Director
Alex Weil Director
Betty Cohen Creative Director
Corey McPherson Nash Agency
Charlex Production
Turner Network Television Client
New York, NY

Hal Aronow-Theil, Stephen Vardy
 Art Directors/Designers
Ray Chiste Technical Director
Steve Besner Director
In-house Design Firm
Image Mix-Compugraph Designs Design Firm
CBS News Client
Brooklyn, NY

Pat Egan, Eric Eiser Art Directors
Tim Miller Creative Director
Don Duncan Producer
Tomandandy Music
Atlantic Motion Pics Production
 NBC Advertising Client
New York, NY

GANGS, COPS, AND DRUGS
"Crips","Bloods", "Little Mafia", come face to fae with the violent new breed of LA street gangs. A frightening two part NBC news summer special begins Tuesday night.

Sarah Pirozek Art Director/Designer
David Phillips Photographer
Louie Lino (Signal Corps) Music
Venus Envy Design Firm
Bloomingdales Client
Brooklyn, NY

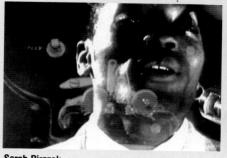  

Sarah Pirozek
   Art Director/Designer/Photographer
Tamsen Martin Editor
Louie Lino (Signal Corps) Music
Venus Envy Design Firm
VH1 Client
Brooklyn, NY

Russ Hardin Art Director
Tom Booth Producer
Gordon Munro Director
Munro Booth Productions Production
Lord & Taylor Client
New York, NY

Radio

Tom Case Copywriter
Jim Reilly Producer
Liggett-Stashower Agency
Motorists Insurance Client
Cleveland, OH

IN THIS BOX

Maybe you think of radio commercials the way I do. Here's this
fellow jawing at you from a box in your car or next to your
bed. You say, "How can he possibly know what I'm all
about? What I need, what I buy?"

Well, I'm this box and you surely don't know me and I surely
don't know you. So why take advice about insurance when
I say Motorists Insurance is a darn good company?

I would certainly appreciate it if you believed me; but it would
make more sense if you believed other people in the insurance business.

They say Motorists is a darn good company. Heck, I'm just
repeating it. You know what the test is? You call up your
independant Motorists agent--he's in the phone book--and
have a chat about your auto, home, business or life
insurance.

Soon enough, you'll make up your mind about him, about
Motorists.

And now that I think of it, about me.

Motorists. It's the kind of insurance company other insurance
companies would like to be.

They're good. And they're different. Motorists. You know us.

Steve Engle Copywriter
Vicki Blanford Producer
Rhea & Kaiser Advertising Agency
Minneapolis Broadcast Company Design Firm
Rhone-Poulenc Ag Company Client
Naperville, IL

LARVICIDE

MUSIC: (TWANGY COUNTRY-WESTERN INSTRUMENTAL)
RUBY LEE: (MONOTONAL SOUTHERN VOICE) Yesterday my
husband Billy Bob came up to me and said, "Honey, I have
got worms."

After my initial suprise, I said to him, "Sweet thing, you should
see a doctor."

"Not those kind of worms," he replied.

"Budworms and Bollworms. In my cotton."

"Oh," I exclaimed. Heliothis virescens and Heliothis zea."

"That is right," he said, amazed at my entomological
knowledge.

So I said, How about using LARVIN brand thiodicarb
insecticide-ovicide? LARVIN provides effective, long-lasting
control of most lepidopterous pests, including budworms
and bollworms. Even pyrethroid-resistant populations."

"But isn't LARVIN expensive?" he probed.

"Au contraire, LARVIN is competitively priced with other non-
pyrethroid larvicides."

Finally, Billy Bob asked, "Sweet thing, wherever did you learn
so much about insects?" To which I replied, "A woman's
mind is a strange and wonderous thing"

He agreed.

ANNCR TAG: Ask your farm chemicals for LARVIN brand
insecticide-ovicide, and save up to three dollars a gallon on
the LARVIN Red-Hot Rebate.

Jean Craig Copywriter
Len Levy Producer
Knesser/Craig Agency
ARCO Client
Los Angeles, CA

GAS

MUSIC UP & UNDER
JAMES EARL JONES: There are 206 billion trees I'm told in
California. Among them, fruit trees-almond and apricot are he
first to suffer the effects of smog.

SFX: BIRDS CHIRPING
JAMES EARL JONES: There are 18 million song birds nesting in
the state. the mockingbird doesn't handle smog too well. Nor
the finch.

SFX: PEOPLE, CHILDREN, LAUGHING, SHOUTING
JAMES EARL JONES: And, of course, there are 28,662,000
people. Give or take.

For all these reasons, ARCO introduces EC-1, emission control
gasoline, replacing leaded. If all leaded users switched, it
would be like reducing emissions from heavier polluting older
cars by 20%. A series of EC Gasolines for all vehicles is
planned. Gasolines designed to be part of the air quality
solution.

SFX: REPRISE SOUNDS OF BIRDS, WIND, CHILDREN.
JAMES EARL JONES: For the sake of people and all living things,
EC-1 is here. Emission Control Gasoline. The Pure and Simple
Solution. From ARCO.

Kathryn Polk Director
Jeff Nordensson, Jeffery Spencer
Copywriters
Kate Maguire Jensen Account Manager
Nordensson Lynn Advertising Agency
Porter Sound Studio Production
Intergroup of Arizona Client
Tucson, AZ

WATER SAFETY

DON: Summertime's filled with sounds from the pool.
SFX: Light splashing, soft giggle, young child playing in the
water. Total silence.
DON: What you just heard was a young child drowning.
(pause)
Doesn't make a lot of noise, does it. (pause) Listening to your
kids when they're around water isn't enough, you've got to
watch them. Watch them all the time.
Keep a lookout, so you can see what you might not hear.
I'm Don Collier for intergroup, of Arizona.

Kevin O'Donoghue Copywriter
Young & Rubicam New York Agency
United States Army Client
New York, NY

BLUES

BLUES SONG: My friends all got the college loan blues facing
a life of I.O.U's
Not me!
I went to my uncle...Uncle Sam
Signed myself up to be an army man
Got confidence and maturity
And let the army pay for my degree
Now it seems like I can't lose
I got rid of those college loan blues.
I'm being all I can be
Got an edge on life in the army.
ANNCR: Paid for by the U.S. Army.

Mike Hughes Copywriter
The Martin Agency Agency
Waves Recording Design Firm
Wrangler Jeans Client
Richmond, VA

POCKETS

TOM POSTON: Are you wearing your blue jeans? Good. Then do this: put your hands all the way down in your pockets. (pause.) Good. Now take them out. (pause.) Now back in. (Brief pause.) Now out. (Brief pause.) In. (Briefer pause) Out. (Briefer pause.) In. Out. If your having trouble keeping up, you're obviously not wearing new Wrangler American Hero jeans with big, man-sized pockets. Get a pair and you'll be ready for our next commercial when we actually wiggle our fingers.
ANNCR #2: Wrangler American Hero jeans. The most comfortable jeans known to man.

Jan Franks Copywriter
Maureen Thompson Agency Producer
Young & Rubicam New York Agency
Warner-Lambert Company Client
New York, NY

HALLELUJAH

CHOCLAIRS RADIO--HALLELUJAH CHORUS
CHORUS: Oh, good gracious
It,s outrageous
To have to sing
This loud thing
When we'd rather be eating Choclairs!
VO: Choclairs. Light wafers in rich imported milk chocolate...whipped to a creaminess so sublime...everyone is singing it's praises.
CHORUS: HAAAAAAAAAAALLLLLAAAAAAAAAAAAAAY...
CHORUS MEMBER: Psst, the sooner we finish, the sooner we can eat 'em!
CHORUS (QUICKLY): lujah!
VO: Choclairs. A Consuming Passion.

HABENERA

CHOCLAIRS RADIO--HABENERA
CARMEN: I have had many love affairs
But that's all changed
Now I've found...Choclairs!
VO: Choclairs. Light wafers in rich imported milk chocolate...whipped to a creaminess so sublime...everyone is singing it's praises.
CARMEN: Choclairs..I'm yours! (BA-BUM-BUM-BUM)
VO: Choclairs. A Consuming Passion.

ODE TO JOY

CHOCLAIRS RADIO--ODE TO JOY
TENOR SINGER: I have been in love before
But this is something new to me
Never has a chocolate bar
filled me with such sweet ecstacy
CHORUS SINGS UNDER
VO: Choclairs. Light wafers in imported milk chocolate...whipped to a creaminess so sublime...everyone is singing it's praises.
TENOR: Choclairs...my loooooooooooovvvvvvvvvvvvvve!
VO: Choclairs. A Consuming Passion.

Chuck Withrow Copywriter
Sal DeMarco Producer
George Gates Engineer
Wyse Advertising Agency
Commercial Recording Production
The Stroh Brewery Company Client
Cleveland, OH

DANGER THIN ICE

JOE BELL: Joe Bell here, I just happened to be having a Goebel Beer right now and I've got things on my mind. Things like those signs that say, "Danger thin ice. Who brings them in for the summer?" How do they do it? And other things, like why is it that you are always smarter than the people who hire you? Why do windsheldwipers on the drivers side streak and wear out first? And why do grandmothers put those hard silver balls on holiday cookies? Why does the bus going the other way always come first? Is the cure for unemployment daytime television? Pour yourself a Joe Bell and answer this. If the devil sneezed, what would you say? (PAUSE) It is important that everybody believe in something. I believe I'll have another Goebel.
VO: The Goebel Brewing Company
Detroit. Michigan.

TRUTH IN ADVERTISING II

JOE BELL: Joe Bell, here, currently engaged in drinking a Goebel Beer and realizing that this beer is...wet. Also realizing, that's exactly the way I like it. But now I see on TV dryyyy beer. Boy, that's a stumper. Huh uh, when I've got a dry beer, I've got an empty glass. And I know what to do about it. This. (POUR) Listen, you pour yourself a Joe bell I've got a plan here. Beers need gimmicks, right? Right. Well, here's one. Super light, extra dry Goebel. Instead of a third less calories. It's got no calories. And it's really dry. You open it. You get pssst. That's it. Hey. Save a bundle on the ingredients. We could put all the money into advertising. Most beers do that anyway. Goebel super lite extra dry. Might work. But I'm going to stick to the wet one. Goebel Brewing Company. Detroit, Michigan.

BUMPER STICKER

JOE BELL: Joe Bell here, pouring myself a Goebel Beer and wondering about bumper stickers. I'm kind of impressed with anyone who can put his thoughts on major issues into four words. But why share those thoughts with me? Like I'm going to change my mind on nuclear disarmament based on a bumper! And who cares whether they've been to lookout mountain? Or whether or not they love, I mean "heart" their cocker spaniel.
Pour yourself a Joe Bell. I'll tell you what bumper stickers are good for. One, they cover up some rust on your car. Two, they help you decide who to vote for.
If I see a candidate's name on a bumper sticker, and the driver does something stupid, I vote for the other guy. It is a democracy you know.
So vote for Goebel Beer. The right beer for your party.
VO: The Goebel Brewing Company. Detroit Michigan.

Mike Bade Art Director
Lori Korchek Copywriter
Margeotes Fertitta & Weiss, Inc. Agency
NEW YORK NEWSDAY Client
New York, NY

DULUTH

MUSIC: GUITAR PICKING IN BACKGROUND

MALE VO: If you live in New York there are some things you have to know to get by. Like never point to a tall building, open your mouth and say, "look at that"…and if it's yellow, and honks, it won't make change for a twenty. But the most important thing to remember is that you don't live in a city where people strum guitars and talk like this. You have to have a little more on the ball here, and the best way to do that is to read New York Newsday. that's right, the newspaper. Not just because the writers are smart and have lots of Pulitzer prizes, but because New York Newsday knows the turf including all those boroughs some papers don't seem to give the time of day to. And I think knowing a little bit more about where you live means you'll care a little bit more, and then…well, who knows, the next time you're dropping two bits for a New York Newsday you might just tip your hat and smile at a stranger. But if you do…run. After all, this isn't Duluth.

TAG LINE: New York Newsday. Truth, Justice and the Comics.

CLASS TRANSIT

MUSIC: GUITAR PICKING IN BACKGROUND

MALE VO: You know the average New Yorker spends over 523 hours a year riding the subway, which is 523 hours too many to spend counting wooly fibers on the collar of the man who's standing on your instep. At least that's what the folks at New York Newsday think or they wouldn't go to so much trouble putting together such a fine paper every day. Because not only does New York Newsday have an award winning sport's section to keep you riveted all thirty minutes of that ten minute delay, but the city news and business section can tell you and the woman that's reading over your shoulder what's bullish before you pull into the Wall Street station. So, before you get on anything that moves, or even a subway car, drop two bits for your New York Newsday. It's the smartest way in New York to find out what's happening in the other 8,237 hours of the year.

TAG LINE: New York Newsday. Truth, Justice and the Comics.

Steve Engle Copywriter
Vicki Blanford Producer
Rhea & Kaiser Advertising Agency
Minneapolis Broadcast Company Design Firm
Rhone-Poulenc Ag Company Client
Naperville, IL

AT PLANTING

SFX: (SOUND EFFECTS OF SLOOPY CHEWING SOUNDS, UP AND UNDER VOICES)

SAM, THE CYST NEMATONE: Hi there! My name's Sam. I'm a cyst nematone. And these here are my buddies, Robby Root Maggot…

ROBBIE: Yo!

SAM: Louie Leafhopper…

LOUIE: Howdy!

SAM: Arnie Aphid

ARNIE: Hi!

SAM: And Lennie Leafminer.

LENNIE: (SURLEY) Bug off!

SAM: Yes, well, we're here to ask you sugar beet growers to stop usin' TEMIK® brand aldicarb pesticide.

GROUP: Yeah!

SAM: Now we've read where TEMIK® gives you up to one ton more beets per acre than other granular pesticides…

GROUP: Big deal!

SAM: (CLEARS HIS THROAT AS IF UPSET BY INTERRUPTION) And now TEMIK® helps improve the quality of your crop by boosting sugar content…

GROUP: So what!

SAM: (CLEARS THROAT AGAIN) We've even heard that TEMIK® increases net profits up to 37 dollars an acre over other at-planting treatments…

GROUP: Who cares!

SAM: But when you guys use TEMIK®, we've gotta move to another field. And that gets to be a real pain in the…

ARNIE APHID: Yeah, I had to move 23 times last year.

SFX: (CHEWING STARTS AGAIN)

SAM: So come on, fellas. If you promise not to use TEMIK®, we'll promise (PAUSE, AS IF THINKING TO HIMSELF)…not to eat your sugar beets.

SFX: (CHEWING STOPS ABRUPTLY AGAIN)

GROUP: (UP IN ARMS) Hey, speak for yourself…are you kiddin'…we'd starve to death…

SAM: It's just a promise, guys…I didn't really mean it…I had my feelers crossed

(FADE OUT)

ANNCR VO: TEMIK® brand aldicarb pesticide. We keep promises nobody else can make.

SIDE DRESS

SFX: (MULTIPLE CHEWING SOUNDS UP AND THEN UNDER VOICES)

SAM, THE CYST NEMATONE: Hey…it's me…Sam, the cyst nematode. Back again with my buddies Robbie Root Maggot, Louie Leafhopper, Arnie Aphid and Lennie Leafminer.

SFX: (CHEWING SUBSIDES)

GROUP: Hi! (AS IF WITH MOUTHS FULL)

SAM: It's come to our attention that some of you sugar beet growers out there are trying to give us bugs a false sense of security.

GROUP: Yeah!

SAM: Instead of applying TEMIK® brand aldicarb pesticide at planting, you're waitin' to use it as a side-dress application.

ARNIE: Oooh, sneaky!

SAM: Now, we know that a side-dress application of TEMIK® offers unsurpassed contact control of nematodes and root maggots…

ROBBIE: Hey, I'm a root maggot!

SAM: Plus, up to 12 weeks of protection against foliar pests…

ARNIE: Pest?! Who're you callin' a pest?!

SAM: We've even read where TEMIK® gives you up to a ton more beets per acre than other granular products. Not to mention better quality and bigger net profits…

ROBBIE: You weren't supposed to mention that!

SAM: But don't yopu think it's a little inconsiderate to trick us like that. I mean, to let us get all settled in and then hit us with a side-dress application of TEMIK®…

ARNIE: It's not fair!

SAM: So, how 'bout it guys? Why don't you just forget about that side-dress application of TEMIK®…

and…and…take a vacation.

ARNIE: Yeah, a long vacation…

ROBBIE: Like around the world…

ARNIE: In a row boat…

(FADE OUT)

ANNCR VO: TEMIK® brand aldicarb pesticide. We keep promises nobody else can make.

Harold Woodrige Director
BBDO Chicago Agency
River Run Production
Central Telephone of Centel Corporation Client
Chicago, IL

CALL FORWARDING-SNOWMEN

(MUSIC UP AND UNDER)
ANNCR 1: Okay, I'm here to tell you how Call Forwarding from Centel can help fight off abominable snowmen. Now, imagine you're at a friend's house having some of his Aunt Edna's award winning egg salad--you know, the kind with the pickle relish and the onions in it. Meanwhile, people are frantically calling your house to tell you tonight's ski trip is off. But, you're not home to find out, so you pack your gear, grab a map and head up there anyway. Now, your almost at the ski lodge when all of a sudden, a monster jumps out of nowhere, licks your bumper and gets stuck to your car. So what do you have? A 4000 pound bumper and some heavy duty car trouble. But if you had Call Forwarding from Centel, you'd still have your bumper and probably better gas mileage. So when we tell you Call Forwarding can fight off abominable monsters, we really mean it.
ANNCR 2: Call Forwarding from Centel.
Where People Connect.
ALT TAG: (SING) WHERE PEOPLE CONNECT.

CALL WAITING-DOG AND CAR

(MUSIC UP AND UNDER)
ANNCR 1: Okay, I'm here to tell you how Call Waiing from Centel can save your dog and your car. You're at home, trying to kick back, but people keep calling you. Meanwhile, your dog's out running a few errands--using your car. You forget that even though he's a pointer, he's really bad with directions. So he makes a wrong turn, gets lost and trots to the nearest phone to call you for some help. But what does he get? A busy signal. Now, this makes him very nervous and confused. In fact, he panics. So he gets back into the car, drives to Pough-keepsie, finds a new owner, and next thing you know, your out a car and a dog. But if you had Call Waiting from Centel, you'd have been able to point your pointer, and your car, in the right direction. So when we tell you Call Waiting can help you keep important things in your life, we really mean it.
ANNCR 2: Call Waiting from Centel. Where People Connect.
ALT TAG: (SING) WHERE PEOPLE CONNECT.

Anita Danz Copywriter
Zwiren Collins Karo Trusk & Ayer Agency
Leaf, Inc. Client
Chicago, IL

MUSIC STORE

MILK DUDS MUSIC THEME BED--NO LYRICS--PLAYED UNDER ENTIRE COMMERCIAL.
(SFX: LARGE CROWD OF CUSTOMERS IN A MUSIC STORE. CASH REGISTER COMPUTING)
FRIEND: Lisa, you're gonna have to be a little more aggressive.
LISA: What's the problem?
FRIEND: The problem? We're at a two-hour music sale--all tapes are half off--and you're eating Milk Duds candy.
LISA: Yeah, so?
(SFX: SHUFFLING TAPES)
FRIEND: Don't you want to dig through this pile with everyone else?
LISA: Nah--I'm kinda' diggin my Milk Duds right now.
AVO: Milk Duds. Rich, long-lasting caramel, coverd with real milk chocolate.
(SFX: CASH REGISTER SOUNDS ARE LOUDER NOW, AS THE GIRLS ARE IN LINE TO PAY)
FRIEND: So, I see you tore yourself away from Milk Duds long enough to buy a tape.
LISA: Yep.
CLERK (TO LISA): Will this be all?

LISA: That's it.
(SFX: CASH REGISTER TOTALS SALE. CLERK RIPS RECEIPT OFF)
CLERK (PLEASED): Hey, congratulations! You're our thousandth customer!
LISA: Really?
CLERK: You and the friend of your choice win a trip to Florida!
FRIEND: Lisa, this is cool!
LISA: Hmm...wonder who I'm gonna bring.
FRIEND (PATRONIZING): That's alright Lis. Here, have some Milk Duds candy, take your time and think about it. Just remember who is, was and always will be your very best friend.
LISA: Yeah. I don't know if I want to go with Fluffy.
FRIEND: Your cat?!
MUSIC OUT: "Milk Duds can't be rushed. The pleasure can't be rushed."

BASKETBALL

MILK DUDS MUSIC THEME BED--NO LYRICS--PLAYED UNDER ENTIRE COMMERCIAL.
(SFX: CROWD IN A HIGH SCHOOL GYMNASIUM AT A BASKET-BALL GAME. THE CROWD IS PUSHING & SHOVING IN THE AISLES)
FRIEND (PUSHING THRU CROWD): You're a lot of help.
KENNY (FOLLOWING CLOSELY BEHIND BUT NOT PUSHING): What?
FRIEND: I'm fighting our way through the crowd to get good seats, and you're taking it easy with your Milk Duds candy.
KENNY: So?
FRIEND: Kenny, this happens to be the biggest game of the season.
KENNY: Yeah, and I happen to like Milk Duds candy.
AVO: Milk Duds. Rich, long lasting caramel, coverd with real milk chocolate.
(SFX: PUSHING & SHOVING STOPS AS THEY BREAK THRU CROWD)
FRIEND (PROUDLY): Well, I got us to row 10.
KENNY: There's only one seat left in this row.
FRIEND: Looks like one of us is gonna have to find someplace else to sit.
SHARON (VOICE A DISTANCE AWAY): Kenny--up here--Sharon.
FRIEND: Ooh--Sharon Doherty.
SHARON: There's a seat next to me--if you want it.
KENNY (YELLS TO SHARON): Thanks.
SHARON: And, bring your Milk Duds candy.
KENNY (TO SHARON): Be right there. (TO FRIEND): Don't you love basketball?
MUSIC OUT: "Milk Duds can't be rushed. The pleasure can't be rushed."

John Cadley Copywriter
Eric Mower and Associates, Inc. Agency
The Production Company Production
F.X. Matt Brewing Company Client
Syracuse, NY

LOVE/HATE

SFX: SOLO ACOUSTIC GUITAR UP AND UNDER THROUGHOUT
VOICE: All of us who live in Upstate have this sort of...love-hate relationship with winter, right? We slip and slide and curse the snow...but deep inside we wouldn't have it any other way. Because things happon that wouldn't happon without winter. Neighbors digging each other out. Strangers stopping to give each other a push. And all of us laughing at the TV when we see some city paralyzed with two inches of snow. It's the winter that brings us together...that gives us a feeling of...well, of home. Boots piled by the door, the smell of wood smoke, good talk, hardy food...and plenty of Matt's beer. Because Matt's is a lot like Central New York winter--cold and fresh and clean, with all the spirit and character that make living here so special. Pick up some Matt's today. And get the real, honest taste...of home.

JUST EAST OF SYRACUSE

SFX: SOLO ACOUSTIC GUITAR UP AND UNDER WITHOUT
VOICE: Just east of Syracuse, off route 173, there's a little side road that runs between a big, open meadow and a faded horse barn. And just where that road crests, high on a hill, you can sit and watch the sunset. You'll see the colors of the sky changing on the waters of Oneida lake. You'll see rows of golden corn...thick stands of pine trees...and all the other reasons why you live here instead of some big city. And if you follow that road when the sun goes down, you'll come to a little tavern. The clock behind the bar says Matt's in warm, red letters, and that's what a lot of folks are drinking. Because around here, Matt's goes with the territory. There's something in the taste that's as pure and clean and refreshing as the country all around. So the next time you want to remind yourself why you live here, pick up some Matt's. And get the real, honest tasts...of home.

EAST UTICA RESTAURANT

SFX: SOLO GUITAR UP AND UNDER THROUGHOUT
VOICE: There's a little restaurant in East Utica. And well...let's just say it's not the kind of place where the atmosphere's been manifactured somewhere else. This place is strictly one-of-a kind, with all the things that make living around here so special. They don't ask what you want. They tell you. And they're always right. The pasta's fresh, the sauce is thick, the bread's warm...and the hot peppers will set your hair on fire. Just the way the regulars like 'em. On Saturdays it's like the old country--they put the tables together and everybody comes to talk. Sports, weather, local politics. Plenty of local politics. And plenty of fresh, cold beer. They serve it in big, heavy 16-ounce mugs. And most of the time it's Matt's. Because Matt's has the things that make this place so special--honest, natural, with real character. Pick up some Matt's today. And get the real, honest taste...of home.

INDEX